MOVIES
(AND OTHER THINGS)

A COLLECTION OF QUESTIONS ASKED, ANSWERED, ILLUSTRATED

SHEA SERRANO

ILLUSTRATED BY ARTURO TORRES

TWELVE

NEW YORK BOSTON

Twelve
Hachette Book Group
1290 Avenue of the Americas, New York, NY 10104
twelvebooks.com
twitter.com/twelvebooks

First Edition: October 2019

Twelve is an imprint of Grand Central Publishing. The Twelve name and logo are trademarks of Hachette Book Group, Inc.

The publisher is not responsible for websites (or their content) that are not owned by the publisher.

The Hachette Speakers Bureau provides a wide range of authors for speaking events. To find out more, go to www.hachettespeakersbureau.com or call (866) 376-6591.

Print book interior design by Jarrod Taylor.

Library of Congress Cataloging-in-Publication Data has been applied for.

ISBNs: 978-1-5387-3019-5 (hardcover, paper over board), 978-1-5387-3020-1 (ebook), 978-1-5387-1739-4 (special, signed edition), 978-1-5387-1740-0 (special, signed edition), 978-1-5387-5100-8 (special edition)

Printed in the United States of America

Worzalla

10 9 8 7 6 5 4 3 2 1

For my wife and for my sons, whom I love very much.
And for Miklo in *Blood In, Blood Out*
whom I love differently, but nearly as deeply.

CHAPTERS

FOREWORD

I THINK THE DAY I REALLY FELL IN LOVE WITH FILMMAKING was when we shot the nightclub scene for *Carlito's Way*. Brian De Palma was directing, and I was acting with Sean Penn and Al Pacino. That was 1993.

Flashback to 1981, my sixteenth birthday. My mom had saved up all of her single-mom-working-four-jobs cash to get me a ticket to see *American Buffalo*, a play written by David Mamet. It was off Broadway at the time, and it was starring Al Pacino. So I'm in the theater, and Pacino comes out and he's so electric, man. He's powerful. And I'm watching him, and he's spitting all over everyone. It was like I was being baptized into acting with that spit. It was the most exhilarating performance that I'd ever seen, and he was *right* there in front of me. He was so . . . *free*.

I had a similar experience when I watched the movie *Mean Streets*. There were a ton of great things about this film, but Robert De Niro's performance just grabbed me. When I watched it I said "Oh my God. This guy is . . . I don't even know how to describe him." He was the coolest, most dangerous actor I'd ever seen on film. Everything he did felt unexpected. It was like watching a chemistry experiment. You didn't know what the hell he was gonna do, but you knew *something* was gonna happen. He was unpredictable. So I'm watching *Mean Streets*, and I can feel all of this inside me. Then I'm watching *American Buffalo*, and I feel all of that inside of me again. And then finally, in *Carlito's Way* eleven or twelve years later, I'm in scenes with Al Pacino. Now I've had different coin-dropping moments in my life; aha! moments. That was definitely one of them.

De Palma let me have thirty-seven takes in that nightclub scene. Thirty-seven! *Nobody* was doing that at the time. If I do an independent film and I want to do an extra take, I have to prove to them why I want to do an extra take. I have to give a dissertation on why I want to do an extra take. You only get two or three tries to get it right. De Palma gave me thirty-seven. It was fun. That was when I fell in love with cinema.

———

The filming of each movie is different every time. If I'm working with one of the masters—and by that I mean the greats, like Brian De Palma, Baz Luhrmann, Spike Lee, Ava DuVernay—they're all brilliant, but they all have different processes. There might be a long rehearsal time, or a long conversation where the actors get to talk with the director about the characters and share thoughts and opinions. It might come early, or late, or happen in a way you aren't expecting. They all digest the information and transform it into art in their own unique way.

And then you've got the actual script. Sometimes you play with the dialogue, change things to feel more natural. If it's really well written, like *exceptionally* well written, then you just say the lines as they are. But even with something like *Romeo + Juliet*, a movie where I recognized that it was really well done, I still tried to improvise. I tried to add in lines, but Baz Luhrmann knew better.

But each movie is different, and making each movie is different. That's really the only way they're the same.

———

So I did *Freak* on Broadway, and it earned some accolades. And I thought, "I got some accolades. Let me take these accolades and go ask who would be the perfect director to direct a filmed version of *Freak*." And it was Spike Lee. So I said, "Spike, I would like you to direct this. I know it's a big ask. I don't know if—" And he was like, "Yo, I'm down." And he came on and he started planning how he was gonna shoot it and where he was gonna shoot it. And when he shot it, he just allowed for everything to happen.

Like, when I crashed into the camera guy during the show, he kept that in there. He just really caught the magic of what was happening in that theater. He really caught what was happening between me and the audience. And audiences, kind of like for the first time, some of them were seeing themselves represented onstage. Latin people were coming in there, and people of color were coming in there like, "That's my life. That's me. That's who I am." And when you see somebody talking about that stuff, celebrating it as special, it's powerful. Spike captured all of that when he filmed that show.

—

There are some scenes that people always ask me about. The gas station scene in *Romeo + Juliet* is one of them. There were a lot of stunts and tricks with the guns, and I wanted to do them all myself. So we're filming the shootout, and in one part I jump and land behind a car. I roll a couple of times, get up, spin one of my guns around my finger, and then put it back in the holster. That's what you see in the movie. But in real life, I jumped and landed on a mattress. If you watch the scene, you can see that I'm looking to try and make sure that I land on the mattress.

But that scene was a lot of work. I had teachers who taught me how to do the gunplay. I spent three months in my hotel room doing it. At first, I was dropping the guns on my feet. I had all these cuts and black and blue marks. I started wearing Timberlands while I was practicing so I wouldn't get hurt. The neighbors in the hotel started complaining because you could hear the guns banging around each time I'd drop one of them, so I started practicing while I was standing on top of the bed so I wouldn't make any noise. When we finally filmed the scene the crew applauded when we did it. Baz added some cuts in afterward because that's his style and he's a genius. But I did the tricks all myself.

—

There are so many movies that shaped me, or inspired me, or helped me through tough times. *Mean Streets*, *Raging Bull*, *Serpico*, *Stir Crazy*, *Live on the Sunset Strip* with Richard Pryor. There are so many.

Before there was YouTube, I used to go to the Museum of Broadcasting in New York City on Fifty-Third Street. And I was just a kid, but I would go to this museum and see the history of comedy. I'd watch all these comedians. I'd be there for hours and hours, just lose myself. I'd take it all in. I'd get lost in it. Theater and film have different effects on the psyche, I believe, and both of them are good. When you see great theater, you feel like you had that experience. You feel like it happened to *you*, in a weird way. You take it in physically, emotionally, intellectually. When you see a film, it blends your dreams and your reality together. It seeps into your subconscious. It takes the part of you that daydreams—no matter how old you are, it takes the part of you that daydreams and it empowers it.

A good movie makes anything feel possible.
Even your dreams.

AN INTRODUCTION, BY WAY OF EIGHT QUESTIONS

1. What is this book?

It's a book about movies, is what it is. I wrote it because I really like movies. They have been important to me since I was a child. They'll probably be important to me all the way up until I'm dead. Or, at least until they stop making The Fast and the Furious movies. It's a toss-up on which of those things happens first.

2. How does the book work?

It's very simple. The book is 30 chapters long. Each chapter is a different movie question that needs to be answered. Sometimes the questions are silly. Other times, the questions are serious. But they're always answered with (what I hope is) a clear amount of care and respect.

And you don't have to read the book in order. You can go in whatever order you like. You don't have to have read, say, chapter 13 (which is about action movies) to understand chapter 14 (which is about *Selena*).

Oh, also: There's a lot of art in the book. I like including art with the stuff because it helps give everything a slightly firmer shape, and helps place the reader in the same kind of headspace that I was in whenever I was writing a thing. So, for example, there's a chapter written as a press conference held by Michael Myers, the iconic movie monster from the *Halloween* franchise. And that's, of course, a silly idea, but there's a piece of art in there with Michael sitting at a conference table in front of a bunch of reporters and seeing that drawing helps turn it into something

that feels a little more real, which helps it feel a little more substantial.

3. Didn't you do a book like this before?

Yes. It was called *Basketball (And Other Things)*. It came out in 2017.

4. Did you know that you were going to write *Movies (And Other Things)* back when you were writing *Basketball (And Other Things)*?

Yes. I knew I wanted to write *Movies (And Other Things)* as soon as I settled on the title for *Basketball (And Other Things)*. But that's not because we had any kind of grand plan in place to turn the (And Other Things) premise into an actual series or anything like that. Mostly it was because we realized that after *Basketball (And Other Things)* had proven itself to be successful you could put "(And Other Things)" behind basically anything and it sounded like a fine idea for a book. *Basketball (And Other Things)*. *Movies (And Other Things)*. *Rap (And Other Things)*. *Hot Dogs (And Other Things)*. *Roofing (And Other Things)*. *Crossbows (And Other Things)*. *Literally Anything (And Other Things)*. *I Can Do This All Day (And Other Things)*. *You Get the Point (And Other Things)*.

5. Are there any guidelines or rules that you had in place when you were working on this book?

The closest thing to a guideline or a rule is that, generally speaking, I didn't want to spend a ton of time or energy talking about movies that came out before the '80s. There just haven't been a lot of times in my life where someone was like, "Hey, man. What'd you think of Tony Curtis in 1959's *Some Like It Hot*," you know what I mean? (In fact, the only reason I know that that's actually a movie is because Cher mentions it in 1995's *Clueless*.) So I just focused on movies that I liked from time periods that I liked. A few of them are from the '80s, and all the rest of them are from the '90s, 2000s, and 2010s.

6. Wait, I just realized that the reason you're doing the introduction in a question and answer format is because the chapters in the book are all written in a question and answer format. Is that what's going on here?

That's a bingo.

7. Why did you ask John Leguizamo to write the fore-word?

Well, there are two reasons why. For one, I asked him to write the foreword because it made sense because this is a book about movies and he is a movie star who has been in a number of films that I enjoy a great deal (he was brilliant as the uncontrollable hothead Benny Blanco in *Carlito's Way*; he was brilliant as the venom-ous Tybalt in *Romeo + Juliet*; he was brilliant as the charming chop shop owner Aurelio in *John Wick*; etc.).

But that's just a part of it. And not even the most important part of it, really. Because the main reason that I asked him to write the foreword is I have looked up to him and admired him and respected him since back when I was in high school and watched *Freak*, his first one-man Broadway show that ran on HBO.

I thought he was incredible in it. I thought he was smart and I thought he was funny and I thought he was cool and I thought he was talented, and all of those feelings were multiplied by about a billion per-cent because he, like me, had dark brown hair and dark brown eyes and a last name that ended in a vowel. And

I'd for sure seen him in movies and on TV before then (two of the three movies I mentioned above came out before his *Freak* special, as had *The Pest* and *Spawn* and *Executive Decision* and several others). But it was watching him up on stage in *Freak*, carrying the entirety of evening on his shoulders, being a total and complete powerhouse, that made me say to myself, "Wow. I . . . I don't know who this guy is, but I know he's going to be someone who will be in my brain for a long time."

8. Why did you ask Don Cheadle to write the after-word?

Same as with Leguizamo, there are two reasons why. First, because he's fucking Don Cheadle, is why. He was Basher in the Ocean's movies. He was Miles Davis in *Miles Ahead*. He was Mouse Alexander in *Devil Wears a Blue Dress*. He was War Machine in the Marvel movies. He was Montel in *Traffic*. He was Buck Swope in *Boogie Nights*. He was Rocket in *Colors*. He was Earl "The Goat" Manigault in *Rebound*. He was Paul Rusesabagina in *Hotel Rwanda*. On and on and on.

Second, BECAUSE HE'S FUCKING DON CHEADLE, one of the four or five coolest people on the planet. I actually asked him about exactly that when we spoke ahead of time for the afterword. I mentioned the cameo he had in the "D.N.A." short video that Kendrick Lamar made and asked him what it felt like to exist every day as someone who was uni-versally recognized as cool, and of course he gave an answer about how he definitely did not see himself that way, but he did so in the coolest way possible, which was incredible. It was like watching Steph Curry tell you he's not good at basketball as he's in the mid-dle of making 45 threes in a row.

A TRICKY THING TO DEAL WITH when writing a book about movies is knowing how much time should be spent recapping the plot of a movie (or movies) that is (or are) central to a given chapter. For example, this chapter heavily features 2007's *I Am Legend*, 2014's *The Drop*, and 2014's *John Wick*. And I like those three movies very much and enjoy talking about them and writing about them and thinking about them. As such, it would be more than easy to spend, say, two thousand words simply going over what those movies are about and the arcs that each of the main characters travel. But I don't want to do that here. Because I don't think it's necessary here. Because this chapter is less a discussion of each of the actual movies and more a discussion of a broad (but significant) similarity that stretches across them.

Robert Neville is the main character in *I Am Legend*. He is a tough guy. And he comes to own a dog he was not expecting to own. Bob Saginowski is the main character in *The Drop*. He is a tough guy. And he comes to own a dog that he was not expecting to own. And John Wick is the main character in *John Wick*. He is a tough guy. And he comes to own a dog he was not expecting to own.[1] Certainly these are not the only movie tough guys who have owned dogs,[2] but they are the three that I'd like to start this book off with. And so here is the question that this chapter is going to answer: Who was the better tough guy movie dog owner? Was it the military virologist Robert Neville, the brooding bartender Bob Saginowski, or the forced-out-of-retirement iconic assassin John Wick?

——

There are six different categories one needs to consider when determining who is the better tough guy movie dog owner. They are: (1) What dog is the better breed? (2) What relationship origin story is the most emotional and compelling? (3) Which of the three dog owners was the best at protecting his dog? (4) Which dog was trained the best? (5) Which pairing had the stronger bond? And (6) Which guy looked better holding his dog?

So let's handle it this way: Let's go category by category, pick a winner for each, then add up the scores at the end. Whoever has the most category victories is the winner. That's who the better tough guy movie dog owner is.[3]

——

WHAT DOG IS THE BETTER BREED? John Wick's puppy was a beagle named Daisy. Bob Saginowski's puppy was a pit bull named Rocco. Robert Neville's puppy was a German shepherd named Sam. I'm not sure the best way to rank dogs by breed. Best I can

---

1. Despite the hardness with which each of these three guys exist, they all fall deeply in love with their dogs, of course, because dogs are the very best and allow humans to access parts of themselves that are often otherwise unreachable.

2. I toyed around briefly with making this chapter a thing about tough guys who own birds as a way to talk about LL Cool J in *Deep Blue Sea* and Mickey Rourke in *Iron Man 2*, but that would've probably only been interesting to me, Chris Ryan, and like six other people.

3. This is the dumbest thing. I love it a lot. As soon as I started writing this chapter, I said to myself, "This is it. This is the one that I'm going to start the book with."

tell, they all seem pretty great. And even if we take a wider view of the situation and consider each dog in relation to each owner, things end up still mostly even, what with (a) a beagle being a good pick for John Wick because of the irony, (b) a pit bull being a good pick for Bob Saginowski because of the symbolism,[4] and (c) a German shepherd being a good pick for Robert Neville because of the pragmatism.[5] This category feels a lot like a stalemate.

Winner: Nobody.

Score: Robert Neville: 0 / Bob Saginowski: 0 / John Wick: 0

———

WHAT RELATIONSHIP ORIGIN STORY IS THE MOST EMOTIONAL AND COMPELLING? Bob Saginowski meets his dog while walking home late one evening. He's walking all alone and just sort of minding his business and, as he passes a house, he hears whimpering. He stops, listens for the sound again, hears it, then realizes it's coming from a trash can. He opens up the trash can and sees a puppy inside of it. He takes the puppy out and notices that it's been beaten into a bloodied mess. The woman who lives in the house happens to be outside on a back patio smoking a cigarette. She watches Bob pull the dog out of the trash. They take the puppy inside, clean him up, then agree that Bob can take a day or two to decide if he wants to become the puppy's full-time owner.

John Wick meets his puppy via a courier service. It was sent to him from beyond the grave by the woman he loved (she'd recently passed away because of an unnamed terminal illness). She sent it to John because she knew he was going to need something new to love, which is what she explains in the note that arrives with the puppy.

Robert Neville's dog actually started out as a family dog. It was him, his wife, his daughter, and their puppy, and they were, best we can tell, living a happy and regular life. But then a genetically reengineered version of the measles that was supposed to work as the cure for cancer turned lethal, killing nearly everyone on Earth and transforming many of the people who didn't immediately die into zombie-vampire things.[6] During a flashback, we see that as New York City was being evacuated, Robert's wife and daughter were being sent away on a helicopter for safekeeping (Robert is a high-ranking member of the military, which is how he was able to secure seats on the escape helicopter for his wife and daughter). Right before they left, Robert's daughter handed him the puppy she was holding. The helicopter exploded when it was slammed into by another helicopter, killing everyone on board. Robert kept the puppy because it was all he had left after the crash and after the virus outbreak.

If we're looking at all three of those backstories side by side by side, it's clear that there are two prominent themes. Bob Saginowski's puppy serves as the impetus for a new relationship, and for new

---

4. There's a whole thing to be said about how pit bulls are a misunderstood breed, same as Bob Saginowski is a misunderstood human.
5. *I Am Legend* looks a lot different if Sam was, say, a weenie dog.
6. How about this for a crossover theory: What if the virus is how John Wick's wife died? I know the time tables don't exactly match up, but I also know that we're talking about zombie-vampires, so, I mean, let's not get too lost in the nitpicking.

hope.[7] With John Wick and his dog and Robert Neville and his dog, they sit way on the other side of the spectrum. Each dog in those two relationships represent all that remains of each owner's broken and destroyed attempts at love. Each dog is a reminder of the unyielding loneliness and heartache consuming each guy.

So that's what we're looking at. And as strong as the storyline is of Bob potentially finding a proper place for himself in the world, there's just no way that he can win this category. Which means it's a toss-up between a guy who gets mailed a dog by his dead wife and a guy who gets handed a dog by his daughter right before she's killed alongside her mom in a helicopter crash. I vote Wick here. And I understand that Neville lost his wife *and* his daughter, but that all happened during an apocalypse that would eventually go on to claim literally billions of lives. There's something a little more poignant, a little more tragic, a little more gripping about a tragedy that feels like it's singled you out.

Winner: John Wick, though it hardly feels accurate to describe him as a "winner" here.

Score: Robert Neville: 0 / Bob Saginowski: 0 / John Wick: 1

———

WHICH OF THE THREE DOG OWNERS IS THE BEST AT PROTECTING HIS DOG? Well, I mean, this is really a results-based category. Daisy gets killed within the first fifteen minutes of *John Wick*. Robert Neville ends up having to kill Sam himself after she starts to turn into a zombie-vampire in the back half of the movie because she got bitten while trying to save Neville's life. And *The Drop* ends with Bob Saginowski and Rocco waiting to go on a date with a woman that Bob has a crush on the day after Bob has murdered the guy who originally beat Rocco and put him in that trash can.

Robert Neville was certainly a more natural dog owner, and John Wick was the most skilled of all three with regards to avenging, but Bob was the best at protecting his puppy.

Winner: Bob Saginowski

Score: Robert Neville: 0 / Bob Saginowski: 1 / John Wick: 1

———

WHICH DOG WAS TRAINED THE BEST? When I was in college, I had a dog named Tyson that I loved a great, great deal. One night during my junior year, I was playing cards at a friend's house. There were, I think, something like eight other people there. One of them was this guy named Jaime.

Jaime was, to that point, probably the third or fourth sweetest guy I'd ever met in my life. He was also, as it turns out, the third or fourth doofiest as well.[8] But

---

7. During a behind-the-scenes interview, Dennis Lehane, the author and screenwriter of *The Drop*, explained, "Ten years prior to the film beginning, Bob has made a decision that he's going to close himself from humanity; he's gonna close himself off from feeling; that he is never going to engage the world. And the film opens really on the day he engages the world again through this puppy. It's when he finds the dog that he begins to open something up in him."

8. My all-time favorite Jaime anecdote is one day I got a phone call at like 8 a.m. on a Tuesday. I didn't recognize the number so I answered it because this was before I had student loan collectors calling me all the time. Jaime was on the other end of the line. When I realized who it was I said, "Why are you calling me at 8 a.m. on a Tuesday, Jaime?" He very matter-of-factly said, "My friend works at the bus station. They have a *Street Fighter II* machine there. Do you wanna go to the bus station with me and play *Street Fighter II*?"

so while we were all sitting there playing cards, Jaime got up and walked to the kitchen and picked up a piece of pizza and started eating it. Tyson, a well-known pizza enthusiast, walked over and sat in front of Jaime and stared at him while he ate. A guy sitting at the table said, "How much do you wanna bet that Tyson is about to outsmart Jaime and get that pizza from him?" I don't know why I thought that was so funny, but let me tell you: I thought that shit was so fucking funny. I've had that memory in my head for the past fifteen years and will have it in there for another fifteen years, I'm sure. I love Tyson and I love Jaime and I love pizza.

At any rate, Jaime with Tyson is the same way I think about Bob with Rocco. Bob was kind of a dunce in *The Drop*. The only real time we see him trying to train Rocco, it's when they're at a dog park one morning and he's trying to get Rocco to sit, which Rocco does not do. I have no doubt that Rocco will grow up in a household full of love and respect, but I also have no doubt that Rocco, like Bob, is going to grow up and be a bit of a blockhead.[9] So Bob and Rocco are out.

Robert Neville had Sam pretty well trained, but I can't get past Sam accidentally running into a building that ended up being a zombie-vampire nest. That's just too big of a mistake to make in that situation. And Sam is already a fully grown dog by that point. She's really only ever known a world with zombie-vampires in it, which means she's only ever known a world where running into a dark building is, by most accounts, a death sentence. So those two are out as well.

The winner here is John Wick and Daisy, because consider this: John Wick receives Daisy one evening. By bedtime, he's already gotten her house-trained (we see Daisy wait until the next morning before she sprints outside to use the restroom). It only took him a few hours to train a puppy not to pee or poop in the house. That's incredible. I have a French bulldog that is over three years old that still poops in the house on occasion. There's probably poop somewhere in my house at this exact moment.

Winner: John Wick

Score: Robert Neville: 0 / Bob Saginowski: 1 / John Wick: 2

Sidebar: More evidence that John Wick is a master dog trainer: John ends up rescuing a new dog from a kill shelter at the end of *John Wick*. When he takes the dog home, the dog is on a leash and kind of all over the place. *John Wick: Chapter 2* takes place just four days after the original. And we see that John has already trained the new dog to walk perfectly by his side without needing a leash at all.

———

WHICH GUY LOOKED BETTER HOLDING HIS DOG?

John Wick is a very handsome man.[10] As is Robert

---

9. There's a 50 percent chance that Bob is actually really smart and understands that pretending to be a blockhead is the easiest way for him to live his life.

10. It's the second best haircut that Keanu Reeves has ever had in a movie. His first best was the very short cut he had in *Speed*. Semi-related: The best non-Keanu haircut that anyone has ever had in a Keanu Reeves movie was the surfer cut that Patrick Swayze had in *Point Break*. It was, in all manner and in all ways, perfect.

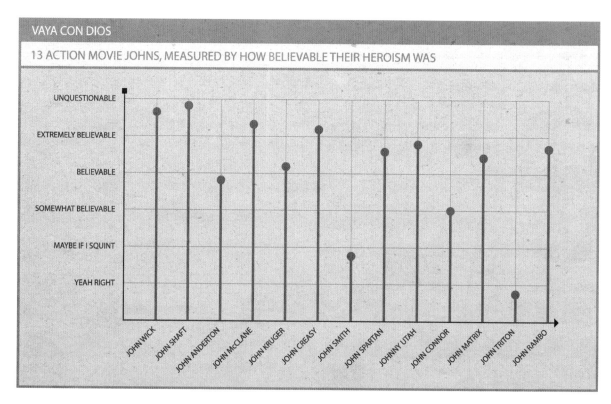

VAYA CON DIOS

13 ACTION MOVIE JOHNS, MEASURED BY HOW BELIEVABLE THEIR HEROISM WAS

Neville.[11] But Bob Saginowski, all quiet and weathered, with that five-o'clock shadow that frames his perfect face like a work of art and with that hunkered-in posture that turns the muscles between his shoulders and his neck into a mountain range—that's a special level of attractive. It's a generational level of attractive. If somebody in heaven was like, "Excuse me, God. I've always wondered this: Where did you get the idea for erections?" God would say something back like, "Oh, man. I just . . . I don't know. I was sitting there one day and I pictured Tom Hardy holding a puppy sitting next to a heating oil tank in a basement and the next thing I knew: malibooyah. Erections." That's what we're dealing with here. John and Robert never stood a chance. Bob wins this category.

Winner: Bob Saginowski

Score: Robert Neville: 0 / Bob Saginowski: 2 / John Wick: 2

———

WHICH PAIRING HAD THE STRONGER BOND? This one feels tricky to measure. Bob Saginowski loved Rocco so much that he was willing to pay Eric Deeds

---

11. My wife and I watched *I Am Legend* in a movie theater during Christmas break the year that it came out. There's a scene in it where Will Smith does pull-ups with his shirt off. When it happened, I leaned over to her and whispered, "Hey. If you ever get the chance to cheat on me with Will Smith, please do it."

$10,000 for him once Deeds started pressing Bob about it. (Eric Deeds was Rocco's original owner. He started leaning on Bob for money after he figured out that Bob loved Rocco.) That's a lot of money. You can go on Craigslist right now and buy a pit bull puppy for, like, $200. Bob could've given Rocco back to Eric, gone on Craigslist, bought forty new pit bulls, and still had $2,000 left over. And that's not even addressing that Bob eventually murdered Eric because he felt like Eric was going to be a continued threat to Rocco.[12]

Robert Neville loved Sam so much that after she died he had a breakdown so severe he (a) started crying when a mannequin wouldn't talk to him, and (b) tried to commit suicide by driving his car into a bunch of zombie-vampires at night. (He'd have died if he didn't get rescued by a woman who just so happened to be out looking for him because she'd heard a radio distress signal that he would put out each day.)

John Wick loved Daisy so much that he was willing to go to war with an entire arm of the Russian mob just to be able to kill the guy that was responsible for Daisy's death, and, so, I mean, if a good way to measure how much you love something is by counting how many of another thing you're willing to kill for it, then John Wick is way the fuck up there, you know what I'm saying? HOWEVER, there's a scene late in the movie where a man asks Wick why he's going so insane about a dead dog and Wick explains that it wasn't just that the dog was taken away from him, but also he had taken from him the opportunity to grieve the loss of his wife. That, to me, makes it clear that the killing spree was due

more to the gigantic hole he had blown through his heart when his wife died than the killing of Daisy.

Robert wins this category.

Winner: Robert Neville

Score: Robert Neville: 1 / Bob Saginowski: 2 / John Wick: 2

———

Given that this has ended in a tie between between Bob Saginowski and John Wick, and given that I do not want to start this book with a question that does not have a proper answer, let's very quickly revisit that first category that ended up getting scored a stalemate and modify it a bit. Let's make it so that rather than looking only at each dog's breed, what we're doing is looking at which dog breed works the best as a philosophical avatar for its owner. If we do that, I think we can, by the tiniest of snouts, nudge this thing in Bob Saginowski's direction. Because those two, when you step back and really look at all the parts and pieces, just seem more cosmically aligned than John Wick and Daisy.

So there it is.

Bob's the winner of this category, so Bob's the winner of the whole thing.

Bob Saginowski is the better tough guy movie dog owner.

---

12. When Nadia, who has just watched Bob shoot Eric in the throat and head, says, "You just fucking shot him," Bob says back, "Yes, I did. Absolutely. He was gonna hurt our dog."

THE QUESTION "WHO GETS IT THE WORST IN *KILL BILL*?" isn't entirely accurate. At least, not within the construct of this chapter, anyway. Because that's not really what I want to ask. What I really want to ask is, "Who gets it the second worst in the *Kill Bill* movie franchise?" That's different in two ways. First, it's different because the phrase "the *Kill Bill* movie franchise" makes it clear that both *Kill Bill: Volume 1* and *Kill Bill: Volume 2* are going to be talked about, not just *Kill Bill: Volume 1*. Second, it's different because it establishes that we're looking to figure out who got it the second worst in those movies, not who got it the first worst, because the first worst is too easy.

And so that's the real question here: Who gets it the second worst in the *Kill Bill* movie franchise?

And I hope that it's obvious here that the entire reason for the meta nature of this chapter intro is that it is a reflection of the way that Quentin Tarantino makes his movies.[1] I also hope it's obvious here that pointing out exactly what I'm doing is also a reflection of the Quentin Tarantino process, because the only thing he seems to like more than making movies that fold over onto themselves is explaining to people in those movies that he's making movies that are folding over onto themselves.[2]

———

The plot mechanics of the *Kill Bill* movies are simple: A woman decides that she no longer wants to be part of a world-class assassination team. She disappears into the wind. The leader (and also her boyfriend) thinks that she was killed on her last mission, and so he sets out to hunt down her killer(s). Alas, he finds her in El Paso, Texas, living under a fake name and preparing to get married, and so he and the other members of the world-class assassination squad kill her, and they kill the man she's about to marry, and they also kill everyone else who happens to be in the room (the woman and her soon-to-be husband were having a wedding rehearsal when the assassins showed up).

Except here's the trick: The woman didn't die in the attack. It looks a lot like she does, and certainly no fault can be placed at the feet of the man or the assassins because they do shoot her square in the head, which is typically a thing that causes people to no longer be alive. But she doesn't. The bullet in her brain sends her into a coma for four years. When she wakes up, she (rightfully) decides that everyone involved in the attack has to die. And so, the two movies follow her as she attempts to kill each person who played a part in the massacre, one by one, in various forms and fashions.

———

There are dozens of characters in the *Kill Bill* universe, but the principal characters are as such:

- **The Bride, otherwise known as Beatrix Kiddo, otherwise known as Black Mamba, otherwise known as Arlene Machiavelli:** She's the star. She's played (perfectly) by Uma Thurman. A big part of the reason she's so motivated is because she was

———

1. Tarantino wrote and directed both of the *Kill Bill* movies.
2. Third on the list of things he likes is "Writing the N word in scripts" would be my guess.

pregnant when she was attacked.[3] When she wakes up, she sees that she's not pregnant anymore. She believes that her baby, like everyone else in the church that day, was killed. We find out at the very end of *Kill Bill: Volume 1* that the baby, a daughter, is alive. When Beatrix shows up to kill Bill in *Kill Bill: Volume 2*'s last big scene, Bill introduces Beatrix to her daughter. It's very moving. (I am going to be as plain and straightforward as I can when I say this because I need for everyone to understand it: Uma Thurman is out and out brilliant as Beatrix Kiddo, and the scene where she meets her daughter for the first time is the very best example of Thurman's acting skill on display. Watching her realize that her daughter is alive is what I imagine it feels like to have someone drive a Chevy Tahoe into your chest at 100 miles an hour.)

- **Bill, otherwise known as nothing else but Bill:** The leader of the Deadly Viper Assassination Squad. He's played (perfectly) by David Carradine. Carradine infuses Bill with such a confident stillness that I feel comfortable in describing him, despite his waifish physique, as "terrifying" and "very unsettling."[4]

- **O-Ren Ishii, otherwise known as Cottonmouth:** She used to be in the Deadly Viper Assassination Squad, but she left and became the head of the Tokyo Yakuza, which I assume was a promotion. As head of the Tokyo Yakuza, she travels with a bodyguard army called the Crazy 88. She's played (perfectly) by Lucy Liu.

- **Vernita Green, otherwise known as Copperhead:** A member of the Deadly Viper Assassination Squad. When we see her, she's living in a quiet neighborhood in Pasadena, California, mother to a four-year-old daughter named Nikki. She's played (perfectly) by Vivica A. Fox.

- **Elle Driver, otherwise known as California Mountain Snake:** Another member of the Deadly Viper Assassination Squad. She is second in command to Bill. She wears an eye patch over her right eye because it was snatched out by Pai Mei, a kung fu master who she temporarily trained under and had a cantankerous relationship with.[5] She respects Kiddo, but only in a way that ever manifests itself as hate or anger or jealousy. She's played (perfectly) by Daryl Hannah.

- **Budd, otherwise known as Sidewinder:** Another member of the Deadly Viper Assassination Squad. He's Bill's brother. He's gross. He's like when Lisa changed Chet into that slime monster in *Weird Science*, but real. He's played (perfectly) by Michael Madsen.

The person who gets it the worst in the *Kill Bill* movie franchise is Beatrix Kiddo. She has the highest number of very bad things happen to her, including but not limited to: being the victim of an attempted murder while she was pregnant and at her wedding rehearsal; having her fiancé murdered; having her new friends murdered by her old friends; spending four

---

3. This is why she decided she no longer wanted to be in the Deadly Viper Assassination Squad.
4. Christoph Waltz does a very similar thing as the villainous Hans Landa in *Inglourious Basterds*.
5. She eventually poisons him.

years in a coma, during which she was raped (what I have to assume was) multiple times; believing her child was murdered inside of her; sitting inside of a truck called Pussy Wagon for thirteen hours while she tried to talk her legs into working again after they'd atrophied during her coma;[6] getting into multiple fistfights; getting beaten and ridiculed by Pai Mei during her training period with him; nearly getting her arm snapped in two by Pai Mei; flying across the ocean to get a Hattori Hanzo sword (flying fucking sucks); getting her back sliced open by a Hattori Hanzo sword during her fight with O-Ren Ishii; getting called a "silly Caucasian girl" during her fight with O-Ren Ishii;[7] getting shotgun blasted in the chest with rock salt; getting spit on; getting buried alive and left to die; finding out that the child she thought was dead is actually alive;[8] and having to kill the father of her child.

But who gets it the second worst?

———

AN ASIDE: WHO GETS IT THE WORST FROM THE CRAZY 88? There aren't actually eighty-eight people in the Crazy 88, that's the first thing you should know. It's closer to forty people. Second, Beatrix ends up having to fight them all before she can fight O-Ren. She cuts arms off and legs off and feet off and even a head off. There's a lot happening, truly, really, definitely.[9]

Out of all of the people who she takes on, the four who get it the worst are: (4) The guy who gets stabbed through the guts and then used as a human shield by Beatrix. (3) The guy who throws two axes at Beatrix. She catches one, dodges the other, then throws the first one back at him, hitting him dead center in the forehead. He beats out the decapitated guy because I just really feel like it has to suck more to get killed with your own weapon than it does to get killed with someone else's weapon. (2) The guy who gets his eyeball plucked out of his head. Everybody remembers Elle Driver getting her eye snatched out by Beatrix, but nobody remembers that she did it to him first. (1) The last guy who she stares down. It ends up being this very child-looking fellow. She doesn't even bother to kill him. She slices his sword to bits, sees him surrender, then grabs him and spanks him with her sword. I figure it has to be extremely deflating to be seen as such a non-threat that a person you're trying to kill decides the only thing you need is to be spanked.[10]

———

6. My first-ever experience with any sort of extended universe was seeing the Pussy Wagon truck in a Missy Elliott video after *Kill Bill: Volume 1* had come out.

7. There's something uniquely hilarious to me about being in a life-threatening sword fight with an ultra assassin and taking the time to pause the fight for a second to call her a "silly Caucasian girl."

8. I know this seems like a good thing, and it probably is, but there's also a part in the scene where Beatrix realizes that she's missed out on the first four years of her daughter's life and somehow becomes even angrier than she was when she thought the little girl was dead.

9. A neat thing is the camera switches to black-and-white during a long stretch of the fight. That's because there was so much blood in that scene that the MPAA threatened to give the movie an NC-17 rating if Tarantino didn't rein things in a bit. Turning everything black-and-white was just a sneaky way to do that.

10. I'm not sure if O-Ren's main bodyguard, a sadistic seventeen-year-old named Gogo Yubari, is a member of the Crazy 88 or not. If she is, you can slide her into the number-two spot in this top four. She gets a table leg with three large nails in it slammed into her foot, which is then pulled out and slammed into the side of her head.

O-REN ISHII GETS IT BAD. She gets the top of her head chopped off, and getting the top of your head chopped off is definitely somehow worse than getting your whole head chopped off.[11] You probably also have to add in whatever it was that she was feeling as she was watching Beatrix mow through all her bodyguards. (I imagine it felt a lot like how Blazers fans felt during that game seven against the Lakers in the 2000 playoffs when Portland gave up the fifteen-point lead in the fourth quarter.) And you probably also have to add in whatever regret she might've been feeling with her decision to not have one single person on her payroll carry a gun.

If we give everyone here a How Bad Did They Get It? score, O-Ren scores a 77 out of a possible 100.

VERNITA GREEN GETS IT BAD. Beatrix shows up at her house unannounced, punches her in the face, kicks her in the vagina, starts a knife fight with her that stretches through a few rooms, pauses for a moment when Vernita's daughter comes home from school, then eventually throws a knife into Vernita's heart from across the kitchen after Vernita tries to sneak-shoot her with a gun she had hiding in a cereal box that she grabbed while she was pretending to make an afternoon snack for her daughter.

As far as deaths go, a knife to the heart is certainly less dramatic than getting the top of your head sliced off. What makes it worse, though, is after Beatrix bends over and pulls the knife out of Vernita's chest, the camera angle they shoot the scene from shows us that her four-year-old daughter, Nikki, is standing there staring at her dead mother. And that's bad for any number of reasons, not the least of which being that Vernita dies knowing that her daughter is watching her die, which has to feel worse than the actual dying part of dying.

A quick story: My twin sons and I were outside playing basketball in the driveway one day when they were, I think, probably nine years old. A tree branch was hanging down low in front of the backboard and we kept hitting it when we were shooting so I went into the garage and pulled out a ladder and set it up under where the branch was. As I climbed the ladder, another dad who was walking past our house with his daughter shouted something to me about having a tree-trimming tool at his house that I could borrow if I needed it. I'm not sure why, but it really bothered me the way he said it,[12] and so I said back to him in a semi-curt way, "I don't need a tree trimmer. I'm fine." Then I reached up, grabbed ahold of the branch, and started yanking down as hard as I could.

It was harder to break off than I was anticipating, but also easier to break off than I was anticipating too, if that makes any sense, and so when it snapped away from the tree I lost my balance entirely. I fell backward off the ladder and landed flat on my back. And mind you, I was something like seven feet in the air when this happened. I hit the ground and it sounded like a small cow had been dropped down to Earth from a helicopter.

---

11. My wife and I have been arguing for fifteen years about whether or not it hurts to get your head cut off. She thinks that it does. I think that it does not. I think that it happens so fast that your brain doesn't have time to register anything other than it maybe saying, "Oh fuck. My head isn't on my body anymore."

12. I actually know exactly why it bothered me. It's because I'm an idiot.

I thought I was dead, but the dad was still there watching and my sons were still there watching so I just popped up, threw the branch into the yard, then said, "There you go, boys. All clear," Then I grabbed the ladder and I carried it back into the garage.

Anyway, I say all of that to say: I was desperately embarrassed that my sons saw me fall off a ladder in front of another dad. I can't even imagine how embarrassing it'd be to get a knife thrown into your chest in front of your child.

Vernita scores an 81 out of a possible 100.

BUDD GETS IT BAD. He gets bit in the face three times by a black mamba, an extremely venomous snake, and dies on the floor while Elle Driver, who set Budd up to die by snakebite, reads a bunch of facts to him about the black mamba.

Right here feels like a good spot to write out several interesting snake-based things I learned while working on this chapter. (1) Vernita Green's code name is Copperhead. A copperhead snake is "an ambush predator," meaning that it typically lies in wait after finding an advantageous spot. Vernita, in a manner of speaking, tries to ambush Beatrix by pretending to make her daughter a snack and then pulling a gun out of a cereal box and shooting at Beatrix. (2) Bill drives a car called De Tomaso Mangusta. *Mangusta* is how you say "mongoose" in Italian, and the most popular trait of the mongoose is its ability to fight and defeat venomous snakes. (3) The name of the assassination group is the Deadly Viper Assassination Squad. The Black Mamba, which is Beatrix Kiddo's code name, is not technically a viper. That makes sense since she

didn't want to be in the gang anymore. (4) The California Mountain Snake, which is Elle Driver's code name, also isn't technically a viper, nor is it even venomous. If you want to get clever and find a movie tie-in, you can point out that the California Mountain Snake is a coral snake mimic. Coral snakes are venomous and deadly. The California Mountain Snake is just a knock-off version. And Elle Driver is just a knockoff version of Beatrix Kiddo.

Anyway, Budd scores an 84 out of a possible 100.

BILL GETS IT BAD. Several bad things happen to him. First, his girlfriend leaves him. And not only does she leave him, but she fakes her death to leave him, which is maybe the most literal way a person has ever tried to ghost someone. Second, when he accidentally finds her in El Paso he learns that not only is she alive, but she's also (a) getting married to some yo-yo who owns a record store, and (b) is pregnant.[13] (There's a quick line at the end of *Kill Bill: Volume 2* where he says that he mourned her for three months before finding her. That means in three months Beatrix was able to relocate, start a new life, fall in love, and get engaged. That seems fast.) So you've got all of that stuff that's already happened, and then there's the thing where he absolutely has the chance to kill her all the way when she's in the coma, and then finally there's the thing where Beatrix, whom he still loves, hits him with the Five Point Palm Exploding Heart Technique that explodes his heart in his chest. So with Bill it's less about his death and more about all of the emotional baggage that he had sitting on his shoulders all the time.

---

13. I would like it stated for the record that none of these things justify him trying to kill her. Thank you.

Bill scores an 88 out of a possible 100.

ELLE DRIVER GETS IT BAD. Very bad. So bad, in fact, that she's the one who gets it the second worst in the *Kill Bill* movie franchise. She gets one of her eyes ripped out of her head by Pai Mei for being disrespectful, then gets her other eye ripped out by Beatrix Kiddo during their big fight. And worse than that, Beatrix doesn't kill her, because Beatrix knows how much more painful it's going to be for Elle to be alive after getting bested by Beatrix, whom Elle extremely hates. (My favorite thing is to imagine Elle meeting up with some of her friends a few weeks after her fight with Beatrix and someone asking her what happened to her one good eye and Elle saying that it was yanked out and then one of her friends being like, *"Again?!"*) Also, she chases after Bill's affection and praise for the whole movie, but he never really gives it to her because he only loves Beatrix. Also, Beatrix throws a can of Budd's tobacco spit at her during their fight, and I know that that's just a dumb, tiny something, but it's definitely not a something you'd want to have happen to you.

But so Elle really checks off all the boxes here. She has a very violent fistfight with Beatrix like Vernita did. She has the gruesome thing happen to her like what happened with O-Ren. There's the whole irony angle to her fate like how it was with Budd. There's the emotional turmoil like what soaked Bill's wretched heart. And, worst of all, Beatrix leaves her alive so she'll have to sit with all of that in her brain and in her spirit forever.[14]

Elle scores a 92 out of a possible 100. She gets it the second worst in the *Kill Bill* movie franchise.

---

14. When they get around to making *Kill Bill: Volume 3*, it will be twenty years in the future from when *Kill Bill: Volume 2* ended and it's going to be Nikki, Vernita's daughter, hunting down Beatrix for killing her mother. And Elle's going to be the one who trains her to be a killer.

GIVEN THAT, AS I AM WRITING THIS BOOK, The Rock has been the biggest movie star on the planet for over half a decade now, it would probably make for a good introduction if I had some sort of anecdote to plug in here about how the idea for this chapter came up during a purposeful brainstorming session after, say, The Rock cohosted the 2016 MTV Movie Awards or while I was sitting in a theater getting ready to watch one of the seven movies that he put out between 2016 and 2018.[1] Because if that were the case, it'd be a natural way to get into a conversation theorizing the ways that, despite the manner in which the internet has atomized and/or fragmented the traditional Hollywood star-making infrastructure, The Rock has still been able to permeate movie culture entirely.

That's not the way the idea happened, though. Instead, it was an accident. The illustrator and I were texting each other late one night during the spring of 2016. He mentioned in passing that he loved The Rock. I told him that I, too, loved The Rock. Then we spent, like, maybe twenty-five minutes sending pictures of The Rock to each other as responses, during one of which I wrote something close to, "Not only do I wish The Rock was in even more movies, I wish we could put The Rock in movies that have already happened." There was a brief bit of radio silence, and then Arturo replied, "We can." And it's been a running joke ever since.

(I don't remember exactly what time of the night it was when this was happening, but I know it was somewhere between 1 a.m. and 4 a.m.)

(It's always hard to say exactly when an event happened during that block of time because it all seems so similar.)

(I also know I stopped texting him back after he sent me a GIF of The Rock having sex with a woman up against an office desk.[2])

At any rate, that's how the idea came to be, and what the idea is: The Rock has been in a lot of movies.[3] Let's put him in more. And let's figure out if the movies are better, the same, or worse with him in there.

1987's *RoboCop*, except with The Rock Instead

What this movie's about: A cop who is a robot.[4]
Who gets replaced: RoboCop.

This one's sneaky. Part of me absolutely feels like it's a no-brainer of a winner, but I think that's just because the word "RoboRock" sounds interesting. Because when I really think about it—when I really and honestly consider it—a bigger part of me feels like it wouldn't work out. I remember reading a thing one time about how Arnold Schwarzenegger was one of the people

---

1. He had *Central Intelligence* (kind of funny), *Moana* (excellent), *The Fate of the Furious* (very good), *Baywatch* (a lot of people hated it but I liked it), *Jumanji: Welcome to the Jungle* (good), *Rampage* (bad), and *Skyscraper* (pretty bad). And that definitely seems like a lot, but only until you remember that he was in five (!!!!!!!) movies in 2013 alone. His films grossed nearly $1.5 billion globally that year.
2. It was spliced from a scene in a TV show on HBO called *Ballers*.
3. He was in thirty-seven between 2001 and 2018.
4. I have to believe that this was the exact pitch for this movie when the writers were shopping it around Hollywood.

considered for the original RoboCop role, but that he was passed over because he was too much of a hulking mass. And that makes sense, because RoboCop is, by its very nature, a slender creation. It's really the only way it works. You need a thin guy in the suit, otherwise everything becomes way too ridiculous.[5] And that's the main problem we'd run into with The Rock as RoboCop. He's just too big.

Also, and this is important, too: The Rock is wildly charismatic. You need the opposite of that from whoever's going to play RoboCop. You need a person with reverse charisma.

Better, Worse, Same: Worse, surprisingly.

1987's *Predator,* except with The Rock Instead

What this movie's about: Several very muscular men are trapped in the jungle with an alien who, in addition to being even more muscular, is also a hunting enthusiast. **Who gets replaced:** Arnold Schwarzenegger's character, Dutch, leader of the group of men being hunted.

Likely what you're thinking here is: "Arnold should not be the one who gets replaced here. That's a mistake, and a wasted opportunity. Arnold for The Rock is basically an even exchange. What you should do is replace the actual Predator with The Rock. Then it'd be really interesting." And I might agree with you there, except there are two issues with that, one of which is immature and dumb, the other of which is serious and nuanced.

The immature and dumb issue: Swapping out Predator for The Rock does, on paper, sound like fun. I mean, you're talking about Prime Era Arnold Schwarzenegger vs. Prime Era The Rock. That's really a transcendent pairing. The only thing is, it's just too dangerous of a proposition, and what I mean by that is picture this: Okay, we remove Predator from *Predator* and replace him with The Rock, right? And let's say all the other parts of the movie stay the same. Let's say (1) Arnold is still leading a team of mercenaries through the jungle. (2) They're all still being hunted by an alien (only this time it's an evil alien version of The Rock, which is already an HFS[6] situation because for as many movies as The Rock has been in, we've still not seen him as a full-blown bad guy yet). And (3) it ends with that big fight to the death between the two of them.

Okay, so if that happens, if after 110 minutes of already redline max level action, a Prime Era Arnold and a Prime Era The Rock fight each other in a South American jungle, it'd be a fucking testosterone hurricane. It'd be like when the crowd is emptying out of

---

5. *RoboCop* is stuffed fat with silly scenes and even sillier moments. My favorite tiny one that happens: While showing off another potential robotic law enforcement machine (the giant, cumbersome, terrifying ED-209) to a boardroom full of suits, the motherboard malfunctions. The ED-209, which was only supposed to scare everyone, ends up shooting a guy in the chest 100,000 times with high-caliber bullets. It turns his chest into spaghetti. There are pieces of him everywhere. He is as dead as anyone has ever been dead, or will ever be dead. That much is clear. And still, after this very obvious massacre, there are a few seconds of silence, and then someone in the background shouts, "Somebody wanna call a goddamn paramedic?!" My best guess is that paramedic was then going to call a janitor, because janitors always have buckets, and that's what they were going to have to carry that guy out of the room in.
6. Holy Fucking Shit, as it were.

an arena after a UFC event and all the guys are walking around with rage erections hoping to pick a fight with someone. That's why it has to be Arnold who gets replaced here. There's just no way that a bunch of UFC rage erections can ever be considered a good thing.[7]

The serious and nuanced issue: As much as I love The Rock, swapping him out here for Arnold isn't a dead-even trade. No action star has ever flattened out the emotion spectrum better than Arnold Schwarzenegger. It's largely the reason a movie like *Predator* even works (and also, more obviously, why the Terminator became such an iconic movie character). Make no mistake, The Rock would be a solid stand-in, but he always emotes just a little too much for him to fit absolutely perfectly here. So:

Better, Worse, Same: Slightly worse.

1991's *Double Impact*, except with The Rock Instead

What this movie's about: Chad and Alex, twin brothers separated at birth after their parents are murdered, grow up on separate continents without knowledge that the other exists. Chad, raised in a loving home in Los Angeles, becomes a very nerdy and highfalutin adult, which you know because he parts his hair on the side and wears black silk underwear. Alex, raised in an orphanage in Hong Kong, becomes a very gritty and cool adult, which you know because he slicks his hair back and gives advice like, "Don't fuck up." Eventually they meet and then join together to defeat big players in China's crime underworld.

Who gets replaced: This was that one movie where Jean-Claude Van Damme played both brothers. So, in a very rare treat, The Rock actually gets swapped into two roles here. He's playing Chad *and* Alex.

Figuring out if the change here makes the movie better or the same or worse is a matter of math, really. If you swap out Jean-Claude Van Damme for The Rock, that means you don't get to look at Van Damme, who is more handsome than The Rock (and more handsome than every other action movie star, truly), so that's a negative. But that's really the only one I can think of. All the rest of the things are positive, the four most important of which being:

1. Chad, who runs a martial arts studio that (for some reason) also has a side room where women just stretch all day, has a scene early in the movie where he does the splits while wearing tights as he explains the importance of flexibility. The switch means you get to see The Rock do that now, which, I mean, come on. We've gotten to see The Rock make friends with a giant gorilla, defeat an earthquake, defeat a drug cartel *and* government bureaucracy at the same time, turn into a mega scorpion, barbecue human flesh,[8] commit suicide by jumping off a building, give a courtroom speech so compelling that he was cleared of all of the criminal charges he was in

---

7. We came dangerously close to this in 2011 when Vin Diesel and The Rock fought in *Fast Five*.

8. *Pain & Gain* was incredible.

court for, and be the literal tooth fairy. It's time for us to see him do the splits.[9]

2. There's a scene in the middle of the movie where Alex imagines his girlfriend having an affair with Chad. Now it's The Rock imagining his girlfriend is having an affair with The Rock, and that means we get to see The Rock having sex on the big screen. Thus far, the only sex scene we've gotten from The Rock was the one I mentioned earlier from *Ballers*. It was serviceable, but just didn't carry the panache of a movie sex scene. It felt a lot like how we had to settle for Kobe and LeBron playing against each other in the All-Star Game because we never got them in the Finals.

3. The movie ends with Chad having to fight a character named Moon. Moon is played Bolo Yeung. Bolo Yeung is the guy who played Chong Li in 1988's *Bloodsport*. That means in this new version of *Double Impact* we get to see The Rock fight Bolo Yeung, and that's basically the same as getting to see The Rock in *Bloodsport* too, and that's just great.

4. JCVD's version of Chad, all goofy and meek and doe-eyed, gets scrapped. In The Rock's version of *Double Impact*, we get two cool brothers instead of the nerdy brother/tough brother conceit. It'd be like when you put two mirrors in front of each other and they just reflect the reflection for infinity, except these mirrors have muscles and also your significant other wants to sleep with them. **Better, Worse, Same:** Better. Definitely.

1991's *My Girl*, except with The Rock Instead

What this movie's about: It's a coming of age story about an eleven-year-old girl named Vada. Many things about Vada are normal (she develops a crush on a teacher; she has a best friend who seems to be the only one who can appreciate how special she is; she's a below-average poet), but many things are not (she lives in a funeral parlor; she has somehow convinced the local doctor to see her repeatedly without ever charging her; she might be a real and actual genius). The most famous scene in the movie is when her best friend, Thomas J., gets stung to death by bees in the woods.

Who gets replaced: Thomas J.

Three things here:

First: This movie, while obviously built with one very specific goal in mind,[10] has aged surprisingly well, particularly if you watched it the first time as a child. While researching for this chapter, I went back and read through a bunch of the reviews that ran when it first came out. The most well-placed and well-pitched one was by Roger Ebert, who wrote that while *My Girl* was not without its errors, it remained "a movie that has its heart in the right place." (I agree with this, obviously, which is how it ends up in a book chapter about The Rock nearly thirty years later.) The

---

9. It was because of this scene that I spent a not insignificant stretch of my young life thinking that women were attracted to men who could do the splits. And while that very well may actually be a true thing, one thing I can say for certain is that women are not attracted to me telling them I can do the splits.

10. To make you cry.

most impactful review I read, however, was by a writer named Laura Adamczyk. She covered it in 2016 for a recurring featuring at *The A.V. Club* called "Memory Wipe" where people rewatched old movies and then wrote about them. Her review ended with this kicker, which was especially smart and powerful: "I wouldn't find a kindred spirit in gritty, realistic angst until Lauren Ambrose smoked, screamed, and photographed her way through *Six Feet Under* as Claire Fisher. But by then, I knew more about death and illness. And I could finally see that films like *My Girl* aren't fondly beloved for their veracity, but for their ability to let young people try on life's most devastating emotions before they have to live with them." This, I would argue alongside Adamczyk, is an exactly right view of *My Girl*.

Second: Macaulay Culkin played Thomas J. in *My Girl,* and a funny thing to think about is how he was able to outsmart two genuine career criminals when they were trying to break into his house in *Home Alone*[11] only to end up getting killed by bees in a freak accident a year later.[12]

Third: If we're replacing Macaulay with The Rock for the Thomas J. role, well, my friend, then let me tell you: You're going to need more than a nest of bees if you want to kill The Rock at the end of this movie. You're gonna need a fucking nest of bears.

No children die in The Rock's version of *My Girl*. As such:

Better, Worse, Same: Significantly better.

> ### 1994's *Shawshank Redemption*, except with The Rock Instead

What this movie's about: A man in prison and all of the things that go along with that.

Who gets replaced: Clancy Brown's character, Captain Byron Hadley, the hardest screw that ever walked a turn at Shawshank State Prison.

No redemptions here, sir. *Nobody* is escaping Shawshank under The Rock's watch.

Better, Worse, Same: Worse.

> ### 1997's *Titanic*, except with The Rock Instead

What this movie's about: A poor young man (Leonardo DiCaprio's Jack) and a supposed-to-be-rich young woman (Kate Winslet's Rose) fall in love after meeting on a boat. The boat hits an iceberg, causing it to sink down to the bottom of the ocean. Try as they might to live, only Rose survives. Jack freezes to death in the ocean as they await rescue.[13]

Who gets replaced: Rose, the hapless debutante.

---

11. *Home Alone* is Culkin's most everlasting movie performance. It's not his best, though. His best is as Henry in *The Good Son*.
12. I guess that's not so much "funny" as it is "sad."
13. They actually allude to how Jack is going to die in exactly this way when Jack and Rose first meet. Rose is about to jump off the back of the boat and kill herself because she's so upset with how her life is turning out. Jack sees her and intervenes. After a couple moments of chitchat, he tells her that if she jumps he's going to have to jump in after her. She says that he'll be killed if he does so. He tells her he's a good swimmer. She says that the fall alone will kill him. And he says, "It would hurt. I'm not saying it wouldn't. To tell you the truth I'm a lot more concerned about that water being so cold."

The boat still sinks, but nobody dies because everyone that was on the *Titanic* just piles onto The Rock's back and he fucking swims the rest of the way to New York. "A finer vessel than this one hath never existed," remarks a gentleman sitting atop one of The Rock's latissimus dorsi muscles as they pull into port. "Here, here," proclaims another, raising a glass of champagne into the crisp night air.

Better, Worse, Same: Better.

2007's *P.S. I Love You*, except with The Rock Instead

What this movie's about: A man (Gerry, played by Gerard Butler) finds out he has a brain tumor and is going to die. He arranges to send his wife (Holly, played by Hilary Swank) posthumous letters and gifts from him after his death at scheduled times and locations.[14] The letters and gifts are supposed to help Holly get over his death (and eventually they do), but a lot of times they seem to have the opposite effect.

Who gets replaced: Gerry.

The movie mostly stays the same all the way up until the end. In the original version, the last thing Holly receives is a letter that urges her to not be afraid to fall in love again. In The Rock's version, though, the last thing Holly receives is a gorgeous black dress. It shows up to her house via a courier service on the one year anniversary of The Rock's death. And there's a small note with it that reads:

```
Wear this tonight . . .
xoxo,
The Rock
```

She reads the note. And she looks confused. And the camera holds on her for a beat. Then it cuts away to a wide shot of the cemetery where The Rock was buried a year prior. It slowly starts to zooms in, closer and closer still to his gravesite. It pulls all the way up to it so that all you see on the screen is grass and tombstone. And it just sits there for fifteen seconds. Everything is perfectly still. You hear a tiny bird chirping in the background. The sunlight is at that perfect angle where all the colors of everything get blurred into a warm hue. A soft breeze blows a couple of leaves across the top of the grass nearby. And it's perfect and calm and serene and beautiful. AND THEN WE SEE A HAND PUNCH UP THROUGH THE EARTH. And The Rock climbs right up out of the grave. He dusts himself off a little. And despite having been dead in a coffin for fifty-two weeks, he's looks fantastic; he looks awards-show fresh, even. He looks at the camera. Smirks a bit. Then he says, "Brain tumor? More like *lame* tumor." Then he does that one eyebrow raise thing he used to do when he was a wrestler. Cut to black. Roll credits.

Better, Worse, Same: Better.

---

14. This is a very sweet thing to do, but I imagine it'd also be wildly traumatizing.

WERE THE JURASSIC PARK RAPTORS JUST Misunderstood?

THE FIRST DINOSAUR THAT GETS SHOWN IN *JURASSIC PARK* is a raptor. And the first thing we see her do is kill a man in front of his coworkers. It happens, quite literally, in the opening scene of the movie.

The situation: A group of handlers on a small island near Costa Rica are transporting a raptor from a temporary cage into a more permanent paddock. They slide the cage up against the edge of the paddock[1] and a guy climbs on top of the cage and raises up the door.[2] The hope, of course, is that the raptor will run out of the cage and into the paddock, same as a monkey would exit a smaller cage to enter a larger sanctuary. The raptor is more violent than they're anticipating, though.[3] She thrashes around, knocking the guy off the top of the cage and also knocking the cage backward, creating a small open space between the cage and the paddock.[4] She grabs ahold of the guy by his legs, drags him into her cage with her, and it's a wrap for him after that. He gets mauled to death (and possibly eaten). And so the point is established quickly: The raptors are the enemy.[5]

The movie continues forward in the same way, reiterating how dangerous and vicious raptors are whenever it can. There's a scene, for example, just a handful of minutes later where Dr. Alan Grant explains to a child at a dinosaur excavation site that raptors don't kill you before they eat you, they maim you so you can't run away and then they eat you while you're still alive. And there's a scene after that where Dr. Grant and several others are on a behind-the-scenes tour at the park. He's given a newborn dinosaur to hold. And he's very sweet and tender with it. Then he finds out it's a raptor, and he reacts like he's been told he's holding a stick of plutonium.

The first time we hear from the grizzled and gnarly game warden at the park, he says of the raptors, "They should all be destroyed." (He walks up on the group as they watch a cow get dropped into the raptor paddock and then shredded to ribbon.) We're told that they're "lethal" at just eight months of age; that they can run upward of sixty miles per hour; that they're "astonishing" jumpers; that they are extremely intelligent; that they hunt in highly organized packs; that they're overseen by "the Big One," a raptor of such might and ferocity that, upon being introduced to the existing group of raptors, she killed all but two in a show of power as she took over the pride. "That one," says the game warden, "when she looks at you, you can see she's working things out."

More things happen during *Jurassic Park* to really bang home the point (the most telling of which being that Dennis Nedry, the corrupt IT guy who hacks the park's security system so that he can smuggle out

---

1. The people who push the cage up against the paddock are called the "Pushing Team," which is hilarious to me.
2. He's called the "Gatekeeper," which is also hilarious to me. I keep picturing some recruiter trying to sell him on the job, being very mysterious and mystical about the situation. And then when he asks what the Gatekeeper is actually responsible for, the recruiter is like, "Huh? Oh, basically you just open a gate."
3. This should not have been a surprise, given that IT'S A FUCKING RAPTOR.
4. I have a lot of questions about this scene, the most relevant of which being: You mean to tell me you've unlocked the science behind re-creating creatures that have been dead for tens of millions of years but you can't figure out how to make a cage that doesn't require a person climbing on top of it to open a gate?
5. This paragraph is the most amount of times in my life I have used the word "paddock."

some dinosaur embryos, makes absolutely certain not to affect the electric fences that held the raptors in place), and by the end of the movie we're left with at least one unquestionable thought: The *Tyrannosaurus rex* might be the big-ticket item during a dinosaur renaissance, but it's the raptors that are the most deadly, the most unforgiving, the most evil, and who we should fear above all.

But let me offer you a counterpoint: What if they're not? What if the raptors in *Jurassic Park* were just misunderstood? Because think on this: Between the release of *Jurassic Park* in 1993 and today,[6] four more movies have been added to the *Jurassic Park* franchise.[7] And over the course of those movies, the reputation of the raptors has shifted completely.

In 1997's *The Lost World: Jurassic Park*, the raptors were still presented as villainous, though only situationally so; mostly, they just wanted to be left alone. In 2001's *Jurassic Park III*, the raptors hunted a group of humans, but only because one of the humans had stolen a raptor egg. (A piece of evidence to show how nonthreatening the raptors were: After the humans gave them back the stolen raptor egg, the raptors left. They didn't even bother to bite them or scratch them or anything. They just scooped up the egg and ran away.) In 2015's *Jurassic World*, raptors were not only working in conjunction with humans to stop a hybrid super dinosaur, but sacrificing their lives to do so.[8] And by 2018's *Jurassic World: Fallen Kingdom*, a human (Owen Grady, played by Chris Pratt) and a raptor (Blue, played by Blue) were basically a buddy cop duo. (There's a part where Grady says to Blue, "Hey, girl. You thinking what I'm thinking," right before they tag team up together in a fight.)

———

The illustration to the right is a picture of two raptors getting baptized by John the Baptist. This being a chapter about raptor redemption, it made sense to do something like for the accompanying art. However, three pages from now there's another illustration. And it doesn't have anything to do with raptors or redemption. It's Leatherface from the *The Texas Chainsaw Massacre* getting a massage. I wish I had a good explanation for why we did it, but I don't. It's just a thing I wanted to see Arturo draw. So there you go.

(An extremely tenuous linking relationship between the two could be that the raptors and Leatherface have very violently killed a number of people. Also, Leatherface is ugly and so are the raptors. Also, Leatherface had a family so I guess that means he was a pack hunter like the raptors were.[9])

———

---

6. February 11, 2019.

7. At the moment, a sixth movie—*Jurassic World III*—is supposed to be released in 2021.

8. Watching *Jurassic World* in a theater in 2015 is one of my five favorite ever movie theater experiences. The part at the end where Blue, the star raptor of the movie that you think has been killed, comes running back on screen to join in the big final dinosaur fight is perfect.

9. I'm doing a lot of work here to talk myself into this idea.

There are nine things that the raptors do in *Jurassic Park* that we have to be able to explain away if we're going to successfully argue the position that they're misunderstood and not actually terrible murdering monsters. Let's do them in the order that they happen. There's:

The time that one raptor in the start of the movie that I was talking about at the beginning of this chapter kills that guy. You could go a few different directions. You could say that the raptor was scared and just acting out of self-preservation. You could say that she's a wild creature and wild creatures aren't meant to be caged and so since they aren't meant to be caged then anything that happens while people are trying to cage them is beyond the creature's control. You could say that she was simply trying to discipline the gatekeeper for not doing his job very well and that maybe this is all just a case of the meaning of an action getting lost in translation, like that one scene in *Smallfoot* when the Yeti tries to take care of the human but he's so much bigger and stronger than the human that he accidentally knocks a few of his teeth out when he touches his face. I'm going with that one. I'm going with the lost in translation defense here.

The time the raptors kill Ray Arnold (Samuel L. Jackson's character). These are the facts that we know, because these are the facts that we are shown: (1) Ray Arnold decides he's going to try to make his way across the compound from the control room to the maintenance shed because he knows that's where he has to go to get the power to come back on. (2) Ray Arnold heads out into the wild knowing that the power is out, and that many dangerous dinosaurs are roaming around ungoverned. (3) Ray Arnold dies.

That's it. Those are all the facts. Everything else is just speculation. What we don't know, because what we are not shown, is: Who's the dinosaur responsible for Ray's death? When we see Ray, he's already dead. We don't ever see the actual attack. We're left to assume that it's the raptors because it's a raptor who we see running around in the maintenance room. But what about the *Tyrannosaurus rex*? Or that one dinosaur with the neck that opens up like an umbrella that killed Dennis Nedry? Why are they not suspects? And besides, think about any movie where someone is wrongfully accused of murder. It's almost always that same kind of situation as what we've found the raptors in here. A guy comes home from work or the bar or whatever and finds his wife dead on the floor. He bends down near her and he can't believe what he's looking at and everything is terrible and the police show up and are convinced it was him who did it and you're sitting there like, "Man, if I was one of those cops I'd know he wasn't the killer." And look at you now. Doing exactly that with the raptors.

The time the raptor chases after Dr. Ellie Sattler in the maintenance room to try and kill her. This happens after Dr. Sattler is able to turn the power back on to get the park's security systems operational again. And that's key here because I don't think the raptor was trying to kill Dr. Sattler. I think the raptor was trying to celebrate with Dr. Sattler. It was probably scared and knew that the *Tyrannosaurus rex* was out there somewhere and it just wanted everything to go back to normal. It was smart enough to make its way to the maintenance shed because it knew that's where you had to go to turn the power back on, but it didn't have the kind of physical dexterity needed to prime the pump that needed to be primed before everything could be switched back on. The raptor saw Dr. Sattler do it, and when she realized that the power was back and that the humans were going to make everything safe again she just wanted to give Dr. Sattler a hug. And you can say, "Shea, that thing was clearly trying to attack her. Did you even look at her face?" And to that I would say, "I have a friend I've known for several years who looks quite menacing. It's just the natural state of his face. His eyebrows are turned downward and his mouth is in a constant snarl and he has an aggressive haircut. Everything he does looks more ill willed than it actually is. When he goes in to give you a hug, it looks like he's going to strangle you. But he's a sweetheart. Just like these raptors are."

The time the raptors teamed up to kill the game warden. Two things: First, assuming the raptors are acting maliciously here, this one's really on the game warden. They make a big fuss about how he's supposed to know more about raptors than anyone on the planet, but he doesn't remember that the raptors' basic hunting strategy is to have one raptor be a decoy while another raptor sneak attacks you from the side? He has to wear a lot of the blame here. It's like, you don't blame the sharks if a guy who works with sharks for a living decides one day to hop into the shark tank wearing a belt made of chunks of fish and they accidentally eat him.

Second, the raptors were operating out of self-defense here. The park was in disarray; the raptors were scared; one of them noticed that a guy who had been arguing since the beginning of the movie that all the raptors should be killed was suddenly in their area

with a gigantic raptor-killing gun. What else would you have them do there? Lie down and die?

The time the raptors tried to kill and eat the two children (Tim and Lex) in the kitchen. The one raptor goes charging at Lex's reflection in the kitchen, but that's only because she saw that Lex looked like she was trapped in a cabinet when Lex was trying to hide. And the other raptor chases after Tim as he goes running toward the freezer in the kitchen, but actually the raptor was trying to help Tim because Tim had hurt his leg and was hobbling and the one thing we definitely do know for sure about raptors is that they are very protective of their young and so maybe that's what was going on here?

The time the raptor tried to kill and eat Tim and Lex and Dr. Grant and Dr. Sattler as it chased them into the control room. The one raptor tried to break into the control panel after Tim and Lex went in there with Dr. Grant and Dr. Sattler, sure, but, again, she probably thought the children were in danger because Dr. Grant had a gun.

And let's not forget that earlier in the movie Dr. Grant was handling a newborn raptor. The full-grown raptor chasing them probably caught that scent on his hands as well. I think seeing the gun and smelling the infant raptor was more than enough to establish probable cause regarding a perceived intent to harm.

The time raptors tried to kill and eat Tim and Lex and Dr. Grant and Dr. Sattler as they chased them through the ductwork. It looks like the one raptor tries to bite Lex's legs off as she's dangling from the ductwork in the ceiling. But I don't think the raptor was actually trying to bite her. I think the raptor was

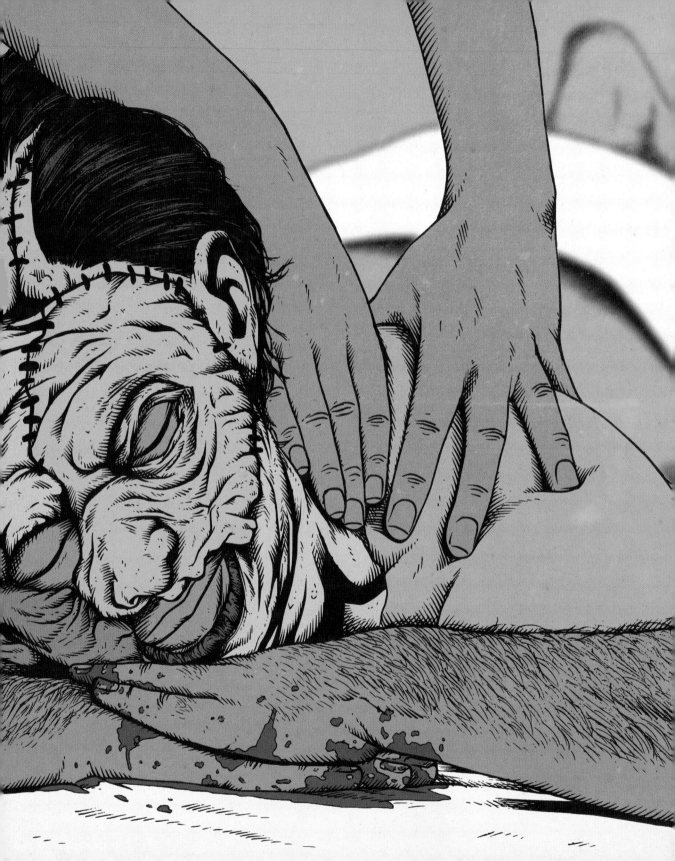

trying to help up back up into the duct so that she wouldn't fall. She was trying to give her a boost.

The time the raptors tried to kill and eat Tim and Lex and Dr. Grant and Dr. Sattler as they chased them into the foyer area where the dinosaur skeletons were hanging from the ceiling. The two raptors jump on the floating dinosaur skeletons in the foyer area as they chase everyone, but, yet again, I think this was more a case of them trying to save the kids than anything else, like how a mom climbs up into a tree to rescue a kid who's climbed too high. (And if not that, then maybe the raptors thought the humans were playing a game and just wanted to join in. Like, maybe they realized that the humans couldn't understand their raptor language and so they were trying to bond by playing whatever it was that they thought the humans were playing?)

And the time the raptors tried to kill and eat Tim and Lex and Dr. Grant and Dr. Sattler when they had them surrounded in the foyer area. The two raptors surround the children and Dr. Grant and Sattler in the foyer area, but, one last time, I suspect that's because they still thought that Dr. Grant and Dr. Sattler were going to hurt the children. Because think on this: The *Tyrannosaurus rex* comes in and attacks and kills one of the raptors during the standoff. And the second raptor, who easily could've picked off one of the humans in the group while they're distracted and then gotten away easily if she'd have wanted to do that, didn't use that time to kill any humans. Instead, she attacked the *Tyrannosaurus rex*, and she did so because the *Tyrannosaurus rex* was suddenly the biggest threat to the children in the room.

And if you've grown tired of the "They were trying to save the children" angle, then how about this one: John Hammond, the huggable old man billionaire who created the park, makes mention during the tour of the park of how he likes to be there for the birth of every dinosaur because the dinosaurs always imprint on whoever the first person (or dinosaur) is that they come in contact with. So what if everything the raptors do in the movie is because of that? What if they kept picking up scents of Hammond on everyone and panicked and thought that the people harmed Hammond somehow? They went the hardest after the kids, which makes sense because the kids had the most of Hammond's scent on them from when he was hugging them. And they went the second hardest after the game warden and Dr. Sattler, which also makes sense because they spent all that time with him in the control room when everything was on lockdown. We can't ignore that that's a possibility here, too.

So you take the kids angle, and the Hammond angle, and the lost in translation angle, and the way the general raptor arc changed over the course of the film franchise, and I think it's easy to say: The *Jurassic Park* raptors were just misunderstood.

WHAT'S THE ORDER OF THE

GANGSTER
MOVIE MOMENT

FICTIONAL DRAFT?

PART 1

IS *PULP FICTION* A GANGSTER MOVIE? It feels like it is, but also it feels like it isn't. And I think it's Ray Liotta's fault.

Liotta wasn't in *Pulp Fiction*, but he was in *Goodfellas*, the minute-for-minute greatest gangster movie that's ever been. And there's this line that he has in there that is exactly perfect, and because it's so exactly perfect it has aged into archetype, reframing everything, at least instinctually (and possibly intellectually). What I mean is: The line happens right near the beginning of the movie. Liotta's character, Henry Hill, is standing at the back of a car at night in the woods and he takes a couple steps toward it to close the trunk (there's a dead body inside of there, because there's always a dead body inside of there). As he reaches up to slam the trunk shut, we hear him start to narrate the scene. "As far back as I can remember," he begins, and if you need for me to finish that line for you then I fear you may have purchased the wrong book.[1]

But because he describes himself as a "gangster" there, and because *Goodfellas* is an all-time top-level brilliant movie, the phrase "gangster movie" since then has (for me, anyway) come to mean something close to, "A movie where some people, likely Italian though occasionally not, participate in various mafia and mafia-adjacent things." But I'm not so sure "gangster movie" means exactly that, really. Because do you actually need the mafia (or a version of the mafia) in a movie for it to be a gangster movie? No, right?

And it's more than just saying, "Well, if the crime is organized, *then* it's a gangster movie," because if that's the case then what about, say, the Joker and his crew in 1989's *Batman*? They were very organized, but nobody would ever call *Batman* a "gangster movie." And it's also more than just saying, "Well, if there are gang members in a movie, then it's a gangster movie," because if that's the case then what about, say, 1978's *Grease*? Danny Zuko and the rest of the T-Birds were a gang, but nobody would ever call *Grease* a "gangster movie." And I know that those are extreme examples, but they're examples nonetheless.[2]

So it's more than that. It's more subtle than that. It's more intricate than that. There are so many parts and pieces to peruse.[3]

The best explanation I got for what is or is not a gangster movie while I was working on this section of the book came from a friend of mine I worked briefly with. He said, "A gangster movie is a gangster movie when you know it's a gangster movie." And that's a bit vague, sure, but it's also very specific. I knew exactly what he meant when he said it, as I'm sure you right now

---

1. "As far back as I can remember I always wanted to be a gangster."
2. A fun aside: Henry Hill talks about wanting to be a gangster as he's dealing with a dead body in a car. Jules Winnfield, who works for crime boss Marsellus Wallace in *Pulp Fiction*, refers to himself (and his partner) as gangsters while he's on the phone with Wallace talking to him about what to do with a dead body they have in their car.
3. Is *Gangs of New York* a gangster film? (Maybe, but probably not.) Is *New Jack City* a gangster film? (Absolutely.) Is *Training Day* a gangster movie? (No.) Is *Snatch* a gangster movie? (Barely, but yes.) Is *Belly* a gangster movie? (Yes.) Is *Blood In, Blood Out* a gangster movie? (It has gangs and also it has what amounts to the movie version of the Mexican mafia in it, but no.) More, more, more.

know exactly what he meant when you read it.[4] And so that's going to be the general guideline for the movies that are eligible to be discussed during these next three chapters, because these next three chapters make up the Gangster Movie Moment Fictional Draft, a thing where we're selecting moments from gangster movies similar (in spirit, anyway) to how the NBA selects players on draft night each summer.[5]

———

There are five rules in place to (hopefully) help make sure the Gangster Movie Moment Fictional Draft is robust and interesting.

1. **THE FRANK COSTELLO RULE:** There are going to be thirty picks in this draft. And thirty sounds like a lot, but definitely it is not, and that's a thing you figure out when you start writing down all of your favorite gangster movie moments and you get to twenty or twenty-one picks and realize you've only gone through two movies. So, as a way to prevent the draft from being overwhelmed by a single movie, this rule establishes the edict that no movie can be used more than twice in the draft. If you want to use the texting scene from *The Departed* and the "My theory on Feds" scene from *The Departed*, then go for it. But that's it. No other

scenes from that movie are eligible after it's been mentioned twice. It's like that with all the movies.

2. **THE *HEAT* RULE:** *Heat* isn't a gangster movie. It's a heist movie. (*Reservoir Dogs*, however, which uses a heist gone wrong as the catalyst for the plot, *is* a gangster movie. Go figure.)

3. ***THE GODFATHER* RULE:** The history of gangster movie cinema stretches all the way back to early 1930s. But our draft, same as the NBA's draft, has age restrictions. No movie that came out before *The Godfather* (1972) is eligible.

4. **THE ROBERT DE NIRO RULE:** Robert De Niro is, no question about it, the greatest gangster movie actor of all time. His catalog is just too deep, too strong, too undeniable. That being the case, even if you stick strictly to the Frank Costello Rule (no movie can be used more than twice) you likely still end up with an extremely De Niro–heavy final draft order. Really, even if you modify the Frank Costello Rule and make it so that you can use each movie once, you're still going to end up with a bunch of De Niro picks. (I mean, you HAVE TO have that scene in *The Godfather: Part II* when Vito Corleone slices up Don Ciccio, and you HAVE TO have that scene in *Casino* when Ace Rothstein has his hoodlums smash the guy's hand to bits after they catch him and his friend cheating, and you HAVE TO have

---

4. There's a book I like called *The Ultimate Book of Gangster Movies* by George Anastasia and Glen Macnow. In it, they walk front to back through what they argue are the hundred best gangster movies of all time. They tackle the topic of figuring out what is or isn't a gangster movie in the foreword, eventually settling on a similar verdict, saying they chose to go with "U.S. Supreme Court Justice Potter Stewart's inarguable characterization of pornography: 'I know it when I see it.'"

5. We did a similar thing in *Basketball (and Other Things)*, except we were picking basketball players from movies and TV shows. It's always one of my favorite things to do. It makes me feel like Kevin Costner in *Draft Day* when he was trying to figure out who to draft for his Cleveland Browns. I always respected that he chose Vontae Mack with the first pick. It took guts to do that, what with several seemingly bigger and better players available. I didn't make a Vontae Mack–style pick anywhere in the *Basketball (and Other Things)* draft, but I'm going to do it somewhere in here.

the scene in *A Bronx Tale* when Lorenzo stands up to Sonny for the first time, and you HAVE TO have the scene in *The Untouchables* when Al Capone bashes the guy's head in with a baseball bat, and you HAVE TO have the grave scene in *Once Upon a Time in America*, and you HAVE TO . . .) So here's the rule: Robert De Niro is off the table. He can't be the primary character of any scene that gets chosen. He can be a side character or a background character, but not the main one. And I know that that sucks a lot, but an easy way to think about it is by remembering how they didn't include Michael Jordan in the NBA JAM video game. That's what this is. The greatest basketball player of all time got left out of the greatest basketball game of all time. The greatest gangster movie actor of all time got left out of the greatest gangster movie moments draft of all time. Same thing.

5. **THE KLEINFELD RULE:** I understand that death is more necessary a part of gangster movies than nearly every other part. I get that. I really do. But I just don't want to waste a lot of energy thinking about the way many of my favorite movie characters died in their movies. So death scenes, same as De Niro, are off the table here, too. And to be clear, I'm *only* talking about the deaths of key characters. Moments or scenes where someone is killing an inessential person are fine. So, for example, Tony dying at the end of *Scarface* would not be an allow-

able pick (neither would Tony killing Manny, for that matter[6]), but Frank Lucas shooting Stringer Bell in the head in front of everyone *would* be fine.[7]

No. 30 Pick: The "Look in your heart" scene from *Miller's Crossing* in 1990.
Main Characters in the Scene: Tom Reagan and Bernie Bernbaum

Sometimes I'll watch a movie and say to myself, "I bet if I was 20 percent smarter I'd have really liked this." *Miller's Crossing*, which is about a lot of things but really it's about comeuppance, is one of those movies. And I don't want for it to seem like I didn't like *Miller's Crossing*, because I did, it's just that maybe I'd have liked it more if I'd have worked harder in college, is what I'm saying.

At any rate, the scene that gets drafted into the thirtieth spot here is the one where Tom Reagan, a gun-for-hire trying to prove his worth to a new crew, is tasked with killing Bernie Bernbaum, a low-grade bookie played to jumpy brilliance by John Turturro.[8] Tom is walking Bernie out into the woods to shoot him in his head,[9] and Bernie, as he should be, is in a total panic. And he's just begging and pleading and crying the whole time they're walking. He pleads to Tom's sense of center ("Tommy, you can't do this! You don't bump guys!"), and he pleads to Tom's sense of logic ("I

---

6. Should Manny have seen this coming? He should have, right?

7. I know the character that Frank Lucas shoots in the head right here isn't really named Stringer Bell (his name is Tango), but it's just that Idris Elba is always going to be Stringer Bell.

8. John Turturro has, for many years, been one of my favorite actors. He has this odd ability to tune in perfectly to whatever frequency it is that a role needs.

9. "Now you know how to do this, right? You gotta remember to put one in his brain. The first shot puts him down, then you put one in his brain. Then he's dead. Then we go home."

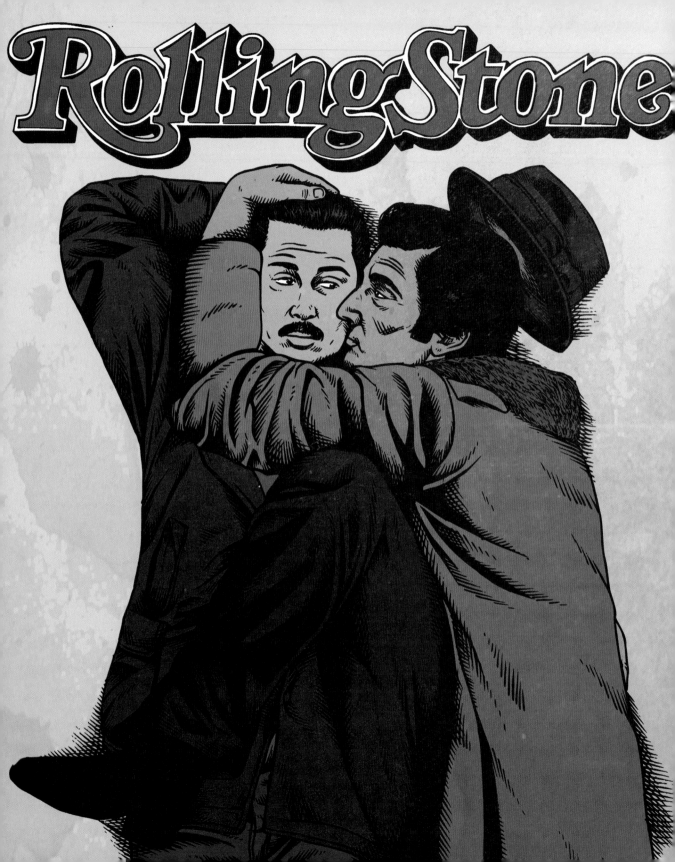

never killed anybody! It [was] just a little information!"), and he pleads to Tom's sense of reason ("I'm just a grifter, Tom! I'm a nobody!"), and he pleads to Tom's sense of heart ("I'm praying to you! I can't die! I can't die! Out here in the woods! Like a dumb animal!"). And as they walk—it's over a full minute—Bernie becomes more and more hysterical, and Tom becomes more and more distant, isolated, withdrawn. It's this great balance between the two of them.

Bernie, who is such a wreck that his legs won't work anymore, drops to his knees and he just keeps crying out, "I'm praying to you! Look in your heart! I'm praying to you! Look in your heart!" And Tom brings his gun up, and he aims it square at Bernie's forehead, and the camera pulls in tight on Tom, and then it cuts to Bernie, whose eyes are closed and his hands are raised in mercy, and then it cuts back to Tom, and the music builds, and Builds, BUILDS, and then . . . *BANG!* The gunshot.

And the camera moves back to Bernie to show his dead body, only except Bernie's not dead. Tom shot into the ground next to him. Bernie opens his eyes slowly and realizes he is still alive, and his whole mood changes. "Tom," he begins, before Tom cuts him off. "Shut up. You're dead. Get that?" says Tom.

And Tom keeps talking and Bernie keeps interrupting him but eventually they get through it. And they have this whole talk afterward about how Tom wants Bernie to ditch town and disappear so he can stay alive, and Bernie agrees but of course he doesn't and ends up fucking up everything. But it's no matter. It's that moment in the woods when Turturro turns on

the big acting engines that really feels special. And so it's the moment that starts off this draft.[10]

No. 29 Pick: The "fuggedaboutit" scene from *Donnie Brasco* in 1997.
Main Characters in the Scene: Donnie Brasco

Joseph Pistone, an FBI agent working undercover as Donnie Brasco, is sitting in a room with two unnamed FBI technicians. (One of the technicians is played by Paul Giamatti. Giamatti had three unnamed roles in 1997. He was an FBI technician in *Donnie Brasco*, a bellman in *My Best Friend's Wedding*, and a hotel clerk in *The Break*. It was a big unnamed year for him.) They're all sitting there listening to tape that Brasco has secretly recorded. During a break, Giamatti's character, in this very sweet way, says to Brasco, "Hey, can I ask you something?" Brasco agrees. Giamatti says, "What's 'fuggedaboutit'? What is that?"

Brasco, who by this point is plugged all the way into gangster life, smiles a tiny smile at the naivete. Then he goes through several different meanings the word can have, each one based on context and tone. "It's like, uh, if you agree with someone, you know. Like, 'Raquel Welch is one great piece of ass.' *Fuggedaboutit*. But then, if you disagree, like, 'A Lincoln is better than a Cadillac.' *Fuggedaboutit*. You know. But then, it's also like if something is the greatest thing in the world, like, 'Mingia, those peppers . . . *fuggedaboutit*.' But it's also like saying, 'Go to hell,' too. Like, you know, like, uh, 'Hey, Paulie. You got a one-inch

---

10. Tom ends up killing Bernie later in the movie because Bernie tries to blackmail Tom with his own pretend death. Tom should've shot Bernie in the woods the first time. It'd have saved everyone a lot of trouble.

NEVER RAT ON YOUR FRIENDS AND ALWAYS KEEP YOUR MOUTH SHUT

ROBERT DE NIRO'S BEST GANGSTER MOVIE ROLES, CHARTED

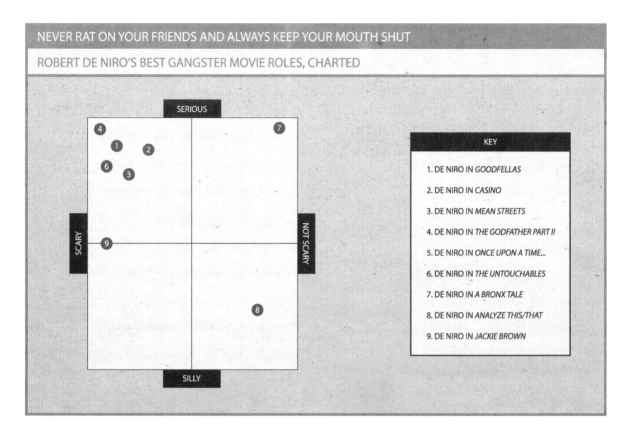

KEY

1. DE NIRO IN *GOODFELLAS*

2. DE NIRO IN *CASINO*

3. DE NIRO IN *MEAN STREETS*

4. DE NIRO IN *THE GODFATHER PART II*

5. DE NIRO IN *ONCE UPON A TIME...*

6. DE NIRO IN *THE UNTOUCHABLES*

7. DE NIRO IN *A BRONX TALE*

8. DE NIRO IN *ANALYZE THIS/THAT*

9. DE NIRO IN *JACKIE BROWN*

pecker.' And Paulie says, '*Fuggedaboutit.*' Sometimes it just means, 'Forget about it.'"

It's a scene that touches on the intricacies and thoroughness of gangster life, but also one that hints at the occasional ineptitude of the people who are supposed to be catching the criminals. (I don't understand how the two guys you have whose job is to parse the recordings Brasco is bringing in can't on their own figure out what "fuggedaboutit" means. Remember that one scene in the TV show *The Wire* when Caroline is listening to the phone calls via wiretap and is translating all the slang that's being used? The FBI should've hired her for

the Brasco case. That shit would've been down in six weeks.)

> **No. 28 Pick:** The bar fight scene from *Legend* in 2015.
> **Main Characters in the Scene:** Reggie and Ronnie Kray

The way you get my money is you say you've made a gangster movie where Tom Hardy is playing twin brothers, one of which is a former boxer, the other of which is a paranoid schizophrenic, both of which are capable of barbarism. Then you say that the twin brothers get into fight with eight other men at once in a bar. Then you say that the boxer brother is wearing brass knuckles during the fight, and that the paranoid schizophrenic brother is using two hammers during the fight. Then you say that, after the other men have been beaten, the paranoid schizophrenic brother is going from person to person, smashing in kneecaps with one of the hammers while the boxer brother drinks a beer and watches. And that's when I say, "That sounds great, thank you. How much are tickets? Are they $100,000 each? Because if so, then that's quite the deal. I'll take ten please."

> **No. 27 Pick:** The "I wanna shoot you..." scene from *New Jack City* in 1991.
> **Main Characters in the Scene:** Scotty Appleton and Nino Brown

Ice-T plays a cop named Scotty Appleton who goes undercover to infiltrate a crime syndicate run by Nino Brown (Wesley Snipes), a brilliant criminal tactician with a black heart. (His most dastardly moment is discussed at a later point in the draft.) When Scotty and Nino finally have their big fight scene at the end of the movie, Scotty beats Nino senseless. And as Nino is lying on the floor in a pile of trash,[11] Scotty takes the gun out of his partner's hands, points it at Nino, then, and he's so overcome by the moment he's shaking, he growls, "I wanna shoot you so bad my dick's hard,"

which has got to be the most anyone has ever wanted to shoot anyone.

> **No. 26 Pick:** The "Aw, man, I shot Marvin in the face" scene from *Pulp Fiction* in 1994.
> **Main Characters in the Scene:** Vincent Vega, Jules Winnfield, Marvin

This will either be a thing where you read it and say (a) "YOU ARE A MASSIVE IDIOT," or (b) "YES ME TOO," but: I've never really cared for *Pulp Fiction*. It's a good movie, sure, of course, definitely. But as an entire product, or as a piece of work to be consumed in its entirety, it's just never been a movie where I felt like I needed to sit down and watch it again and again and again from front to back.

If I'm scrolling through the channels on TV and it happens to be on a part that I enjoy—the "Say 'what' again" scene; the scene where Mrs. Wallace dances with Vincent Vega; the Winston Wolf scene; any scene that involves a conversation at a table, especially a diner table, etc.—then yes, absolutely, no doubt, I will stop and watch it for a few minutes. But if it's not one of those, then I don't. It's less a movie in my head and more a collection of YouTube clips, if that makes any sense. It's a Highlight Reel Movie.

The Marvin scene is unequivocally great, though. *Pulp Fiction* is a gangster movie.

---

11. SYMBOLISM!

WHAT'S THE ORDER OF THE

GANGSTER MOVIE MOMENT

FICTIONAL DRAFT?

PART 2

. . . CONT'D

No. 25 Pick: The diner scene from *A History of Violence* in 2005.

Main Characters in the Scene: Tom Stall, otherwise known as Joey Cusack; a couple of hoodlums

In *A History of Violence*, Viggo Mortensen plays Tom Stall, an unassuming diner owner in Small Town, America. One night, as the diner is preparing to close up, two street toughs come in and start causing trouble. Stall, who's hoping to avoid any sort of confrontation, meekly gives in to their demands, offering them whatever little money that the diner happens to have earned that night. When it looks like one of the men is going to kill a waitress, though, everything about Tom changes. His eyes tighten; his bones strengthen; his menace gets increased by 100,000 percent. He smashes one of the men in the side of the head with a pot of hot coffee, hops over the diner counter, grabs a gun that the coffee'd bad guy dropped, fires several shots into the second man's chest, then spins around and shoots the first guy in the top of the head.

The whole fight takes eighteen seconds, but it ends up turning Tom's life into madness. Because, as it turns out, he's not really Tom Stall. That's just a fake name he gave himself years ago. His real name is Joey Cusack, and he's a former hit man for a mob operating in Philadelphia. The mobsters see Tom on the news being celebrated as a hero, and so several of them go there and terrorize him and his family, all while he tries to keep pretending that he's Tom. The diner scene is not my favorite scene in the movie,[1] or even my second favorite scene, really.[2] But it's the most important one because it functions as the thrust of the plot. That's why it's getting drafted here.

No. 24 Pick: The bathhouse fight from *Eastern Promises* in 2007.

Main Characters in the Scene: Nikolai Luzhin; two Chechen hit men

This is the Viggo Mortensen section of the GMMFD, it would appear. He plays Nikolai in *Eastern Promises*, and there's a scene in it where two people try to attack him in a bathhouse, and it's a four-minute-long fight that Nikolai does entirely naked. And listen, I don't want to be too direct here, but, I mean, if you've got the opportunity to draft Viggo Mortensen's dick, then you draft Viggo Mortensen's dick. You don't want to overthink things and end up taking a Darko Milicic dick when a Carmelo Anthony dick was there on the table.

---

1. My favorite scene is when he ends up back in Philadelphia at the end of the movie. He's sitting across from his gangster brother, who had to suffer through the blowback of Tom/Joey leaving. Tom says that he's there to make peace. His brother says no, that he has to die, and then a guy standing behind Tom tries to strangle Tom with a piece of thin rope or wire like an idiot instead of shooting him in the back of the head like a non-idiot. Tom, of course, fights his way out of the room, killing two of his brother's men on the way out, one of which he stomps in the throat.

2. My second favorite scene is when Tom finally admits that he's Joey. He holds on to that lie for long enough that you really start to feel like maybe it's all just a big case of mistaken identity. Hearing him say he really is Joey is very satisfying.

No. 23 Pick: Gina and Manny during the car ride from *Scarface* in 1983.
Main Characters in the Scene: Gina Montana, Manny Ribera, Tony Montana

No. 22 Pick: The baby-carriage-down-the-stairs scene from *The Untouchables* in 1987.
Main Characters in the Scene: Eliot Ness; George Stone; Walter Payne

This is the scene that happens after Tony sees Gina at the club dancing with Fernando, a handsy and unlikable guy who invites her into the restroom so they can do cocaine and kiss in a bathroom stall.[3] Tony busts in and throws Fernando out of the restroom and has a big fight with Gina and then tells Manny to drive her home. While Manny and Gina are in the car, we get to see the two of them talk through the events of the evening, and it's this sweet, tender scene where Manny is explaining that Gina is the only good thing Tony has left in his life. (His point is magnified here because, as Manny and Gina are riding home, the camera is cutting back and forth between them and Tony, who is sitting in the club all alone while two guys get ready to try and murder him.)

As they're talking, Gina says that she likes Fernando, that "he's a fun guy and he's nice. And he knows how to treat a woman, all right?" Manny, the most personable and charming person in *Scarface*, absorbs what she says, measures it up against what he's seen that night, then asks, "*He* knows how to treat a woman?" She says yes. And Manny, in the best and most adorable way possible, says back, "By taking you to the *toilet* to make out?" It's a great line, and one of the movie's most purely pleasant moments, and watching it again after knowing what happens to him later makes it feel surprisingly tragic.[4]

Four things here:

1. The baseball bat scene is ineligible on account of the Robert De Niro rule.

2. There's a scene in *The Untouchables* where Sean Connery's character, Jimmy Malone, tricks a bad guy into giving up some information in a clever way. He picks up a dead guy and starts to interrogate him in front of the bad guy he's hoping will eventually talk. (The bad guy Malone's hoping will eventually talk doesn't know that the guy Malone is holding up is already dead.) Malone makes a big deal about Dead Guy refusing to talk, then shoots him in the head, making Bad Guy think he's just killed Dead Guy for not talking. Bad Guy immediately begins talking. It's a neat trick, and the interrogation was the only other scene I considered picking here. The baby carriage part is just a little more iconic, though, which is why it gets the nod.

3. It's surprising how inert *The Untouchables* feels when you rewatch it. There's just no real get-up-and-go to it. *Public Enemies*, which starred Johnny Depp as the famed bank robber John Dillinger, has the same sort of feel.

4. That baby carriage really feels like it was tumbling down those train station steps for, like, forty-five minutes straight.

---

3. This sounds like a terrible date, but also it sounds like kind of an excellent date.
4. Manny and Gina would've made for a great couple, I suspect.

MOVIES (AND OTHER THINGS)

> **No. 21 Pick:** Bullet Tooth Tony's introduction from *Snatch* in 2000 and Rory Breaker's fire extinguisher story from *Lock, Stock and Two Smoking Barrels* in 1998.
> **Main Characters in the Scene(s):** Bullet Tooth Tony; Rory Breaker

I'm cheating here. Sorry. I just really, really, really, really like the scenes they do in gangster movies where they introduce new characters, and I especially, especially, especially, especially like when they do it for characters who are supposed to be threatening or terrifying.

With Bullet Tooth Tony, twin sisters introduce him into the *Snatch* universe by telling a story about how one time he got shot six times in the chest and never even went down to the ground. Immediately after that, they cut to Tony's phone ringing in his car, then the camera cuts to a different angle to show that he's in the middle of crushing a guy's skull by smashing it with a car door over and over again.

With Rory Breaker, a guy introduces him into the *Lock, Stock and Two Smoking Barrels* universe by telling a story about how he one time spit alcohol on a guy in a bar and then set him on fire in front of everyone because the guy was interrupting his viewing of a soccer match. (The best part of the story is that Rory, moments before he set the guy on fire, took the bar's fire extinguisher off the wall and set it outside so that nobody would be able to quickly rescue the guy as he burned.)[5]

Nobody has ever introduced me with a cool story like either of these. The closest I've gotten is one time one of my neighbors was talking to a different neighbor and I came up in the conversation and one of them said to the other something like, "Yeah, you remember him. He's the guy who fell backward into the bush that one afternoon because he thought a bee was gonna sting him in the head."

> **No. 20 Pick:** The opening scene from *Belly* in 1998.
> **Main Characters in the Scene:** Buns; Sin; Mark; a black light

Belly is not a very good movie. But the opening scene, which shows Buns (played by DMX right before he became a global star) and Sin (played by Nas, four years after he'd become a true rap icon), and Mark (played by Wee-Bey from *The Wire*, four years before he shot Detective Greggs) and one other person robbing a nightclub, is unforgettable, and kinetic, and massive, and auspicious, and exactly the kind of thing you're hoping to see when you sit down to watch a movie starring DMX and Nas directed by Hype Williams.

> **No. 19 Pick:** The part from *Carlito's Way* in 1993 when Carlito doesn't kill Benny Blanco after they get into an argument at the club.
> **Main Characters in the Scene:** Carlito; Benny Blanco; Pachanga

First, let me say that John Leguizamo is fantastic as the fiery, aggressive, disrespectful, confrontational

---

5. The guy who played Bullet Tooth Tony in *Snatch* (Vinnie Jones) plays a similar character in *Lock, Stock and Two Smoking Barrels.* There's even a scene where he bashes a guy's head in with a car door. (Guy Ritchie directed both movies.)

Benny Blanco. He's the best part of the movie, which is not often a thing you say about someone other than Al Pacino in an Al Pacino movie.[6]

Second, same as with the new character introductions thing that I mentioned earlier, I really enjoy the part in gangster movies where someone either does a thing or does not do a thing and it ends up having some big effect later on, and that's exactly what happens here. Benny and Carlito get into an argument in the club, and then it moves into the bowels of the club, where Benny tells Carlito that he should just go ahead and kill him right there because if he ever sees Carlito again he's going to kill him. Carlito bonks him in the head, sending him tumbling down a flight of stairs, then has two of his henchmen leave Blanco in the alley instead of killing him because Carlito is trying to not be that kind of person anymore.

And then, of course, Benny ends up killing Carlito later during the movie's big finish, because that's how these sorts of things always work out.[7]

No. 18 Pick: The Li'l Zé origin story from *City of God* in 2002.
Main Characters in the Scene: Li'l Zé

This is a dumb thing, but it's a true thing: I didn't watch *City of God* until 2018 because the first time I saw the cover I was led to believe not that it was a gangster movie of the highest order,[8] but that it was "a foreign language movie about a boy who wants to be a photographer," which is how it was described to me by a person that I later realized was terrible at describing movies.[9]

At any rate, I'm going to talk more about it in the next chapter because a different scene from it lands in the GMMFD Top 10, but for this part just know that there's a three-minute scene in it where we get to watch a young boy sprint headfirst into the role of murdering psychopath and it is, at once, exhilarating and terrifying and electric and devastating.

No. 17 Pick: The torture scene from *Reservoir Dogs* in 1992.
Main Characters in the Scene: Mr. Blonde; a cop who gets kidnapped and then has his ear cut off while getting tortured to death

---

Six things: (1) This part of Mr. Blonde's monologue: "Look it. I'm not gonna bullshit you, okay? I don't really give a good fuck what you know or don't know, but I'm gonna torture you anyway. Regardless. Not to get information. It's amusing to me to torture a cop. You can say anything you want. I've heard it all before. All you can do is pray for a quick death, which you ain't gonna get." (2) The dancing. (3) The part where Mr. Blonde talks into the ear after he cuts it off. (4) The shot of the cop where you see him realize that Mr. Blonde is deranged. (5) The part where Mr. Blonde walks out to the car

---

6. Pacino is, at best, the third best part of *Carlito's Way*, losing out to Leguizamo as Benny Blanco and Sean Penn as the slimy and loathsome lawyer David Kleinfeld. It's Pacino's accent that does it. He's never quite able to pin down exactly what he's supposed to sound like.

7. Do you think that if Carlito had killed Benny he'd have made it out of the movie alive? There's no chance, right? Carlito was forever fated to a catastrophic end, is what it feels like to me, and what Carlito alluded to when he got pulled into that drug deal with his cousin.

8. It's so fucking good.

9. This same person one time recapped *The Lion King* by saying, "It's about a lion who makes friends with a pig and a ferret."

to get the gasoline to set the cop on fire. (6) The part where he taunts the cop while he's holding the lighter.

No. 16 Pick: The .50 caliber scene where Sharice lights everyone the fuck up from *Smokin' Aces* in 2006.[10]
Main Characters in the Scene: Sharice Watters; Georgia Sykes; a whole bunch of other people

---

When Sharice (Taraji P. Henson) hits that first guy in the chest with a shot from the big gun and he goes flying across the room like he's just been hit by a fire truck doing seventy miles per hour. [Pretend there's one of those wide-eyes emojis right here.]

No. 15 Pick: The craps game in *A Bronx Tale* in 1993.
Main Characters in the Scene: Calogero, otherwise known as C; Sonny; Frankie Coffeecake; JoJo the Whale; Eddie Mush

---

You've got "Ain't That a Kick in the Head" by Dean Martin playing as the soundtrack to the scene. You've got C delivering drinks to the guys playing craps in the basement. You've got Eddie Mush begging for money so he can get in on the game, which he gets and then immediately loses. You've got Sonny quarterbacking the room, his megawatt charm overpowering everything and everyone. You've got C getting pulled into the game by Sonny, who asks him to roll the dice for him because he suspects he's good luck.

You've got Sonny, proudly and with a great fatherly flair, puffing his chest out after he has his handler place a large bet on C rolling a winner. You've got JoJo the Whale, Eddie Mush, and Frankie Coffeecake getting put in the bathroom because Sonny thinks they're bad luck. You've got C misunderstanding the game, then people laughing at him, then Sonny protecting him from their jabs. You've got C saying, "Come on, gimme the two-two on the hard four," and then Sonny playfully telling him, "Aye, don't get cocky," and then laughing to himself. You've got the music fading out into the background without you noticing, and then it comes busting back on when C rolls another winner, on his way toward eventually rolling eleven winners in a row, each time he and Sonny cheering bigger and louder and bigger and louder. And you've got Sonny, after C has finished playing and is heading home, stopping C, handing him (what appears to be) a $100 bill for his time, then C looking at it and asking, "That's it?" It's all just so very, very great. In a movie that crawls around within the minutiae of a neighborhood's gangster ecosystem, this single scene might be its most informed.

No. 14 Pick: The human shield scene in *New Jack City* in 1991.
Main Characters in the Scene: Nino Brown; Scotty Appleton; Gee Money; a little girl

---

Three things here:

1. Remember in the previous chapter where I said that we'd talk about Nino's most dastardly moment later in the draft? This is that moment.
2. What happens is Nino Brown is attending a wedding with some of his gangster pals. At the end of the wed-

---

10. *Smokin' Aces* is only juuuuuuuuuuust barely a gangster movie, but it's a gangster movie nonetheless.

ding, some men pretending to be part of the cleanup crew attempt to assassinate him and his friends. He realizes it's a hit right before it happens, and so he tries to take off running. The bullets start spraying all around him before he can get away, though, so what he does is grab a little girl who's nearby and uses her as a human shield so he can escape.[11] He makes it out of the shootout alive.

3. For all of *New Jack City*, Nino positions himself as a fearless, ruthless gangster with ambitions of building a true empire. And he does a really great job of selling that version of himself. We find out at the end of the movie, however, that it's an entirely conditional thing. Nino is able to operate as the alpha male in a situation only when his side of the equation is stacked fat with support. As soon as he finds himself in a one-on-one type situation—like when he and Scotty fistfight with no one else around—he turns into a super worm, and a weasel, and a coward. It's a very complex, advanced take on a gangster kingpin, and I don't think Wesley Snipes has ever gotten enough credit for pulling it off as convincingly as he did.

No. 13 Pick: The "My theory on Feds" scene in *The Departed* in 2006.
Main Characters in the Scene: Dignam; Ellerby; Sullivan

Mark Wahlberg is generally a good actor, but he's a top-level brilliant actor when he's asked to play one of two types of roles: (1) A dumb person who thinks he's smart, like in *Boogie Nights* or *Pain & Gain* or *Rock Star*; or (2) An angry person who gets to be mean, which is what he is (and what he does) in *The Departed*, perhaps the scene-for-scene greatest performance of his career.[12] He plays Staff Sergeant Dignam, one of two people who oversees a department that has situated a mole inside of Frank Costello's criminal organization. He has several great lines in the movie,[13] but none are better than the one he delivers at the end of a briefing session he's holding with a room full of other law enforcement officers. After he's already been hassled about not sharing the name of a person he may or may not have working undercover, a guy sitting down offers a gentler approach. He asks Dignam, "Without asking for too many details, do you have anyone in with Costello presently?" Dignam stares at him for half a second, then, with several truckloads of contempt piled on top of each of his words, responds back, "Maybe. Maybe not. Maybe fuck yourself." Then he turns his gaze away from him and aims it out at the entire table as the camera pulls in tighter on his face. "My theory on Feds is they're like mushrooms," he says, before rolling his eyes over back to the person who asked him about Costello. "Feed 'em shit and keep 'em in the dark."

---

11. Fortunately, she does not get shot. Her father does, though.
12. The out and out greatest performance of his career was in *Boogie Nights*, obviously. But he doesn't have to carry *The Departed* like he did in *Boogie Nights*. He gets to show up for a few minutes, put up a few thirty-five-footers off the dribble, and then disappear. It's like talking about the difference between someone's best overall season and their best single-game performance.
13. His second best: "I'm the guy who does his job. You must be the other guy." His third best: "If you had an idea of what we do, we would not be good at what we do, now would we? We would be cunts. Are you calling us cunts?"

WHAT'S THE ORDER OF THE

GANGSTER
MOVIE MOMENT

FICTIONAL DRAFT?

PART 3

... CONT'D

No. 12 Pick: The "Either you're somebody or you're nobody" scene from *American Gangster* in 2007.
Main Characters in the Scene: Frank Lucas; his brothers; an empty sugar shaker; Tango[1]

Frank Lucas is holding court in a diner in Harlem. He's talking to his team about important business principles, and he goes on to explain how in this world you can only be one of two things: a somebody or a nobody. While he's giving his sermon, he spots Tango, a drug dealer who owes him some money, out on the street. He excuses himself from the table, leaves the diner, then walks up on Tango.

Frank asks Tango for his money, Tango bucks back at the idea, and so Frank pulls a gun out and puts it to Tango's forehead. Tango doesn't flinch. "The fuck are you gonna do, Frank?" asks Tango, knowing that they're both standing on a crowded street, which means there are witnesses everywhere. "You gonna shoot me in front of everybody? Huh? Come on," says Tango. And so Frank comes on. He pulls the trigger, exploding Tango's brains out of the back of his head. He reaches into Tango's pocket, takes the money he's owed, then walks away, leaving the body on the middle of the sidewalk. Then he goes back to the diner, sits down with his brothers (who are in all caps TOTAL shock), and asks, "So what was I saying?" It's the single most electric moment of the entire movie, and also a wonderful use of Denzel's ability to be terrifying without ever raising his voice.

No. 11 Pick: When Joe Pesci puts that guy's head in a vise from *Casino* in 1995.
Main Characters in the Scene: Joe Pesci; Tony Dogs; a vise

Three things:

1. Joe Pesci is such an overpowering, overwhelming tidal wave of a personality that he has never appeared (to me) to be a character in a movie, he's only ever been Joe Pesci in different clothes. That's why I wrote his name in the Main Characters in the Scene section up there as "Joe Pesci" rather than the actual name of his character in *Casino* (Nicky Santoro). He appears two more times in the draft. He's "Joe Pesci" each time.

2. In the scene, Pesci ends a two-day-long torture session of a guy named Tony Dogs by putting his head in a vise and squeezing the vise shut until Tony's head is so compressed that his left eye pops out of his skull. (Pesci is torturing Tony because he wants Tony to rat out someone.) My favorite thing about the scene is when Tony finally ends up ratting, Joe Pesci responds by getting even madder, shouting at him, "Charlie M? CHARLIE M?! YOU MADE ME POP YOUR FUCKING EYE OUT OF YOUR HEAD TO PROTECT THAT PIECE OF SHIT?! CHARLIE M?! YOU DUMB MOTHERFUCKER!" It's funny in the most terrifying way a thing can be funny.

3. Martin Scorsese actually put this scene in the movie as a trap of sorts. He knew that the rest of the movie was already very violent, and so he

---

1. See? It feels weird calling him "Tango" and not "Stringer."

dropped this scene in there because he wanted the people in charge of deciding such things to focus on it when they were figuring out what needed to be cut out and what could stay in. He thought for sure they'd cut it out. It's like when I'm at the store with my wife and I know she's going to suggest we eat something healthy for dinner so I just come in way over the top beforehand and ask her if we can eat an ice cream cake for dinner that way it seems like a compromise when I offer up enchiladas afterward.

No. 10 Pick: The trash can basketball scene from *Paid in Full* in 2002.
Main Characters in the Scene: Ace; Mitch; Rico

Ace, Rico, and Mitch, three friends on the drug dealer come up in Harlem in the eighties, are sitting around a table one night eating Chinese takeout together. As they eat, Ace crumples up one of the takeout bags and shoots it into a small wastebasket on the other side of the room. Rico watches him do it, then immediately challenges him to do it again, betting him $5,000 he'll miss the next shot. Ace, demure and almost always only concerned with being invisible, declines the bet. Rico continues to pester him, making fun of him for always saving his money. Mitch, sensing that Ace is slightly uncomfortable, inserts himself into the exchange, saying he'll take the bet.

Mitch crumples up a different bag, mimics doing a few basketball moves, then fires up a shot. He makes it, celebrates with Ace, and collects his money from Rico. Rico challenges him again, this time upping the amount of the bet. Mitch accepts, but misses the shot this time. There's a beat of silence, and then Rico asks for the money, only for Mitch to tell him that he doesn't have enough to cover the bet.[2] And this is where the scene gets good, and interesting, and why it's such a high pick.

In nearly any other situation, this is the part of the gangster movie where things get way too serious, way too quickly, eventually ending up with someone shot dead. And they make it seem like that's about to happen here, too. (The air in the room fills up with tension very quickly when Mitch hears that Rico can't pay him.) Only except but it doesn't. The three are able to get through it without bloodshed. And so a dinner together that looks like it's headed toward a clichéd catastrophe ends up being this sweet, charming, unexpected moment that has several tiny pieces to it that show just how much all three of the guys care about each other.[3]

No. 9 Pick: The texting scene in *The Departed* in 2006.
Main Characters in the Scene: Billy Costigan; Frank Costello; Colin Sullivan; Sergeant Dignam; Captain Ellerby

---

2. Ace lends Mitch $5,000, which is enough for Rico to calm down. This has always bothered me. Mitch wasn't short on the money. After their initial bet, Mitch had $10,000 in his possession (his original $5,000, plus the $5,000 he'd just won from Rico). When they bet the second time, Rico tells him to "double up," setting two wads of money on the table. Assuming each wad is $5,000, that means the total of the new bet is $10,000, which Mitch was in possession of.
3. Of course, their relationships all turn to muck later in the movie.

This is when Costello is selling some fake microchips to some Chinese men while the police are trying to catch them in the act, and so the scene is jumping back and forth between the criminals and the police. We get a bunch of great things here. We get: (1) The line from Costello about automatic guns not adding inches to your dick and the line from Dignam about being the guy who does his job. (2) Sullivan, the crooked cop, twisting in the wind as he tries to figure out which of the people in Costello's crew is working with the police. (3) Costigan, the guy who's working with the police, texting from his phone while it's in his pocket, which is so much more difficult than it looks. (4) Captain Ellerby asking if he can talk to the video operator for a second and then punching him in the face. And (5) Costello tossing a bunch of racism into the air just to make things a little spicy.

No. 8 Pick: The "Shall I shoot you in the hand or foot?" scene from *City of God* in 2002.
Main Characters in the Scene: Li'l Zé; the Runts; Steak with Fries

---

You know what I loved[4] about *City of God*? I loved[5] that there were several times during the movie where I was watching a thing unfold its way toward something truly horrifying and said something like, "Well, there's no way they're about to let *this* happen," and then whatever the thing was that I thought was not going to happen happened every goddamn time. And there's no better instance of that then the "Shall I shoot you in the hand or foot?" scene.

In it, Li'l Zé, a highly vicious gangster, corners two young boys, one somewhere close to six years old and the other close to ten years old. He tells them he's going to shoot each of them in either the hand or the foot. (He's doing this as retaliation because the boys belong to a group of kids that stole from a store under Li'l Zé's protection.) The six-year-old starts to cry before eventually offering up his hand (the ten-year-old also chooses his hand). Li'l Zé looks at their hands, then shoots each of them in the foot. And were that not horrific enough,[6] he then calls over a young member of his gang named Steak with Fries and demands that he kill one of the boys. And listen, if you've not seen the movie, you're likely sitting there right now, as I was, saying to yourself, "There's no way Steak with Fries actually shoots and kills one of those children." But he does. He fucking does.

No. 7 Pick: The "Say 'what' again" scene from *Pulp Fiction* in 1994.
Main Characters in the Scene: Jules Winnfield; Vincent Vega; Brett; the word "what"; a Bible passage

---

Pulp Fiction is still a gangster movie.

---

4. Hated.
5. Hated.
6. There are few things as unsettling as watching a child contemplate where he wants to be shot.

No. 6 Pick: The success montage from *Scarface* in 1983.
Main Characters in the Scene: Tony Montana; Gina Montana; Elvira Hancock; Manny Ribera

Scarface has three main sections in it. There's the first section, which is where we watch Tony walk toward becoming a drug kingpin (this one ends with him and Manny killing Frank and the crooked cop). There's the third section, which is where we watch everything unravel for Tony (this one ends with Tony and everyone he cares about dead[7]). And there's the middle section, which is a success montage showing Tony rocket his way to power. The success montage stitches together the first section and the third section. And a thing I didn't notice (or realize) until recently is the time allotments for each.

   That first section takes over 103 minutes of the movie's 170-minute runtime, and that makes sense because climbing your way up from a refugee camp to a position of true criminal power and true criminal prestige seems like a very long journey. That third section takes around 60 minutes, and that makes sense because it's always easier to lose everything quickly than to gain everything quickly. And that middle section, which is the only part of the movie where we get things to go smoothly for Tony and the only part of the movie where we get to see Tony be happy, is barely three minutes long, and I don't think I need to point out the symbolism here.

No. 5 Pick: When Kay tells Michael that the child he thought she miscarried was actually an abortion from *The Godfather: Part II* in 1974.
Main Characters in the Scene: Kay Corleone; Michael Corleone

"Oh. Oh, Michael. Michael, you *are* blind. It wasn't a miscarriage. It was an abortion. An *abortion*, Michael. Just like our marriage is an abortion. Something that's unholy and evil. I didn't want your son, Michael. I wouldn't bring another one of your sons into this world. It was an abortion, Michael. It was a son. A son. And I had it killed because *this* must all end!" I gasped. I was watching the movie by myself at home and that part happened and I literally gasped.

No. 4 Pick: The blackjack scene from *Goodfellas* in 1990.
Main Characters in the Scene: Joe Pesci; a blackjack dealer

(see below)

No. 3 Pick: When Joe Pesci is funny like a clown from *Goodfellas* in 1990.
Main Characters in the Scene: Joe Pesci; Henry Hill

---

7. Except Elvira. She was the only one smart enough to see that hanging around Tony was going to get her killed. I always wondered if she'd tried her hand at any more relationships after she left Tony. Like, was there a point in her life afterward where she was out on a date with some guy and he asked her about her previous relationship and she had to explain to him that her husband was a drug dealer who was murdered? And so then as a way to break the tension her date asked her about her relationship before that and she was like, "He was a drug dealer who was murdered."

I'm not sure if this is a controversial thing to say or not, but Joe Pesci is, by my estimation, the single most electric actor to have ever appeared in a gangster movie ever. I know that technically Marlon Brando is a more skilled actor. And I know that Robert De Niro is more all-around great in gangster movies than Pesci. But there's something about Pesci that, when you need someone to jolt a scene to life, or when you need someone to take a regular thing and turn it terrifying, or when you need someone to call someone a "motherfucker" with so much force and so much disdain that the moon wobbles, Pesci is the first call you make. It's why a scene with a premise as simple as "A guy gets upset while playing blackjack" slides its way up into the top four of this draft, or why a scene with a premise as simple as "A guy pretends to get mad at his friend at dinner" ends up producing the most iconic gangster movie monologue. Pesci did that. Nobody else but Pesci ever could've done that.

> **No. 2 Pick:** The opening scene from *The Godfather* in 1972.
> **Main Characters in the Scene:** Vito Corleone; Amerigo Bonasera

There are a number of reasons why this scene— Amerigo Bonasera asking Don Corleone to kill some men who assaulted his daughter—is so powerful, the two most substantial of which being:

1. **It's expertly acted.** Marlon Brando as Vito Corleone is obviously incredible, and obviously iconic, and obviously undeniable, and obviously essential, and obviously a movie character that will live forever, and obviously that's all very important in these types of situations.
2. **It's brilliantly written.** What stands out most about this scene, and what is most vividly and captivatingly on display in this scene, is the pageantry of gangsterism. It's presented as this noble, very dignified, very refined thing. There are governing philosophies to it; a rigid structure set in place that must be abided by; a carefulness to all its parts that somehow legitimizes the illegitimacy of life that includes cutting off horse heads. That's the whole point of the conversation that Vito and Bonasera have, and why none of Bonasera's early attempts at getting Vito to attack the men who attacked his daughter are successful. Vito is offended by Bonasera asking him to do that; not because he's opposed to criminality, but because he feels like Bonasera has not paid the proper respect to him, and to his position. That's why the scene ends with Bonasera kissing Vito's ring and then calling him "Godfather." Bonasera figures it out. He figures out that Vito isn't interested in money. He's only interested in reverence, and if not that, then at least the ritual.

And I know that this one would've been an ideal number one pick, and certainly it'd have been a safer number one pick than what ended up landing there, and probably it *should've* been a number one pick, really. HOWEVER, it loses out to a sleeper moment. It loses out to . . .

> **No. 1 Pick:** The "Now youse can't leave" scene from *A Bronx Tale* in 1993.
> **Main Characters in the Scene:** Sonny LoSpecchio; Calogero Anello; some bikers

Three things here: the first of which is about *A Bronx Tale* as a total entity, the second of which is about *A Bronx Tale* as it relates directly to me, and the third of which is about the specific "Now youse can't leave" scene.

1: *A Bronx Tale* is a small stakes gangster movie (especially when measured up against the world-chasing ambition of Tony Montana in *Scarface* or the world-defining class of Vito Corleone in *The Godfather*), but being set up that way has two big benefits. First, it allows for the movie to zoom in hard on the existences of a small number of people. That sort of specificity is always enjoyable, and a very effective way to get viewers to care about characters. Second, it allows for the movie to move in such a way that every tiny thing begins to feel like a gigantic, paradigm-shifting event, because, in a sense, that's exactly what it is. That's one of my favorite things about it.

2: As I write this, my father has driven a city bus in San Antonio for over thirty years.[8] It's a job that he likes and a job that he's good at and a job that he has a great deal of respect for. As such, he carries himself a certain way. And I mention that because Robert De Niro's character, Lorenzo Anello, is a proud, strong, respected bus driver in *A Bronx Tale*. When I watch the movie, my father is who I see whenever De Niro is on the screen. I have to assume that's part of the reason I like it so much.

3: In the selected scene, a group of bikers stops off in Sonny's neighborhood and visits a bar. Sonny walks in and sees that the leader of the bikers is arguing with one of Sonny's men because Sonny's man is telling them that they aren't dressed properly and have to leave. The leader of the bikers tells Sonny that they're only there looking to get a few beers. Sonny decides to let them stay, and then steps outside to talk to Calogero. When the bikers get their beers, they shake them up and spray them everywhere. Sonny sees it happen, cusses to himself, then walks in and says, "That wasn't very nice. Now youse gotta leave." The leader of the bikers tells him to fuck off, and so Sonny stands there for a second deciding what to do. Then he turns around, walks to the door, closes it, locks it, then walks back to the bikers, looks at them with shark eyes and says, "Now youse can't leave." Calogero, who's standing at Sonny's side, narrates what he sees as the camera pans across the faces of the bikers. He says, "I will never forget the look on their faces. All of them; their faces dropped. All their courage and strength was drained right from their bodies. They had a reputation for breaking up bars. But they knew that instant, they made a fatal mistake. This time they walked into the wrong bar." And right then a secret door at the back of the bar opens up and a bunch of Sonny's other men come charging in and kick the shit out of the bikers.

It's literally a perfect scene. It hat-tips so many of the things that are important in these kinds of movies (power, nobility, coolness, viciousness), and it does so in this incredibly smart, clever way, with two incredibly smart, clever, underappreciated characters in the gangster movie canon. I recognize that it's a bit of a gamble taking this moment with the first pick in the GMMFD (I have to assume I could've traded down to, say, the eighth spot, and still gotten it there while also picking up some other assets). But I couldn't resist. It's my Vontae Mack pick.[9]

---

8. To get hyper-specific about the situation: I am writing this right now in my office in downtown San Antonio. My father drives a bus two blocks away from the building I'm in. If I look out the window at exactly the right time each day, I can see him.
9. Told you.

CAN I ASK YOU

A COUPLE QUESTIONS

ABOUT THE MCU?

THE FIRST INSTALLMENT OF THE MARVEL CINEMATIC UNIVERSE, which is a movie universe where the plots and storylines of 22 films about a specific group of superheroes overlap with one another, is the most successful media franchise that has ever existed. And I know that describing something as "the most successful media franchise that has ever existed" can feel a bit nebulous, so let me be a little more specific so that you can get a sense of the scale.

In the entire history of cinema, only five movies have ever had a box office worldwide gross of more than $2 billion: *Avatar*, which is no. 1 on the list, did it in 2009 ($2.7 billion). *Titanic*, no. 3 on the list, did it in 1997 ($2.1 billion).[1] And *Star Wars: The Force Awakens*, no. 4 on the list, did it in 2015 ($2 billion). The other two spots on there? They both belong to movies from the MCU, and one of them (*Avengers: Endgame*) took only 11 days to blow past the $2 billion mark.[2] It's nuts to think about, really, but also cool to think about, too. The three tentpole films in the MCU (Marvel's *The Avengers*; *Avengers: Infinity War*; and *Avengers: Endgame*[3]) somehow all managed to become pieces of monoculture, which is wildly rare.[4] And when you distill all of the rest of this down to its main point, that's what this chapter is really about.

What follows is a conversation that I had with my three sons shortly after watching *Avengers: Endgame* in April of 2019. I'd originally had a different, sillier chapter in the book about several of the Marvel characters, but I replaced it with this one after watching *Endgame* because I thought it was a better way to indirectly talk about not only the expansive and artistic brilliance of the MCU, but also the way that its first installment was able to build itself up into as pure a movie-going phenomenon as has been had since the internet changed all of everything forever.

Two quick notes: (1) Because I don't talk to my sons the same way that I write a book chapter, the footnotes here mostly have the heftier parts of the important information that would otherwise appear in a book chapter about the MCU. (2) I, for obvious reasons, will be identified in the conversation as "Daddy." I asked each of my sons what they wanted to be called because I didn't want to use their real names.[5] The youngest one, a brilliant six-year-old hurricane of Skittles and hair, asked to be called "The King Spider."[6] And the twins, twelve-year-old handsome geniuses, asked to be referred to as "A_Kid" and "Two." So that's what they'll be.

---

1. James Cameron directed both *Avatar* and *Titanic*.
2. *Avengers: Infinity War* is the other.
3. I know that *Avengers: Age of Ultron* was also an Avengers movie but it never felt like it grabbed a hold of everyone the way that the other three did.
4. Two other modern examples of monoculture: the last three seasons of *Game of Thrones* and rooting against the Warriors from 2017 to 2019.
5. I realize that this is silly given that I wrote their names in the acknowledgments, but it just feels different.
6. It took a good 10 minutes before he landed on this name. He spent more time coming up with his fake name here than his mother and I did coming up with his real name when he was born.

DADDY, to the twins: Well, the first question I want to ask you is: Did you like it? We've been watching these movies since you two were babies and this was the one it was all building to. Did you like it? Was it worth it? I really liked it. I thought it was super neat the way that they jumped back in time to the original movies.

A_KID: I liked it.

TWO: It was good.

THE KING SPIDER: I liked it too.

DADDY: Did you understand everything?

THE KING SPIDER: I don't know.

DADDY: That's probably a "no" then. Which is good. Because I also did not understand everything.

THE KING SPIDER: The Avengers killed Thanos. And the people from the other movie came back. Did you see Spider-Man!?[7]

DADDY: I *did*. I was happy to see him. I missed him. Remember the other Spider-Man?[8] I like this new Spider-Man more.

THE KING SPIDER: Me too.

DADDY: Who's your favorite Avenger?

THE KING SPIDER: Aquaman.

TWO: Aquaman's not an Avenger. He's in the Justice League with Superman and them.

THE KING SPIDER: Oh. Then Superman.

TWO: No. You can't pick him. He's in the Justice League, too. You can't pick Superman or Aquaman or Wonder Woman or The Flash or the metal guy. Those are all Justice League people.

A_KID: I like Iron Man the best.

THE KING SPIDER: He's a metal guy.

DADDY: That's a different metal guy.

TWO: I like the Hulk.

DADDY, to TWO: Do you remember when your brother turned into The Hulk?

A_KID: Yes![9]

THE KING SPIDER: I like Spider-Man. And Owen Grady.[10] And Iron Man.

DADDY: How did you feel when Iron Man died? Did you cry? I was trying hard not to cry. A few tears came out.

TWO: How many? Like one?

---

7. Truth be told, this is actually a pretty good way to summarize *Avengers: Endgame*.

8. Every Friday, we do a thing at our house called Friday Family Movie Night. I imagine many families do it. Everyone turns off their personal electronics and we order Chinese food and then put a movie on and sit there and watch it together. Sometimes it's bad, like the time when one of the twins asked to watch *Paranormal Activity*, but mostly it's very good. Anyway, we had a stretch where we watched the three *Spider-Man* movies that Tobey Maguire made. That's who I was talking about here. And for the record, I liked Tobey as Spider-Man. It's just that I liked Tom Holland more. He's my second favorite ever Spider-Man, behind only Shameik Moore as Miles Morales in *Into the Spider-Verse*.

9. When the twins were young—probably around six or seven—Larami and I put them in taekwondo. And they really liked it a lot in the beginning, but then they started sparring, at which point they hated it. One of the boys (the one who's going by the name "Two" in this chapter) was sparring with a kid, but he was a little too nervous to hit the kid so the teacher gave them both these foam swords and said to use those instead. The point was to introduce them to the idea of hitting each other, which, as I type this, I'm seeing how dumb that is. But so the teacher gave each of the kids a foam sword, and then signaled the start of their sparring match. The kid whopped Two across the chest with the sword and Two lost his fucking mind. He dropped the sword, balled his little fists up, did a scream like The Hulk did in the first Avengers movie when he saw all the aliens, and then charged at the kid. He tackled him down and just started pounding on him. It has since been a running joke that Two, if you get him mad enough, will turn into a tinier, more tan version of the Hulk.

10. The Baby loves the *Jurassic World* franchise. Chris Pratt, who plays Peter Quill in the MCU, also plays Owen Grady, star of the Jurassic movies.

DADDY: Like six.[11]

A_KID: That's a lot. You weren't "trying hard not to cry." You were crying.

THE KING SPIDER: Iron Man died!?

DADDY: How did you miss that? It's the biggest part of the movie.

THE KING SPIDER: I don't know. I dropped a candy. I think it was the same time. It went in my seat.

DADDY: Did you find the candy?

THE KING SPIDER: No.

DADDY: Tough break. It was a tough day for you and it was a tough day for Iron Man.

A_KID: I didn't cry.

TWO: Me neither.

DADDY: You cried at Coco but you didn't cry when Iron Man died?

A_KID: That was different. I was younger.

DADDY: Coco came out not that long ago. It was, like, 2017. You were ten. You're only eleven now.

A_KID: Yeah. Ten is younger than eleven.

TWO: [laughing]

DADDY: Ha. I suppose you have a point. I really liked Iron Man. He was my favorite. And he was the most important Avenger. He's the guy who started it all, and the guy who held it all together.[12] He was very charming and funny and had just this perfect mixture of acting ability and sauce to make everything feel believable.[13] I already miss him.

THE KING SPIDER: Are you sure that he died?

DADDY: Boy.

TWO, to The King Spider: They had a funeral for him. Remember when everyone was dressed in black at the end? That's what that was.

DADDY, to The King Spider: Are there any people from any movies that you would be sad if they died?

THE KING SPIDER: I was sad when the bird died in that movie with the spiders.[14] And I would be very sad if Owen Grady died. I would be real sad. I thought the Indominus was gonna eat him.[15]

DADDY: You were sad when a bird died but not sad when Iron Man died?

THE KING SPIDER: The bird was definitely dead. I don't know if Iron Man is dead.[16]

DADDY: Can I ask you a couple questions about the MCU?

A_KID: What's the MCU?

---

11. This doesn't really have anything to do with anything, but the all-time greatest quick little Easter egg in a Marvel movie is when Red Skull, the Nazi villain from Captain America: The First Avenger, makes an offhand remark about how Hitler is overseeing a mining expedition in the desert, which is a sneaky high-five to Indiana Jones and the Raiders of the Lost Ark.

12. Iron Man was the first movie of the MCU's twenty-two movies that made up its initial run. There was actually some uncertainty in place when Marvel started the MCU. People in charge thought that The Incredible Hulk was going to be the universe's marquee figure in the beginning, but Robert Downey Jr. was so undeniably good as Iron Man that he became the central figure.

13. A fun thing: Tony Stark meets Nick Fury at the very end of Iron Man. Fury says to him, "Mr. Stark, you've become part of a bigger universe." It's a neat thing to look back on and realize that Marvel's very ambitious plans to make their own cinematic universe were in play from the start. It's also a neat thing to look back and realize that Nick Fury was actually talking to the audience as well.

14. Eight Legged Freaks. It was on Netflix. We tried watching it one day. A bird gets killed in the first few minutes. The King Spider started crying. We had to turn it off.

15. The Indominus Rex is the main villain dinosaur in Jurassic World.

16. I was mad right here, but the more I think about it, the more sense it makes. He just watched a movie where literally billions of people on earth come back to life. That probably clouds up the permanence of death in a six-year-old's mind. Unless you're killed by a spider, in which case you are dead forever, apparently.

DADDY: It's what they call all of the superhero movies that have, like, Iron Man and Thor and Black Panther and Spider-Man and so on. They're all connected. Same as how Superman and Batman and Wonder Woman are connected. That's a different movie universe.[17]

A_KID: Oh.

DADDY: Remember when they put Thanos in Fortnite for a while? It's kind of like that. Fortnite and the Marvel movies became connected there. It established that they both exist in the same universe.

TWO: Aren't we all in one big universe. Like, *everything* is in it.

DADDY: I don't know. This conversation is getting away from us a little. I'm gonna move us in a new direction. And it doesn't have anything to do with anything, I'm just curious about the way your brains work so I'm gonna ask you a new question.

THE KING SPIDER: My brain is as big as a car. Your brain is as big as a walnut. Like an ampelosaurus.[18]

DADDY: Thank you. Let's say that you were having a birthday party and you were able to invite one member of the Avengers. It would be the real, actual superhero with their real, actual powers. And they were guaranteed to come. Which one would you invite?

THE KING SPIDER: Not the Hulk.

DADDY: Why?

THE KING SPIDER: Because he would destroy everything. He would smash the cake. And the presents.

DADDY: Sure, but he'd also smash the pinata. That would be good. Even if he had a blindfold on it'd still be pretty easy for him.

A_KID: You could invite the smart Hulk. He wouldn't smash your stuff but he'd still be the Hulk. Like from *Endgame*.

DADDY: That's a good call.

TWO: I would invite Thor. Or the raccoon.

DADDY: Why?

TWO: I don't know. I was just saying some names before you asked me.

DADDY: Awesome.

THE KING SPIDER: I would invite Spider-Man.

A_KID: Why?

THE KING SPIDER: Because he's a kid. And he can do flips.[19] And I like his costume.

A_KID: Iron Man is really rich. I'd invite him because maybe he'll bring me a really good present.

DADDY: That's smart. He's for sure showing up with something that no one else is gonna give you.

THE KING SPIDER: I know who I would invite: Sub-Zero.

TWO: He's from Mortal Kombat. He's not an Avenger.

THE KING SPIDER: He could make snow cones for everyone. Like, in the game he has ice. He can make ice. So he could make snow cones instead of freezing

---

17. One of my very favorite things is when two different parts of pop culture get folded over onto each other. (You could've maybe guessed this by looking at the cover of this book.) It happened every so often when I was a kid—I remember being absolutely beside myself when I found out that the Ninja Turtles and Vanilla Ice existed in the same universe; I had the same feeling when Uncle Phil showed up on an episode of *Family Matters*—and happens all the time now. The MCU will, in all likelihood, end up being the finest example of that kind of stream crossing that any of us ever get. It has changed storytelling for the rest of time.

18. The boy can't remember to brush his teeth at night, but he knows about 600 dinosaur facts.

19. Kids fucking love flips so much.

people. Or, I guess if it's hot outside he could freeze them too to help them cool off.

DADDY: I mean, Sub-Zero isn't an Avenger but that's a pretty good answer so I'm gonna give you credit for it.

THE KING SPIDER: Can I really invite Sub-Zero to my birthday party?

DADDY: I think it's important to remember that Sub-Zero is a murderer, son. So no. Because what if he shows up and you're like, "Hi, Sub-Zero. Can I have a strawberry snow cone?" And he's like, "No, but what you can have is this," and then he tears your spine out.

THE KING SPIDER: I like blue snow cones, not strawberry.

DADDY: I think you might be missing the point.

TWO: Aren't all of the Avengers murderers?

DADDY: Huh?

TWO: If you're not gonna invite Sub-Zero because he's a murderer, then you shouldn't invite any of the Avengers either. They killed a lot of people. Some were bad guys, but a few of them probably weren't. Are you inviting murderers to your party or aren't you?

DADDY: It's not the same.

TWO: Why?

DADDY: I don't know. Let's talk about something else. If I was an Avenger, which one would I be? Who do I have the most in common with?

A_KID: None of them.

TWO: [laughing]

DADDY: I don't like how fast you answered that.

THE KING SPIDER: Iron Man. You both have mustaches. And you're both dads.

DADDY: I'll take it. There was only one Avenger I was hoping you all wouldn't choose for me anyway.

A_KID: Hawkeye.

DADDY: Yes!

TWO: Hawkeye was the weakest. He was just a guy with a bow and arrow. And not even a magic bow and arrow. It was a regular bow and arrow.

A_KID: Why didn't they make it magic? Everything else was magic. Thor can control lightning but Hawkeye can't get some magic arrows that never run out?

DADDY: That's a strong point. It was the same with Black Widow. They were both pretty weak. Iron Man didn't have any powers but at least he had cool equipment. Like Batman, but better.

TWO: Falcon, too.

DADDY, to Two: Can I remind you of something before we move on?

TWO: Yes.

DADDY: Several years ago, your brother and you and I went to this thing called Avengers Live. It was a live-action play basically where they had people pretending to be the Avengers and they were all fighting bad guys and whatnot. Anyway, when all the Avengers came out, the only one you were interested in was Falcon. You stared at him the whole time. Your eyes were so big and excited. You tapped me on my shoulder and asked who he was. I told you he was Falcon. A few minutes passed and then you tapped me again. You were like, "Daddy, is he a good guy?" You were so taken with him. It was the cutest thing. It was the first time in my life that I was ever like, "Dang, I wish there was a Mexican Avenger." You've got 250 superheroes in *Avengers: Endgame*. We can't get one Mexican? I'm gonna just start telling people that Tony Stark is Mexican. His full name is Antonio Stark.

THE KING SPIDER: That's a lie. You're telling a lie.

DADDY, ignoring The King Spider: Okay, let me switch it up a little: Hawkeye and Black Widow don't have any powers. We can agree on that. But does that make them the *least* impressive Avengers or the *most* impressive Avengers? Because, I mean, it's easy to survive an alien fight when you're an actual god. But Hawkeye and Black Widow were just normal people. It's like the difference between beating a video game when you have infinite lives and infinite bullets versus beating a video game when you have one life and one bullet.

A_KID: I guess that makes sense.

TWO: I don't know if there's a way to make it so that two regular people are more impressive than Thor or Captain America or Ant-Man.

THE KING SPIDER: I would invite Ant-Man to my party so he could turn small. And he could make the ants clean up.

A_KID: I don't understand Ant-Man. How does he shrink? Shouldn't he die? Because his body isn't special. He gets in the suit and the suit shrinks. Shouldn't he, like, be crushed?

DADDY: Like if you filled a bag with ice cream and then squished the bag down real small and the ice cream started spilling out?

TWO: I don't think it's like ice cream.

A_KID: [laughing]

THE KING SPIDER: I'm gonna have ice cream at my party.

DADDY: You know there's not a real party, right? We're just talking about stuff right now.

TWO: It's those particles. The ones they used to go back in time. The particles can make you small without hurting you.

THE KING SPIDER: I want a birthday party.

DADDY: No, no. You're gonna have a birthday party. But it's just that this one we're talking about right now is a fake thing. I'm just making it up. For the conversation.

THE KING SPIDER: You're telling more lies.

DADDY: Okay. I think that'll do. Thanks, boys.

RACE-FORWARD FOOTBALL CAMP

WORK OR NOT?

IN 2000, DENZEL WASHINGTON STARRED IN *REMEMBER THE TITANS,* a very great and enjoyable movie that, per IMDB.com, was about: "The true story of a newly appointed African-American coach and his high school team on their first season as a racially integrated unit." And this will either come as a great shock to you or no shock at all, but *Remember the Titans* isn't precisely a true story. Parts of it were fudged a bit to make it a more enjoyable experience.

Some of the changes were small changes, and when you hear them you go, "Oh. Well, I suppose that makes sense, what with Disney being in charge and all." (For example, in the movie, a brick gets thrown through a window into Denzel Washington's home. In real life, it was a toilet that was thrown the window.[1]) Some of the changes were medium changes, and when you hear them you go, "Oh. Well, I mean, I guess technically that *does* make it a more powerful moment." (For example, in the movie, one of the white coaches replaces a white player with a black player during a game because the white player can't cover an opponent. In real life, that player swap happened during the days between games.) And some of the changes were gigantic changes, and when you hear them you go, "Wait. What the fuck? Why'd they do *that*?" (For example, in the movie, Gerry Bertier, the team's All-American linebacker, gets into a car crash before the championship game and is paralyzed from the waist down. In real life, he got into the accident when he was driving home from an awards banquet after the season had already ended. He played in the championship game.)

So, again, it's not precisely a true story, but it is still an upper tier sports movie, and perhaps the best football movie that's ever been.[2]

———

In *Remember the Titans*, Denzel Washington is selected to coach a high school football team during the school's first year of integration.[3] The players quickly form into two separate packs based on race,[4] so Denzel comes up with a plan: He decides that when the team is away at football camp, he's going to arrange it so that the black players and the white players have to interact with each other as often as possible.

He makes it so that they have to sit with each other on the buses, and that they have to eat together in the cafeteria, and that they have to room together in the dorms, and that they have to talk to each other and learn facts about each other to report to the group. And there are problems at first, for sure—fights and arguments and such break out. But by the end of the camp, mostly all of the players like each other and get along and no longer appear to feel the same sort of racial animosity that was present before camp.

1. You can always tell how much someone hates by how big of an object it is that they're willing to figure out how to pick up and throw at you.
2. Others on that list include *Any Given Sunday, Friday Night Lights, Invincible, Rudy, The Replacements, Little Giants, The Longest Yard, Brian's Song, The Waterboy, Necessary Roughness, The Program,* and *Varsity Blues.*
3. This wasn't a true thing either. In real life, the school was integrated five years before the 1971 football season.
4. Every time I watch a movie like one of these where it's the white people against the black people, I always say to myself, "Where the fuck were the Mexicans during all of this?"

And that's the beginning of what this chapter is about. The idea is to figure out if Denzel's race-forward football camp actually worked long-term for the players, or if it was more one of those situations like when you say you're going to start eating healthier and then after two days of salads you realize you don't know where to find healthy food so you're just like, "Fuck it. I guess let me go ahead and grab a couple of these Wendy's junior bacon cheeseburgers for dinner today." And the way we're going to do that is by looking at which actors played which characters, then digging around through the other movies that those actors were in to see if there are some obvious examples of it having worked or not worked.

Here's an easy example to understand: Ethan Suplee plays Louie Lastik in *Remember the Titans*. And Louie Lastik is this very funny, very charming offensive lineman who is the most open-minded of all the players on the team. To wit, he's the first white guy to join the black players when they all meet up, and he's the first white guy to make friends with the black players, and he's the only white guy whose first interaction with Denzel is a polite and accommodating one. He's already pretty well situated as a person, and so you would think that attending the race-forward football camp would only strengthen his general good feelings toward everyone. But it doesn't. It actually radicalizes him. And the way you know this is because Ethan Suplee also plays a hateable and loathsome neo-Nazi named Seth in *American History X*.[5] So if you ask, "Did Denzel's race-forward football camp work for Louie Lastik?" The answer is, "No. No, Denzel's race-forward

football camp did not work for Louie Lastik because Louie Lastik became a neo-Nazi in 1998."

———

Here are two questions you may have asked yourself while reading the section above this one:

Question 1: Wait. Didn't *American History X* come out before *Remember the Titans*? Wouldn't that mean that actually the race-forward football camp helped a great deal?

Question 2: And are we talking about if Denzel's race-forward football camp worked for Louie Lastik, or are we talking about if Denzel's race-forward football camp worked for Ethan Suplee?

And here are two answers to go along with those two questions:

Answer 1: You are correct. *American History X* did come out before *Remember the Titans*. But for this exercise, we're going to use the date that a movie is set in to determine if the camp worked, not the date that it was released. *Remember the Titans* is, for nearly the entirety of it, set in 1971. So any movies that Ethan Suplee was in that were set after 1971 would be eligible to be used as proof in an argument for or against the race-forward football camp working for Louie Lastik. Any movies set before 1971, however, would not. So that means *American History X* is eligible, meanwhile something like *Cold Mountain*, where Suplee plays a confederate soldier who becomes a deserter, would not be eligible because it was set in 1861.

---

5. It is a true testament to Suplee's talent as an actor that he was able to play both of these characters convincingly.

Answer 2: We're talking about the characters, not the people who played them. Just picture it like if we took all of the movies that Ethan Suplee was in and replaced all of his characters with Louie Lastik. It goes like that for everyone.

—

Not counting Louie Lastik, there are eight key players on the team who attended Denzel's race-forward football camp that we need to look at, as well as one non-player. We have:

- **Sheryl Yoast:** She's the nine-year-old daughter of Bill Yoast, Denzel's main assistant coach. (She's played by Hayden Panettiere.)
- **Julius Campbell:** He's a co-captain of the team and a star player for the defense. (He's played by Wood Harris.)
- **Gerry Bertier:** He's the other co-captain of the team. He's also a star player for the defense. (He's played by Ryan Hurst.)
- **Petey Jones:** He's the player I mentioned earlier who takes the place of the white player who's too slow to keep up with the person he's supposed to be covering one game. (He's played by Donald Faison.)
- **Alan Bosley:** He's the white player who gets his spot taken by Petey. (He's played by Ryan Gosling.[6])
- **Jerry "Rev" Harris:** He's the quarterback. They call him "Rev" because he really loves Jesus. (He's played by Craig Kirkwood.)

- **Ray Budds:** He's Gerry Bertier's best friend. He's also very racist. Bertier eventually has him kicked off the team because he intentionally misses a block that leads to Rev getting injured. (He's played by Burgess Jenkins.)
- **Ronnie "Sunshine" Bass:** He's the backup QB who has to step in after Rev gets hurt. He's the very handsome and gentle-spirit hippie of the team. (He's played by Kip Pardue, which is funny because if I was writing a movie and had to come up with the name of a character described as "very handsome and gentle-spirit hippie" I would almost certainly land on "Kip Pardue.")
- **Blue Stanton:** He's a fun lineman who just wants everyone to relax. (He's played by Earl Poitier.)

—

Right at this moment, we are nine chapters into the book. And I would hope by now that you would understand that while each chapter definitely has a core question it's trying to answer, answering that core question is, in many cases, not the actual point of the chapter. The actual point of each chapter is some version of some kind of insight about some kind of thing. And while I generally like to leave those things to be discovered by the reader at whatever pace it is that the reader happens to discover them, I want to state it very clearly and plainly here: The actual point of including this chapter in *Movies (And Other Things)* is to celebrate Denzel Washington, perhaps the most purely talented actor and undeniable movie star that we have

---

6. This was the first real role for Gosling. He's mostly a background character. Watching *Remember the Titans* now after he's become one of the biggest stars in the world is a real treat.

ever gotten. Everything about him is mammoth. His stare feels like words and his words feel like monologues and his monologues feel like you're standing under a mega waterfall and looking up into the stream. Never one single time has a movie been worse off because Denzel Washington was in it. Never will it.

> **Did Denzel's race-forward football camp work for Julius Campbell (played by Wood Harris)?**

Wood Harris's most famous movie role wasn't even a movie role, it was when he played a high-ranking drug dealer in West Baltimore named Avon Barksdale for five seasons on HBO's *The Wire*. But it's a smaller role on a different HBO show that I'm leaning on here to get our answer. In 1997, Harris had a bit part as a correctional officer on *Oz*, a show about a fictional prison called Oswald State penitentiary. He appeared in exactly one episode, and when he did, it was to give a handgun to a prisoner named Kareem Said, a black nationalist who blew up a warehouse owned by white people. So no, Denzel's race-forward football camp did not work for Julius Campbell. (Can I say very quickly: I love Wood Harris so much. He has this remarkable ability to toggle back and forth between being earnest and being cool. It's why he's able to so perfectly deliver the "Attitude reflect leadership, captain" line in *Remember the Titans* but also

the "They gotta fight for life" line in *Creed* but also the "I'm just a gangsta, I suppose" line from *The Wire*. He has been a good actor for 100 percent of his career.)

> **Did Denzel's race-forward football camp work for Ronnie "Sunshine" Bass (played by Kip Pardue)?**

Yes. Kip Pardue was in a movie called *Beyond Valkyrie: Dawn of the 4th Reich*, and in that movie he and his friends killed a bunch of Nazis, and I know that this breaks the "we're using when the date that movie was set in, not the date that the movie was released" rule, but killing Nazis will always earn you enough goodwill to supersede certain rules.[7] Speaking of which . . .

> **Did Denzel's race-forward football camp work for Gerry Bertier (played by Ryan Hurst)?**

Ryan Hurst was in a very bad movie in 2002 called *Lone Star State of Mind*, and there's a part in it where he says, "Don't shoot me! I love your people. Ricky Martin's great. Yo quiero Taco Bell," which, I mean, that's somewhere between him being racist and him being ignorant, so that's a pretty bad start. And if you take that and then add it together with how he was Opie Winston in *Sons of*

---

7. A few days after we'd turned this book in to be sent off to the printer, Kip Pardue was fined by the actors' union because he'd been accused of on-set sexual harassment. When I saw the news clip, I searched for other actors I've mentioned in this book to see if anyone else had also been accused of anything similar. Several of them had been, including Kevin Spacey, Arnold Schwarzenegger, Sylvester Stallone, Ben Affleck, and Morgan Freeman. I'd known about Spacey beforehand (which is why he is only mentioned in the chapter where I was listing Oscar winners). I had not known about Schwarzenegger, Stallone, Affleck, and Freeman (which is why they are mentioned slightly more). I hope there are not others that I've missed here. Apologies to everyone, if so.

Anarchy, which was a TV show about an all-white motorcycle gang, it starts to look a lot like the race-forward football camp didn't work for Bertier. But, same as with Pardue, I'm going to cheat here and say that it did work, and the reason I'm going to do so is because Hurst also has a movie in his filmography where he kills Nazis (in his case, it's when he showed up for a small role in *Saving Private Ryan*). So Bertier is a yes. Denzel's race-forward football camp worked for him. (Can I say very quickly: I love Ryan Hurst so much. Watching him die in *Sons of Anarchy* was several miles past heartbreaking.[8])

Did Denzel's race-forward football camp work for Ray Budds (played by Burgess Jenkins)?

Fuck Ray Budds.

Did Denzel's race-forward football camp work for Sheryl Yoast (played by Hayden Panettiere)?

Sheryl didn't seem to be very racist at all, which makes sense given that (a) she was just nine, and (b) her dad, while not all the way racism-free, seemed to be much less racist than most everyone around him. (She was mad at Denzel a couple times in the movie, but generally speaking it was because she felt like Denzel getting the head coaching job had cost her dad his chance at getting into the Virginia High School Hall of Fame, which is both very sweet and very preposterous. No nine-year-old would ever care about that. They're oblivious to everything further away from them than their arms can reach. You're doing good if you can get a nine-year-old to notice that someone has just set your head on fire.) At any rate, Hayden Panettiere played the leader of a clique of popular high school girls in 2009's *I Love You, Beth Cooper* that had a non-white member in it so, at the very least, Denzel's race-forward football didn't not work for her.

Did Denzel's race-forward football camp work for Blue Stanton (played by Earl Poitier)?

Yes. He was good friends with a white guy in *Drumline* and he was best friends with a white guy in *Little Chicago*. Being good friends with someone the opposite race of you is an easy way to know that Denzel's race-forward football camp worked. Speaking of which . . .

Did Denzel's race-forward football camp work for Petey Jones (played by Donald Faison)?

Yes. Donald Faison was in *Clueless*, and his character was a high school student who was part of a mixed race clique. And Donald Faison was in *Can't Hardly Wait*, and his character was a drummer in an otherwise all-white high school band. And Donald Faison was in *Scrubs*, and

---

8. It was also a perfect TV scene. They played it expertly, giving you these tiny bits of hope along the way; just enough so that you'd be all the way wrecked when he finally died.

his character was married to a Dominican woman[9] and his best friend was a white guy.[10] (Can I say very quickly: I love Donald Faison so much. He is endlessly funny, but also able to pack real and legitimate emotion into even the tiniest of spaces. Were I allowed to choose between any of the people mentioned here in this chapter to hang out with for an afternoon, it'd be Faison.)

> **Did Denzel's race-forward football camp work for Jerry "Rev" Harris (played by Craig Kirkwood)?**

Probably the best one to use here is when he had a recurring part on a TV show called *Running the Halls*, which was a knock-off version of *Saved by the Bell* that NBC tried to slide in behind *Saved by the Bell: The New Class*. It was about a group of kids who attended a boarding school. Most of them were white. And Rev didn't seem to actively hate any of them. So yes, Denzel's race-forward football camp worked for him.

> **Did Denzel's race-forward football camp work for Alan Bosley (played by Ryan Gosling)?**

This is the trickiest of all of the entries. Because he's in a movie called *The Slaughter Rule* and his best friend is Native American. And also he's in a movie called *Half Nelson* and he plays a drug-addicted middle school teacher who befriends one of his black students. And also he's in a movie called *The Place Beyond the Pines* and he has a kid with Eva Mendes. And also he's in a movie called *Murder by Numbers* where he and a friend drive around in a parking lot looking for someone to murder and they settle on a white woman, and I figure if a potential killer is out looking for a person to murder and the potential killer settles on someone who's the same race then maybe you could look at that as the worst way to prove that the potential killer isn't racist.[11] HOWEVER, he was also in a movie called *The Believer* where he played a very violent neo-Nazi, and I'm pretty sure that outweighs everything else. So no, Denzel's race-forward football camp did not work for Alan Bosley. (Can I say very quickly: I love Ryan Gosling so much. He just has a confident stillness to his whole essence that is very interesting. And I really like that thing he does where he lets all of the emotion fall out of his eyes and turns them blank. It's a neat trick.[12])

---

9. A small thing about the *Scrubs* inclusion here is that his character, Turk, had a hard time remembering if his wife was Dominican or Puerto Rican.
10. Two roles that someone could use to argue the other way: When he was Wedgie Rudlin in *The Boondocks*, and when he starred in *Homie Spumoni*, a movie that somehow managed to be offensive to several different races and ethnicities all at once.
11. It seems like accusations of racism would be a secondary concern in that situation, though.
12. I remember everyone making a big, big deal about his performance in *La La Land* because he was singing with Emma Stone, and I definitely understand the fuss because watching Ryan Gosling and Emma Stone sing to each other is something that checks off a lot of the boxes on the list of things that I am interested in. But the most exciting part about him being in a movie where he was singing was that it reminded someone to start circulating a video of the time he performed Jodeci's "Cry For You" as part of a group on the Mickey Mouse Club when he was a preteen.

WHO'S IN THE

REGINA GEORGE

CIRCLE OF

FRIENDS?

SUPPOSE THAT WE TOOK ALL OF THE CHARACTERS who have ever appeared in a high school movie and enrolled them all at the same school. I'm talking everyone from *House Party*, *Rushmore*, *Superbad*, *Booksmart*, *The Breakfast Club*, *Dazed and Confused*, *Napoleon Dynamite*, *Easy A*, *Election*, *Stand and Deliver*, *Clueless*, *10 Things I Hate About You*, *Freedom Writers*, *Dangerous Minds*, *Dazed and Confused*, *Carrie*, *Bring It On*, *Cooley High*, *Heathers*, *Ferris Bueller's Day Off*, *Pretty in Pink*, on and on and on, until you've gotten every person from every high school movie that's ever been.

Suppose they all now attend a school called Movie High School. Suppose that they all have classes together and eat together and exist together, meaning they all have the opportunity now to begin to form new social circles in this new social setting. Suppose, for example, that Taylor Vaughan from 1999's *She's All That* could become friends with Malcolm from 2015's *Dope*,[1] or that Johnny Lawrence from 1984's *The Karate Kid* could become friends with Lara Jean from 2018's *To All the Boys I've Loved Before*.[2] And suppose that after a few months of all of the characters from all of the high school movies being around each other, *Regina George*, the big bad at the center of 2004's *Mean Girls*, climbed her way up to the top of social hierarchy where she belongs. Suppose that all of those things are true, and suppose that none of the logistical problems you might be imagining for such a campus are relevant.

That being the case, I ask this question: Who's in the Regina George circle of friends? There were six seats at each cafeteria table in *Mean Girls*. If we delete the friends that she had in that movie and start populating them with kids from Movie High School, who gets to sit with her? Who takes up those five extremely valuable seats?

———

The "circle of friends" notion here is something that, in other situations, I might assume should not be explained. But given that this is a book, and given that explanations are, in one form or another, either directly or indirectly, in some instances overt and other instances discreet and more brilliant instances symbolic or allegorical, inseparable from the very nature of (most) books, here is one: The phrase "circle of friends" is used to mean "a group of people that a person hangs out with regularly."

The group of people I regularly hung out with in high school was as follows:

There was Johnny. He was handsome and charming and occasionally angry. (I liked him because he seemed unafraid of every person and every situation.) I remember one time when we were trying out for the basketball team in middle school he said he could tell I could run fast because my forehead was too big for my body, which is a very funny joke that I refused to acknowledge was very funny.

There was Eddie. Eddie was a big-time dork in middle school but sometime between eleventh and twelfth grade he grew into himself and somehow, inexplicably, unpredictably, undeniably became

---

1. This would never happen.
2. Neither would this.

almost cool. I feel like he maybe started trying to get people to call him Edward, but I can't say for certain. What I can say for certain, though, is that if he did, we did not oblige him.

There was Brian. He was the one white kid in our group, and one of the very few in our neighborhood. A lot of girls liked him because, per the girls, he kind of looked like a tougher version of Jonathan Taylor Thomas from *Home Improvement*, which at the time was just about the nicest specific compliment I'd ever heard anyone say about anyone.

There was Cassie. She was the tiniest one in the group but also the most ferocious. I *think* she liked Eddie and I *know* that she hated me.

There was Mark, otherwise known as Marky, occasionally known as Marcus. He wore this big brace on one of his legs because he'd gotten into a very bad car crash with his older brother during (I think) his sophomore year. Mark was the funniest and most interesting person in the group. He was also unreasonably strong, though nobody ever figured out why because he never worked out or even exercised at all. I remember one time we were play-fighting at his house and he picked me up clean off the floor and tossed me across the room. A theory was floated that he was part ape, but we could never figure out a way to test the validity of the statement.

And there was Joaquin. He was tall and thin and looked a lot like Ethan Embry in *Can't Hardly Wait* and so of course he was the most popular person in our not-very-popular group. A girl that I liked chose him over me, which made me secretly not like him, but then he and I learned how to do a portion of the dance that Usher does in the "My Way" video together and so that made me like him again.

There were other people who floated in and out of orbit—there was Ryan, a tall and kind of weird kid who was mostly nice; there was Miguel, who I was very close with in middle school and then drifted away from in high school because he transferred schools after ninth grade; and there was Max, who was attractive and talented but we all made fun of because one time he took a picture with his shirt off and you could tell he was trying to pull the skin on his stomach down to give himself a six-pack[3]—but by and large, that was it. That was the group. That was my circle of friends.

———

Some quick notes before we continue:

- *Mean Girls* came out in 2004.
- It starred Lindsay Lohan as Cady Heron and Rachel McAdams as Regina George.
- Cady was a sweet and likable teenager who, because of the jobs that her parents worked, had only ever been homeschooled.
- Cady ends up attending a proper high school starting her junior year, and that's how we meet Regina.
- Regina is the most popular person at the school.

---

3. We all swore this was the nerdiest thing and then each tried to do it in private on our own.

- She's the leader of a group of girls called the Plastics, the three of whom are universally viewed as the apex of the school's popularity pyramid.
- Regina is wholly evil. She is manipulative, and mentally abusive, and conniving, and dazzling in that specifically intimidating way that only the most effective bullies can be.
- Cady gets roped into a conspiratorial plan by someone who hates Regina to infiltrate the Plastics and disintegrate them from within.
- Things start out well but then go sideways quickly—Cady, hesitant to even participate in Regina's undoing, eventually becomes fully invested in the mission, so much that Cady's not only able to shove Regina off her perch, but also take her spot there.
- There's a scene in *Mean Girls* where Regina gets hit head-on by a bus doing forty miles per hour and not only does she not die, but she's back at school within the next week in hopes of capturing the title of Queen of the Spring Fling.[4] That's the kind of powerhouse we're talking about here.
- Given that *Mean Girls* is presented as a funny high school movie about young women, and given that pretty much every "funny high school movie about young women" is often incorrectly categorized as only exactly that, it's become easy to disregard the case that *Mean Girls* is art, and it's become easy to disregard the case that Regina George is a top-level movie villain. But the very real truth is: *Mean Girls* is truly exceptional, and Regina is the most lethal, most devastating, most unstoppable, most interesting, most complicated, most compelling, all-in-all best high school movie character that has ever been. Which is why she is at the center of the conversation this chapter is having.

> **Some Marquee Names Who Seem Like They'd Be Included in Regina's Circle of Friends, but Ultimately Would Not Be**

Johnny Lawrence from 1984's *The Karate Kid*: He'd get to sit with her for a while, yes, but only up until he loses to Daniel LaRusso at the All-Valley Karate Tournament, at which point he would be dismissed. (Daniel LaRusso, by the way, while charming, is too wormy and unkempt to be part of Regina's circle. He doesn't get a permanent seat at her table either. You could maybe make a decent case for Ali, the girl Johnny and Daniel were ultimately fighting over, to be included, but she's likely too decent of a person for Regina.)

Veronica from 1988's *Heathers*: She feels like another obvious pick for the circle—she's talented, beautiful, smart, capable of thriving in the highest rung of the social order, etc.—and, truthfully, she very well might be perfect for it. It's just that, despite Regina clearly being a bad person, I can't even in this fake exercise convince myself to put Regina's life at risk, which is exactly what we'd be doing if we allowed Veronica a seat at the table. So Veronica is out. (Incidentally, each of the three Heathers from *Heathers* are also out, and obviously J.D. is out too.)

---

4. The Spring Fling is a big dance that happens at the school every year.

MOVIE HIGH SCHOOL

Malcolm Adekanbi,
Dope

John Bender,
The Breakfast Club

Laney Boggs,
She's All That

Napoleon Dynamite,
Napoleon Dynamite

Evan,
Superbad

Max Fischer,
Rushmore

Regina George,
Mean Girls

Angel Guzman,
Stand and Deliver

Cher Horowitz,
Clueless

Isis,
Bring It On

Johnny Lawrence,
The Karate Kid

Lara Jean,
To All the Boys...

MOVIE HIGH SCHOOL

Juno MacGuff,
Juno

Christine McPherson,
Lady Bird

Preston Meyers,
Can't Hardly Wait

Emilio Ramirez,
Dangerous Minds

Christopher Reid,
House Party

Veronica Sawyer,
Heathers

Ron Slater,
Dazed and Confused

Tre Styles,
Boys n the Hood

Zeke Tyler,
The Faculty

Andie Walsh,
Pretty in Pink

Kyle Lee Watson,
Above the Rim

Rita Watson,
Sister Act 2

Amanda from 1998's *Can't Hardly Wait:* She's a little too sentimental, is all. She was the most popular girl at her school and somehow ended up dating Ethan Embry's character, Preston Meyers. And, I mean, listen: This is not an admonishment of Ethan Embry. He *is* handsome, and he *is* cool, but he's definitely only handsome and cool in an unexpected way, which is not the same as being handsome and cool in a regular way (like, say, Heath Ledger in *10 Things I Hate About You*), or in an obvious way (like, say, Josh Hartnett in 2000's *The Virgin Suicides*). So Amanda is out. (And I know these two movies aren't connected in any real or significant way, but since they both came out around the same time I'm going to take this opportunity to go ahead and nix everyone from 1999's *American Pie*.)

Zack Siler in 1999's *She's All That*: Extremely popular and extremely handsome and extremely perfect, yes, but he's out for the same reason that Amanda is out.[5] (Dean Sampson Jr., Paul Walker's character from this movie, is a much more likely candidate for inclusion in Regina's circle. He's the one who set the bet in place that Zack couldn't take a nerd and turn her into a prom queen.) (Taylor Vaughan, Zack's original girlfriend who dumped him to date an MTV *Real World* star, is also a potential pick for the circle.)

Ferris Bueller from 1986's *Ferris Bueller's Day Off*: Remember how in *Mean Girls* there were some inconsistencies in the stories that Regina and Aaron were each telling about who broke up with who? That's what I figure would happen with Ferris and Regina here. They'd date for a little while, then they'd break up after either Ferris made a few too many jokes that Regina didn't like or Regina did something truly mean to someone and Ferris realized he wasn't built for that kind of lifestyle, and then they'd both get caught in the middle of a he-said-she-said about why they broke up.

Biff Tannen from 1985's *Back to the Future*: He's too oafish to ever even exist in Regina's orbit, obviously, so that's one reason he's not getting a seat. A larger problem for him here, though, is that he tried to rape a classmate in front of his friends and also in front of her date. I don't want to put him in anyone's circle of friends, unless we're talking about a circle of friends in prison.[6] (It was always strange to me that George McFly, Marty McFly's father and the guy who punched out Biff when he was sexually assaulting Lorraine, chose to hire Biff later to work for him when they were all adults.)

Isis from 2000's *Bring It On*: Regina needs people in her group that she can control, that she can bend in whatever direction she needs them to bend. And while Isis is many things that would be appealing to Regina, she is not, in any way and for any reason, susceptible to that kind of pressure. (Big Red, the cheer captain from *Bring It On* who preceded Kirsten Dunst's character, would be a much more likely candidate, as would Courtney and Whitney.) (Also: I often wonder what life was like for Isis in her remaining high school and college days after ISIS became a thing

---

5. This movie came out my senior year of high school. I absolutely loved it. There's a part in it where Freddie Prinze Jr. plays hacky sack, which is probably the only time a cool person has ever played hacky sack.
6. As far as Untried Movie Crimes in movies considered to be classics are concerned, Biff attempting to rape Lorraine outside of a high school dance is up there with the guy from *Revenge of the Nerds* pretending to be a girl's boyfriend and performing oral sex on her.

that people in America largely knew about and were concerned with. That was some very bad luck for her. Usually it's like the school year ends, summer happens, then the next school year starts and a kid shows up and they have a new haircut or whatever. Poor Isis had the school year end, then summer happened, then the next school year started and suddenly she was sharing a name with a terrorist organization.)

The Three People Guaranteed to Have a Seat at the Table

Kathryn Merteuil from 1999's *Cruel Intentions*: Rich and merciless and vile and willing to ruin multiple lives just because she's bored. She gets a seat. She'd be perfect. And more than that: We would be looking at unprecedented levels of chicanery if Kathryn was able to convince Regina to try cocaine like Kathryn was doing in *Cruel Intentions*. If you had Regina and Kathryn together all teamed up and vicious and regularly using cocaine, it'd take about two weeks before the hallways in Movie High School looked like some combination of the last ten minutes of *Escape from New York* and the first ten minutes of *Saving Private Ryan*.

Claire from 1985's *The Breakfast Club*: None of the other characters from *The Breakfast Club* would be granted entry into the circle—not John Bender (the criminal), not Allison Reynolds (the basket case), not Brian Johnson (the brain), and not even Andrew Clark (the athlete)—but Claire would. Because more valuable than even her spot as an unquestioned high school princess is her dogged dedication to upholding the status quo. She would be the ideal member for Regina's circle of friends: a subservient debutante who adds value to the group without ever threatening to make a run at the throne. (She would, in effect, be the new Gretchen Wieners.) She gets a seat.

Harry Osborn from 2002's *Spider-Man*: Beautiful and a little dumb and able to be vicious and vindictive when necessary. He gets a seat.

A Bunch of People Who Would Not Be Chosen to Be Part of Regina George's Circle of Friends, but Certainly Not All of the People Who Would Not Be Chosen to Be a Part of Regina George's Circle of Friends

Troy Bolton from 2006's *High School Musical* (too sweet); Roxanne from 1995's *A Goofy Movie* (too young[7]); Olive from 2010's *Easy A* (too resourceful) and Marianne from 2010's *Easy A* (too Christian) and Woodchuck Todd from 2010's *Easy A* (his name is Woodchuck Todd); Steff McKee in 1986's *Pretty in Pink* (too creepy); Joey from *10 Things I Hate About You* (too much of a doof[8]); Cher from 1995's *Clueless* (too oblivious); Tyler Gage from 2006's *Step Up* (too poor); Madison from 2015's *The Duff* (too uninteresting); the human version of Scott Howard in 1985's *Teen Wolf* (too dorky) but possibly not the were-

---

7. Also a cartoon. I assume that would prove more troublesome here.

8. As part of the research for this chapter I spent something like eight straight days watching high school movies back to back to back. I'd almost forgotten how wonderful the poem scene at the end of *10 Things I Hate About You* is. I don't know that it's the finest sixty-second stretch of Julia Stiles's career, but I also don't know that it isn't.

wolf version of Scott Howard in 1985's *Teen Wolf*; Billy Loomis from 1996's *Scream* (too poor, and also too much of a literal murderer); post-injury Boobie Miles from 2004's *Friday Night Lights*[9] (too heart-breaking[10]); any of the Power Rangers from 2017's *Power Rangers* (too preoccupied with saving the world to dedicate the appropriate amount of time and energy into advancing Regina's legacy[11]); Lara Jean from 2018's *To All the Boys I've Loved Before* (too wholesome); any of the vampires from 1987's *The Lost Boys*[12] ("Get in, loser, we're going to kill some children"); Napoleon from 2004's *Napoleon Dynamite* (not enough skills); Darcy from 1999's *Varsity Blues* ("Is whipped cream a carb?"); Tracy Flick from 1999's *Election* (too ambitious); anyone from 1993's *Dazed and Confused*, but especially Ron Slater (too untethered to the high school caste system);[13] Hugo in 2001's *O* (too handsome); Seth from 2007's *Superbad* (too weird looking) and Evan from 2007's *Superbad* (too penis-based); any of the guys from 2012's *Chronicle* who gained powers from the alien ship thing (too odd); any of the guys from 1989's *Dead Poets Society* (too bookish); and all of the people from any high school movie where the school was set in a tough neighborhood, including but not limited to 1988's *Stand and Deliver*,[14] 2007's *Freedom Writers*, 1995's *Dangerous Minds*,[15] 1989's *Lean on Me*, and 1997's *One Eight Seven*.[16]

———

If we stick to the thing earlier about each cafeteria table having six seats, then that means we're still left with two seats to fill, what with Regina getting a seat, Kathryn from *Cruel Intentions* getting a seat, Claire from *The Breakfast Club* getting a seat, and Harry Osborn from *Spider-Man* getting a seat.

I think I'd fill one of those final two spots with Dionne from 1995's *Clueless*. She, same as Claire from *The Breakfast Club*, is someone who adds an instant and prominent value to the group without pulling too much of the spotlight away from Regina. And I know there's a tiny risk here that we might find out after dropping Dionne into the group that Regina, who we already know is homophobic, is also a racist, but I'd like to at least start out the discussion by assuming that she is not.

And with that very last spot, let's go with Ryan McCarthy from 2008's *Never Back Down*, a talented mixed martial artist with perfect teeth, perfect abs,

9. As a rule of thumb here, we can probably eliminate any injured athlete from every movie about high school sports.

10. The scene where he cleans out his locker and he's being very confident and Boobie-ish and then he gets to the car outside and gets in and has a breakdown is so fucking crushing. I've seen *Friday Night Lights* probably fifteen different times, and each time I (a) skip right past the scene, and (b) try with all my might and my heart and my love to will Mike into the end zone on that last play.

11. They sneak a joke early into this movie about masturbating an animal. That doesn't have anything to do with anything, but I thought I should tell you about it.

12. The vampires from 2008's *Twilight* have a better shot, would be my guess.

13. Maaaaaaaaaaaybe Parker Posey.

14. I would all-caps LOVE to see Regina in Mr. Escalante's class—or, better still, working on a group project with Angel as her partner.

15. EMILIO SHOULD STILL BE ALIVE. I WILL NEVER FORGIVE THAT PRINCIPAL.

16. We need a stretch of, like, forty-five movies about high schools with non-white people in them where the students have money and aren't stuck in the middle of some gang dilemma where they have to choose between ratting out another gang member or learning math or whatever.

and the kind of gray morality that would let him feel good about making fun of a kid whose dad died just so he could goad him into a fight so he could beat him up in front of everyone. He's the closest we've ever come to seeing a male version of Regina George.[17]

There you go. That's the lineup: Regina George, Kathryn from *Cruel Intentions*, Claire from *The Breakfast Club*, Harry from *Spider-Man*, Dionne from *Clueless*, and Ryan from *Never Back Down*.

Actually, you know what? I've changed my mind on the Harry from *Spider-Man* pick. His name feels weird in this group. It made sense at the time, and he seemed like a strong pick at the time because of star power, but I don't think it's going to work out well with this mix of people we've built. (This is one of those Shaquille O'Neal in Phoenix situations. They signed Shaq going into the 2009 season and everyone was like, "Oh shit, that's a good idea." But then they started playing actual games and everyone was like, "Oh shit, that was a horrible idea.") So let's cut him. And I know that this is breaking the rules because this is supposed to only be movie characters, but I'm going to drop a new name into all of this, because it's a name that can't be ignored, because it was a performance that can't be ignored.

The final spot goes to Julie Taylor from the TV version of *Friday Night Lights*. She was smart, and she was funny, and she could be mean, and she could be menacing, but she had *just* enough innocence in her that Regina would probably be able to press into shape whenever she really needed to. Also, she was an underclassman, so if we're looking at leg-acy here, she'd be able to slide into Regina's spot as the new leader of the group after Regina eventually graduated.

So there you go for real. That's the lineup: Regina George, Kathryn from *Cruel Intentions*, Claire from *The Breakfast Club*, Dionne from *Clueless*, Ryan from *Never Back Down*, and Julie Taylor from the TV version of *Friday Night Lights*.

That's who's in the Regina George circle of friends.

---

17. That being said, he's still not within forty miles of Regina George.

WHICH  MOVIE HAD THE MORE

INTENSE OPENING,

FACE/OFF  OR

FINDING NEMO?

SEVERAL YEARS AGO—this was back around 2014—I was at the theater with my wife and sons. We were there to watch *Big Hero 6*, which is about a boy who befriends an inflatable robot and starts a superhero team. It was a fun movie (the robot was fucking hilarious[1]), but one that had roots in real and true sadness (the star, Hiro, is a gifted fourteen-year-old robotics enthusiast who's forced into greatness after his mother, father, and brother all die within, like, a ten-minute stretch of movie time). And so I remember watching it, processing that part of it, then realizing how many other animated movie characters have a measure of that kind of gigantic heartache built into their existences.[2]

Simba from *The Lion King* is a good example (he watched his father die, and then was made to believe it was his fault). Bambi from *Bambi* is also an obvious one (his mother gets shot dead). Carl from *Up* is a big time choice here (he had to watch his wife get sick and die, and then he had to realize that she never got to go on her dream trip that he'd promised her decades earlier), as is WALL-E from *WALL-E* (my second favorite animated movie character[3]). There's also Elsa from *Frozen* (I remember watching an episode of *House* one time where we find out that a mom and a dad had a second child solely because they wanted to use the second child's bone marrow to help try and heal their first child because the first child had some rare disease

and I know that's not exactly like *Frozen*[4] but it's what I thought about during that scene where Anna is singing about wanting to build a snowman while poor Elsa is locked away in her room[5]).

And don't forget about Doc Hudson from *Cars* (as I've gotten older, I've become more and more susceptible to feeling badly for people and things that lose their utility as they age). Or Geppetto from *Pinocchio* (he was so lonely that he built a puppet and then tried to wish him into becoming a real boy). Or Ralph from *Wreck-It-Ralph* (he just wanted some friends, or at least some appreciation for his efforts). And so, so, so many others.

Also on that list, and somewhere near the top of it, really: Marlin from *Finding Nemo*. Because, okay, I mean, sure, he ends up saving Nemo after Nemo gets captured by a scuba diver, yes. And that's the part of the movie that everyone focuses on because that's the whole thrust of the movie, of course. And Marlin and Nemo have a wonderful and beautiful and fruitful father-son relationship, absolutely. But you have to remember that those two are, in effect, pushed toward that life by a horrible, horrible, horrible tragedy, which we'll talk more about in a moment.

—

---

1. The single best part is when the kid teaches him how to do a fist bump.
2. I ended up writing an article about sad animated movie characters for a place called Grantland, which is where I was working at the time. I'll always remember that assignment because when I was explaining the idea to one of my then six-year-old sons, he said, "Daddy, don't be mad, but that sounds dumb."
3. Woody is first.
4. Or anything like *Frozen*.
5. There's a good chance I've gotten the plot of this particular episode of *House* wrong.

Face/Off is a silly movie.[6] It stars John Travolta as an FBI agent named Sean Archer who, as a way to find where a massive bomb has been planted in Los Angeles, volunteers himself for a surgery where he'll have his face cut off and replaced with a bad guy's face so he can then pose as the bad guy and trick a different bad guy into telling him where the bomb is. (The bad guy Archer trades faces with is Castor Troy, a globally feared madman played by Nicolas Cage. He and Archer were fighting and Castor got blown backward by the blast from an airplane engine and bonked his head really badly and never woke up again.[7])

The face-swap plan actually works (after the surgery, Sean-as-Castor is dropped into a maximum security prison with Castor's brother, Pollux, whom he eventually tricks into telling him where the bomb is). But the problem is Castor ends up waking up from his coma a day or so after the surgery, calls a few of his bad guy friends, has them kidnap the doctor who performed the surgery, forces the doctor to put Archer's face on him, then kills the doctor and burns down the facility where the surgery took place so that nobody will ever know that the switch happened. So by this point in the movie you've got an FBI agent wearing a criminal's face trapped in prison, and a criminal wearing an FBI agent's face running around in the free world. And everything just sort of plays out from there.

And I know that sounds like a lot (and I also know that it *is* a lot), but that's the most streamlined version of the plot I can come up with.[8] And everything in it is set into motion by the movie's first three minutes, which contains a horrible, horrible, horrible tragedy, which we'll talk more about in a moment.

———

One quick thing about *Face/Off*, one quick thing Nic Cage, one quick thing about face-swapping, one quick thing about *Finding Nemo*, and one quick thing about intense movie openings:

Face/Off: *Face/Off* has aged into this very specific and very hokey kind of reverence. This, most people would assume, is because Travolta and Cage are fucking bonkers in it (and I suppose that *is* part of it). But really it's because John Woo, perhaps the greatest action movie director of all, ripped out the brake lines on the movie and floored it the whole way through. He's beautiful, and it's beautiful.[9]

Nic Cage: Nic Cage had one of the all-time great career stretches during the back half of the nineties. He was in *Leaving Las Vegas* in 1995 (he is uniquely

---

6. And also a great, great movie.

7. As a way to prove how deep into his coma he is, an FBI agent puts a cigarette out on his arm, which to me seems like a very extreme way to prove that point.

8. There's so much other stuff that happens in the movie that I didn't even get to, and won't be able to get to, including but not limited to: Castor shooting an undercover FBI agent and then tossing her out of the plane and then shrugging in celebration like Jordan in the '92 Finals; a shootout set to "Somewhere Over the Rainbow"; a floating prison where all the inmates wear magnetic boots and occasionally receive shock treatment; and Castor dressing up as a priest and fondling a young girl during a choir performance. (He wears the priest outfit as a disguise, but then he dances in it and then joins a choir mid-performance, which, I mean, why put on a disguise if you're not going to try to blend in? It'd be like if you were going hunting and so you put on camouflage pants and shirt but then walked around the woods shouting, "Hey, you fucking deer! Where you at?!")

9. His four best movies: 1989's *The Killer*, 1992's *Hard Boiled*, 1997's *Face/Off*, and 1986's *A Better Tomorrow*.

brilliant here), *The Rock* in 1996 (my favorite thing about *The Rock* is when they spend a bunch of time talking about how hard it's supposed to be to break out of Alcatraz and then Sean Connery does that shit in like two minutes), *Con Air* in 1997 (a masterpiece), *Face/Off* in 1997 (also a masterpiece), *City of Angels* in 1998 (a movie that finally got around to asking: What if angels could fuck?), *Snake Eyes* in 1998, *8MM* in 1999 (two movies I somehow always manage to get confused even though the only thing they have in common is that Nic Cage is in them), *Bringing Out the Dead* in 1999, and *Gone in 60 Seconds* in 2000 (somehow simultaneously beloved and underrated). The part that always jumps out at me whenever I revisit that list is realizing that he won an Oscar for Best Actor for his role in *Leaving Las Vegas* and then was like, "You know what I'm going to do now? A movie where I trade faces with someone." It's the second oddest post-Oscar heat check, losing out only to the time Gwyneth Paltrow won the Oscar for Best Actress with her role in 1998's *Shakespeare in Love* and then three years later she costarred with Jack Black in *Shallow Hal*, a movie about a guy who gets hypnotized by Tony Robbins into seeing the inner beauty of overweight and unattractive people.[10]

Face-Swapping: The idea of switching one person's face with another person's face brings up a number of interesting questions, the most lewd of which being: Wouldn't Sean's wife have noticed when his penis wasn't his penis when she had sex with Castor-as-Sean after Castor had started wearing Sean's face?[11] Or are they penis twins and that's why she didn't notice?

Finding Nemo: In *Finding Nemo*, the guy who scoops up Nemo when he sees him while scuba diving mentions later in the movie that he did so because he thought he was helping him. "I found that little guy struggling for life out on the reef and I saved him," he says, and it took me a good three or four times of watching *Finding Nemo* before I realized that this was (probably) a wink by the filmmakers acknowledging the way that oftentimes when we think we're helping in a situation we're really actually making things a billion times worse than if we'd just minded our business.

Intense Movie Openings: I like them. I like when the beginning of a movie feels like someone's holding a running chainsaw a few inches from your throat. The one from *Mad Max: Fury Road* is wonderful. The café explosion in *Children of Men* is a real ride. The countdown at the start of *Mission: Impossible III* is masterful. The one from *There Will Be Blood* doesn't feel like it's going to be intense but then you get to minute eight or nine of no words at all being spoken and suddenly it feels like you're walking a high wire between two buildings. I don't know if the car ride in *Lady Bird* counts as "intense" but it certainly counts as "goddamn artwork." The jolt from watching the two guys get shot in *Seven Psychopaths* is incredible. The beach scene in *Saving Private Ryan* sent actual former

---

10. Also, he has a friend who has a tail. That's not a joke.
11. This is a point that Bill Simmons brought up one night when we recorded a live podcast about *Face/Off* in October 2017, and I've thought about it every day since, and will continue to think about it every day until I'm buried in the ground.

soldiers into fits of post-traumatic stress.[12] There are a bunch. I like them, is the point.

———

THE HORRIBLE, HORRIBLE TRAGEDIES AT THE START OF EACH MOVIE:

Face/Off opens with Sean Archer at a fair (or something fair-like). He's there with his son and the two of them are having what appears to be a good time being father and son. (His son, Michael, looks to be somewhere around five or six years old.) As they ride on a merry-go-round, Castor Troy sets up a sniper rifle a couple hundred yards away because he plans on gunning down Sean. Castor looks through his scope, sees Sean with his son, thinks on the situation for a moment, then decides to go through with it. He fires a shot that hits Sean in the back. The bullet, what with it being fired from a high-powered rifle, exits Sean's chest and hits his son in the head, killing him.

Finding Nemo opens with Marlin and Coral, fish husband and fish wife, in the middle of a victory lap celebrating their new life together. They're doing so because (a) they've just moved into a new sea anemone at the edge of the reef that has a dazzling view of the wide open ocean, and (b) they are days away from over four hundred of their fish eggs hatching, meaning they are days away from being first-time parents, which is always an exciting time. They're swimming together and flirting together and being happy together and it's just this great, great moment. And

then it's not. After swimming out of the sea anemone, Marlin realizes that all the other sea life on the reef is hiding. He turns around and sees a barracuda not so far away. He tries to tell Coral to get back inside the anemone, but she decides she wants to try and protect her eggs instead. She zips toward them. The barracuda sees her and darts toward her. Marlin tries to jump and fight the barracuda, but the barracuda is too strong. Marlin gets knocked unconscious. When he wakes up, he finds that Coral and all but one of his would-be sons and daughters are dead, food victims of the barracuda.

So that's how each of those movies start. And so that's where we get this particular question: Which movie had the more intense opening, *Finding Nemo* or *Face/Off*?

———

This is a conversation topic that can be settled by digging into three different categories.

1. "WHICH OF THE TWO OPENINGS FEATURED A DAD WHO LOST THE MOST?" This part is a straight-up math situation, is what this is. Prior to being eaten, Coral makes mention of how there were more than four hundred eggs that were potentially going to hatch. So, at the very least, Marlin lost 402 loved ones in during his scene.[13] Sean, however, lost one.

And I get that there's an impulse to argue here that Sean losing Michael likely felt bigger and more substantial to him than Marlin losing his eggs felt to

---

12. This is seriously a real thing that happened.
13. You start with 401 because it's the minimum number you can have that's still "more than 400," and then you add one more for Coral.

him on account of Sean's son having been alive in his arms for several years while Marlin's eggs weren't even hatched yet. And also I get that maybe there's another impulse here to argue that Sean's son getting killed could've ruined Sean's marriage. But still: 402 is just too, too, too many dead things to ignore.

And besides, we know that Sean and his wife were still together six years later after Michael's death because we see it when the movie flashes forward. And also we know that Sean and his wife already had an older child who they loved very much, so it's not like they were all the way childless. And also we know that Sean ends up, in effect, replacing Michael at the end of the movie with a little boy that's approximately the same age that Michael was when he passed. And also we're all kind of ignoring that Marlin lost his wife in addition to losing his children, which is a very devastating multiplier.

All things told, this is a blowout win for Marlin.

———

One of the things I learned while I was researching for this chapter: When two clown fish mate and have a clutch of eggs, it's the dad's job to guard and protect them. I mention it because when the barracuda shows up in *Finding Nemo*, Marlin has no interest at all in guarding or protecting the eggs. He says to Coral, "Coral, get inside the house, Coral." When he sees her eyeing the eggs, he knows that she's going to try and save them. He says, "No. Coral, don't. They'll be fine." All he wanted to do was get back inside the house and hide and cross his fingers (fins?) and hope that the barracuda didn't see the eggs. I love Marlin a lot, but he was soft as fuck here.

———

2. "WHICH OF THE TWO OPENINGS FEATURED A TRAGEDY THAT IS GOING TO CARRY THE MOST COSMIC REGRET WITH IT?" This one is tricky because you're looking at two different types of regret here.

With Marlin, it's clear that moving into a sea anemone on the edge of the reef (which, in addition to its great view, also featured greater risk for danger, what with it being on the edge of the reef and not mixed in with everything else closer near the center) was Marlin's idea and not Coral's. And so I have to imagine there were a lot of nights where Marlin laid there and wondered to himself why he didn't pick a place for them to live that was not in such a barracuda-heavy traffic area. He probably really beat himself up about it, is my guess.

I remember one time when I was coaching middle school football there was a play at the end of a game where I realized that the other team was going to run a reverse. And so what I should've done right there is called a time-out and prepared the team for what was coming (or, at the very least, shouted out to my team what was coming without actually calling a time-out). I didn't, though. I just stood there quiet like an idiot. And sure enough, they ran a reverse and our little cornerback on that side of the field had no idea what to do and we ended up giving up a late-game touchdown that won the game for the other team and lost it for us. That play has eaten me up for years. I can close my eyes and still see our poor tiny cornerback getting blasted into smithereens by the block that sprung the receiver for his score. It's been over half a decade since that play happened and it still hurts. Marlin's thing was like that but instead of losing a seventh-grade football game, over four hundred of his family members died.[14]

With Sean, it's clear that Castor had no intention of killing Sean's son. Castor pauses just enough when he sees Michael through the scope to let you know that he's thinking about possibly not shooting Sean right then. And there's a shot of Castor after he shoots Sean where he realizes he's accidentally hit Michael and there's a real look of dread on his face. And so Sean not only has to live with knowing that his son was killed by mistake, but also he has to know that it happened as a kind of collateral damage. (Sean, an FBI agent, was chasing after Castor, a criminal. Castor decided to kill Sean because he was tired of being chased. Had Sean been, say, a fireman or a schoolteacher or a tax attorney or literally anything else that was not law enforcement-y, Michael probably would still be alive.)

At any rate, I think there are enough of "I should've just . . ." sentences on Sean's side of this that we have to lean this category in his direction.

—

One of the things I realized while I was researching for this chapter: Typically, an actor or actress is two layers deep in acting, and occasionally three layers

deep in acting. After the face-swapping in *Face/Off*, though, both Travolta and Cage are four layers deep in acting, which is tied for the most layers deep in acting anyone has ever gone. Travolta, for example, can't just pretend to be Sean Archer and also he can't just pretend to be Castor Troy. He has to pretend to be Nic Cage who is pretending to be John Travolta who is pretending to be Sean Archer who is pretending to be Castor Troy. Same goes for Cage, except in the other direction (Cage → Travolta → Castor Troy → Sean Archer). I don't know why this is so interesting to me, but I have to assume that if you've made it this far into this chapter then you'll probably find it interesting, too.

—

3. "WHICH OF THE TWO OPENINGS FEATURED HUMANS?" Listen, I really like *Finding Nemo*. A lot. Marlin, while at times cloying, is superb as a character and as a complex creation. But he's still a fucking clown fish. It's easy to watch the beginning of *Finding Nemo* and be like, "Can we just hurry up and get to the sea turtles? Those guys are funny." You can't do that with *Face/Off*, though. You can't watch a child get shot in the head and think anything other than, "Oh my God. Did that kid just get shot in the head?" Because humans are humans and fish are fish.

Face/Off wins this category.

Face/Off wins the whole thing.

Face/Off's opening is more intense.[15]

---

14. It was not "like that," I suppose.

15. My greatest hope is that there's a clown fish version of this same book for sale in underwater bookstores everywhere and they have this same chapter in it except it ends with, "Sean Archer, while at times cloying, is superb as a character and as a complex creation. But he's still a fucking human."

ARE
IN THE

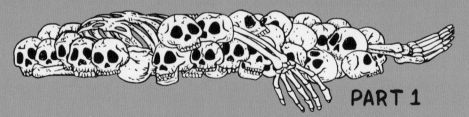

ACTION MOVIE KILLS

HALL OF FAME?

PART 1

DID YOU KNOW THAT THERE'S AN INTER-NATIONAL SCUBA DIVING HALL OF FAME? That's a real thing that actually, truly, honestly is really real. It was founded in 2000 and, per their website, it "honors the pioneers of the sport of scuba diving."[1] There's also a Consumer Electronics Hall of Fame (I am an employed adult who is married with children and have been on this earth for more than three decades and I still don't exactly know what the phrase "consumer electronics" means), and a Burlesque Hall of Fame (I know what "burlesque" means, thank you), and a Robot Hall of Fame (this one is not nearly as fun or interesting as you're imagining it in your head to be), and a Hall of Fame for Great Americans (this one somehow sounds more fake than the International Scuba Diving one).

There are many Halls of Fame, in fact. Many, many Halls of Fame, to be sure. So many, actually, that there's an entire Wikipedia page dedicated to all of the different Halls of Fame. But one that's not on there yet, because I'm just right now making it up, is the Action Movie Kills Hall of Fame, which is what the following two chapters are about.

———

A number of questions about the Action Movie Kills Hall of Fame, and a number of rules regarding the Action Movie Kills Hall of Fame as well:

What is the Action Move Kills Hall of Fame? It's exactly what you think it is: a very specific Hall of Fame that celebrates only the very best kills that happen in action movies.[2] It's not been designed to (directly) celebrate the action movies, mind you. And it's not been designed to (directly) celebrate the action movie heroes either. And it's not even been designed to (directly) celebrate the real humans who played the action movie heroes. It's been designed to celebrate action movie kills. And, yes, sure, of course, a lot of people get killed in action movies, but, same as there are a lot of professional baseball players in the history of the MLB, only the very best, most important ones make it into the Hall of Fame.

Is there a scoring system or something that determines which kills get into the Action Movie Kills Hall of Fame and which ones don't? Not really, no. There's some stuff that can help, definitely. Like, it's helpful if something cool was said either right before or after the kill (like in *Die Hard 2* when John McClane does the "Yippee-ki-yay, motherfucker" callback before blowing up the airplane). And it's helpful if the kill is something that, for whatever reason, sticks in your bones (like in *The Raid 2* when Rama kills Baseball Man and Hammer Girl during their fight). And it's helpful if the kill was either extremely hard-earned (like the pencil scene in *John Wick 2*) or extremely satisfying (like when they finally killed the T-1000 in *Terminator 2*). But mostly, it's all about feel.

---

1. I would like to officially call into question the legitimacy of the mission statement of the International Scuba Diving Hall of Fame, and I would like to do so because Carter Blake, the hero shark wrangler from *Deep Blue Sea*, is *not* in the International Scuba Diving Hall of Fame. And, I mean, if Carter Blake isn't worthy, then who is?
2. It honors the pioneers of the sport of killing people in action movies, if you will.

All of the examples you just gave were from movie sequels. Does a movie have to be a sequel for one of its kills to be eligible for the Action Movie Kills Hall of Fame? What? No. It was just a coincidence. The kill does not have to have happened in a sequel.

Did you actually like *Die Hard 2*? Not especially, no. And I don't think that that particular airplane explosion kill is one that could ever make it into the Action Movie Kills Hall of Fame either. But it's just that I can remember the feeling I had being a kid and watching *Die Hard 2* and hearing the "Yippee-ki-yay-motherfucker" line and realizing that they'd done it as a tie-in to the original *Die Hard*. That was maybe the first time in my life I can remember watching a movie give itself a high-five like that, and so I've just always had it in my head.

Does it matter who gets the kill in the action movie? Like, does it have to be the star of the action movie? No. It doesn't have to be the star. It can be anyone. It can be a sidekick, or a villain, or someone who works for a villain, or a nobody, or an anybody. As long as the scene ends with someone's family having to make funeral arrangements, then you're good to go.

Okay, but so are there any rules at all in place here that govern if a kill is or isn't eligible? It seems like there should be rules. There actually are some rules, yes. They are:

- **THE NUMBERS RULE:** Much the same way that heaven has a capacity limit, so too does the Action Movie Kills Hall of Fame. There have just been too many hall of fame–caliber kills that have happened in action movies to make

it feasible for them to all be included here. That being the case, we're going to cap it. The inaugural class of the Action Movie Kills Hall of Fame only has nineteen spots available. So eighteen kills will make the cut, and then all the other kills will have to cross their fingers and hope they make it in on the next go-round whenever it is that I revisit this idea because I've run out of other ideas.

- **THE KILLING SPREE RULE:** Any of the kills that happen during a killing spree are, of course, on the table. HOWEVER, the entirety of a killing spree is not. So, let's say you wanted to pick the kill from the hardware store scene in *The Equalizer* where Denzel hangs the guy with barbed wire. That's fine. That's an okay thing to do. What you can't do, though, is select the entire scene, no matter how great it is. It has to be one specific kill that gets picked.

- **THE OVERSEAS RULE:** Kills that happen in foreign films are absolutely eligible. We think of action movies as a distinctly American thing (and maybe they've become exactly that), but the Action Movie Kills Hall of Fame is globally inclusive. Just think on it like the NBA: The talent overseas is just too great to ignore.

- **THE SUPERPOWERS RULE:** A superhero movie is not an action movie. It's just not. So any kill that has ever happened in a superhero movie is out. And maybe you're thinking, "Well, that's fine. Lots of superhero movies don't even have kills, and the ones that do have kills usually aren't interesting beyond the relationship that the audience has with whoever it is that's being killed." But to that I would say, "Sure, but what about the Magic Trick Kill that the Joker does in *The Dark Knight*? Or the 'Some motherfuckers are always trying to ice skate uphill' kill in *Blade*? Or the 'Walk away from that, you son of a bitch' kill from *Iron Man* 3?" There are more, for sure. And losing them all sucks. But rules are rules.

- **THE ACTION MOVIES RULE:** This is an extension of the superpowers rule above: The movie that a kill happens in has to, above all else, feel more like an action than any other kind of movie. And I know that that's a hazy discussion to have, yes, but that's because hall of fames are, by their own design, hazy. It's what makes them so much fun (and also, at times, so infuriating). And here's a good example of how tricky this rule can end up being: A kill from 1989's *Tango & Cash*, which is a movie about two cops trying to solve a crime, would count. But a kill from 2012's *End of Watch*, which is also a movie about two cops trying to solve a crime, would not count. And the only reason is because one feels like an action movie and one does not.

- **THE STARTING POINT RULE:** There has to be a rule in place that, unlike the one above, is absolutely firm and inarguable. As such, let's make it so that no kills that happened in any action movie before 1982 are eligible. And I'm going with 1982 as the date because that's the year that *48 Hours* came out, and *48 Hours* is often cited as the first Buddy-Cop movie, and Buddy-Cop movies are among my very favorite subcategories of action movies, right up there with Avenging A Loved One Who's Been Kidnapped Or Murdered action movies and Forced Into Action action movies.[3]

Let's go.

AN ACTION MOVIE KILLS HOF INDUCTEE:
When John Matrix kills Bennett by throwing a goddamn steam pipe through his chest in 1985's *Commando*.

Have you ever heard of the foot-in-the-door sales technique? It's a trick that you do where you offer up some easy-to-say-yes-to thing so that the person you're talking to feels comfortable and like they're in control of the situation. You do it once or twice before you get to the real thing you want them to agree to. That's what I'm doing right now. I'm starting this with a pick that is Action Movie Unquestionable (Schwarzenegger! John Matrix! Bennett! The post-death quip![4] *Commando*! The golden age of action movies!) because the next pick is one that (probably) some people won't see coming.

---

3. I'm going to break this rule one time during the induction ceremony.
4. "Let off some steam, Bennett."

Perhaps an unexpected pick for the inaugural class of the Action Movie Kills Hall of Fame, but it's one that absolutely has to be made for three reasons:

1. Jet Li is marvelous. He showed up in 1998's *Lethal Weapon 4* as a hit man and it was obvious to everyone that he was going to be in our movie lives for a long, long time. He has this tiny moment during the movie where Riggs aims a gun's laser beam at his chest and Li, with so much lordliness that you can somehow *hear* his body filling with disdain, brushes it away like you would a gnat. It's fantastic, and exactly the kind of thing only a movie star with real weight can pull off.

2. Following *Lethal Weapon 4*, six of Li's next nine movies were new era action movie classics. There was *Romeo Must Die* (we got the vertebrae kill scene that they delivered to us in x-ray vision, which was a truly great moment[5]), *The One* (secretly brilliant), *Kiss of the Dragon* (he gets in a fight while N.E.R.D.'s "Lapdance" plays, and this feels like a good spot to point out that nobody has ever married fight scenes in action movies to rap music better than Jet Li), *Cradle 2 The Grave* (he fights an entire octagon full of cage fighters[6]), *Unleashed* (he's a human who's actually a dog), and *War* (JET LI VS. JASON STATHAM).[7] And . . .

3. Despite all of those things, no action movie star has ever been as underappreciated as Jet Li. (Second place on the Underappreciated Action Movie Stars list is Wesley Snipes.) (Third place is Jackie Chan.) (Fourth place is Michelle Rodriguez.) (Fifth place is Carl Weathers.) (I can do this for a long time, if you'd like.) (But the point is you have to go a long way down the list before you get to a white man action movie star who is underappreciated.)

Jet Li has always unofficially been a hall of famer. Now he's officially one too.

In *Death Hammer 3: . . . And Hammers for All*, the follow-up to 2017's surprisingly successful *Death Hammer 2: Hammergeddon*, we tag along with Detroit cop John Hardest as he takes down a corrupt senator named Tom Murphy and La Muerte, a shadow organization whose slimy tentacles reach all the way up to the most exclusive and powerful corners of the American government.

---

5. The first time this happened in a movie was in 1974's *The Street Fighter*, a karate exploitation movie starring Sonny Chiba.

6. Also, DMX stars in this movie with him, and let me tell you: If the people who made *Cradle 2 The Grave* were trying to satisfy all of the things twenty-two-year-old me wanted in a movie, they fucking nailed it.

7. The other three—*Hero*, *Fearless*, and *The Warlords*—were not action movies.

In the movie's final scene, John Hardest tears through an office full of henchmen to finally get to Tom Murphy. Murphy begs for his life, screaming, "You can't kill me. I'm a United States senator!" To which Hardest responds by smashing a hammer into Tom Murphy's head with so much rage and fury that it explodes. Hardest stands over the body for a second, then says, "You've just been impeached." Then he looks up, sees an American flag in the corner of the office, raises his right hand above his heart, then says, "I pledge allegiance to the Flag of the United States of America. And to the Republic for which it stands, one Nation under God, indivisible, with liberty..." He pauses for a second, looking around at all the dead men at his feet. He allows himself a small moment of relief, and the hint of a smile sneaks across his face. ". . . and hammers for all."

AN ACTION MOVIE KILLS HOF INDUCTEE:
When President Harrison Ford snaps Gary Oldman's neck by wrapping a cargo strap around his neck and then opening his parachute as they both dangled out of the back of the plane in 1997's *Air Force One*.

A few notes about this kill: (1) Harrison Ford's bodyguard detail ought to be absolutely ashamed of themselves. (2) Harrison Ford being very handsome and cool while saying "Get off my plane" is at one end of the White Men Telling People To Get Off Things spectrum. On the other end of that spectrum is when the ugly guy who lives on the subway train in *Ghost* yells *"Get off my train!"* at Patrick Swayze. And somewhere in between those two is Clint Eastwood telling the Hmong gang members to get off his lawn in *Gran Torino*. (3) *Air Force One* is not the best Harrison Ford action movie, but it's definitely the campiest Harrison Ford action movie, which means it's my favorite Harrison Ford action movie. (4) Mostly all of the other entries here are listed by their character's names. Not this one, though. *Air Force One* is just one of those movies where you call everyone by their real names. It's like how nobody ever calls Liam Neeson's character in *Taken* by his character name, they just call him Liam Neeson.

AN ACTION MOVIE KILLS HOF INDUCTEE:
When Harry Hart super kills a guy during the church killing spree scene in 2014's *Kingsman: The Secret Service*.

This scene is an incredible piece of art.[8] It's a straight-up free-for-all of murder and destruction that is brilliantly choreographed (it's presented as one long shot) and expertly soundtracked (they used Lynyrd Skynyrd's "Free Bird," a nod that's double clever because the scene happens in a hate group's church in Kentucky and Lynyrd Skynyrd has, since their earliest days and almost without exception, incorporated the Confederate flag into their branding[9]). Harry kills nearly forty people in less than

---

8. Harry hadn't intended on killing a bunch of people when he went into the hate group's church, FYI. He was just there investigating some stuff. But the movie's main bad guy, Richmond Valentine (Samuel L. Jackson), had arranged it so that when he turned a knob on a machine everyone's cell phone would start emitting a high pitched sound that turned everyone into raging lunatics.

9. In 2012, members of the band said they were discontinuing their use of the Confederate flag. They changed their minds after protests from their fans.

four minutes, many of them in exciting and innovative ways. The specific kill from the killing spree that's getting inducted into the Action Movie Kills Hall of Fame is the one where he electrocutes a guy in the face, stuffs a grenade in his pocket, breaks his spine with an elbow blow, breaks his neck by slamming him into a stanchion, then runs away as the grenade explodes. By my count, Harry kills him two, maybe three different times during their fight, and I think it's important that the AMKHOF acknowledges that kind of stat.

(Incidentally: This scene is the finest killing spree scene that we have ever gotten in an action movie. It goes this one for first place, then the one in *Kill Bill* where Beatrix Kiddo fights The Crazy 88,[10] then the nightclub scene in *John Wick*. Some other good ones that are, sadly, going to go unmentioned from here forward: the hallway shootout in *Kick-Ass*; the lobby shootout with Neo and Trinity in *The Matrix*; the restaurant shootout in *A Better Tomorrow*; the bar shootout in *Desperado*; and the catacombs shootout in *John Wick: Chapter 2*.)

Aliens, which came out in 1986 and leaned all the way into the Ripley vs. Xenomorph rivalry, is a full-on action movie.[11] So much so, in fact, that it ends with Ripley, who by that point is absolutely fed the fuck up with the xenomorphs, stepping inside of a power loader exosuit,[12] calling the queen xenomorph a bitch, and then fighting her in hand-to-hand combat[13] before tossing her into the cold emptiness of outer space.

And listen, I have watched a lot of cool people do cool things in movies, but I can't immediately think of three things cooler than walking into a room with a gigantic murdering alien and picking a fight with it by calling it a bitch. I mean, Ripley had just a few minutes before that watched the queen xenomorph literally rip someone in half. It happened several feet in front of her eyes and face. And still, it didn't matter. Ripley survived two full movies of watching pretty much everyone she knew and liked (or loved) getting killed by xenomorphs and was still like, "You know what? Okay. Enough is enough. It's time for me to put these robot hands on you." AND THEN SHE FUCKING PUT THOSE ROBOT HANDS ON HER. Ellen Ripley is untouchable.

> **AN ACTION MOVIE KILLS HOF INDUCTEE:**
> When Ellen Ripley puts on the exosuit and fights the queen xenomorph in 1986's *Aliens*.

To be clear: *Alien*, a wildly important film that came out in 1979, is a horror movie. It's follow-up, however,

---

10. I am not entirely sure that *Kill Bill* is an action movie. If you decide that it's not, then go ahead and slide the nightclub scene in *John Wick* up to second and move the lobby shootout from *The Matrix* up into third. Keanu is great in a killing spree.

11. The way you know this is true is that Ripley has a team of Space Marines with her to battle the xenomorphs. (The best space marine is Private Hudson, a character played by Bill Paxton. He says things like, "Hey, Ripley. Don't worry. Me and my squad of ultimate badasses will protect you." He gets killed, of course.)

12. The exosuit is basically a twelve-foot-tall robot shell that Ripley gets inside of and controls with her body.

13. Or, robot-to-alien combat, I guess?

WHICH KILLS

ARE IN THE

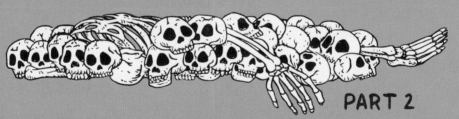

ACTION MOVIE KILLS

HALL OF FAME?

PART 2

... CONT'D.

AN ACTION MOVIE KILLS HOF INDUCTEE:
When Achilles kills Hector in front of his own castle in 2004's *Troy*.

First: I'm still mad at weak ass Orlando Bloom for setting all of this in motion.

Second: As soon as Achilles showed up outside the castle walls, Hector should've known he wasn't winning that battle. He should've just shot an arrow down into Achilles's head and been done with it.

Third: Fuck that one-on-one fighting bullshit. This was like the Ancient Greece version of someone walking to your home, knocking on your front door, then beating you up in front of your friends and family. That's not how that fight is going at my house. You knock on my door to fight, I'm coming outside with six or seven just-got-out-of-jail Mexicans with me. Hector's people deserve a lot of the blame for Hector's death.

AN ACTION MOVIE KILLS HOF INDUCTEE:
When John Creasy puts an explosive in a bad guy's butthole and then blows him up in 2004's *Man on Fire*.

John Creasy is hired to protect Pita, the nine-year-old daughter of a wealthy businessman in Mexico. Creasy gets ambushed one day while on duty. Kidnappers take and then kill Pita.[1] Creasy has a conversation with Pita's mother in Pita's room afterward as they mourn the situation. She asks him what he's going to do. He says, "I'm gonna kill them. Anyone that was involved, anybody who profited from it, anybody who opens their eyes at me." Pita's mom sits with his words for a second, then says back to him, "You kill them all." And that's what the fuck he does.

He loads up on guns and weapons and supplies and then goes hunting. He duct tapes one guy's hands to a steering wheel, cuts off a couple of his fingers, cauterizes each wound with the car's cigarette lighter, shoots the guy in the head, then sends the car off a cliff. He shoots a few people in the chest at a dance party. He explodes an SUV full of bad guys with a rocket launcher. It's a collection of kills that, as Christopher Walken's character describes it in the movie, is a "masterpiece." Creasy's best of the bunch, though, is when he strips a guy down to his boxers, ties his hands to the hood of a car, puts a bomb up a guy's butt, interrogates him, then explodes him into a thousand chunks as he walks away.

And please pay attention to this part because it's important: All of these things would've been cool no matter who it was that the producers of the movie hired to play John Creasy. (Picture Jason Statham in that role, or Jackie Chan in that role,[2] or Sylvester Stallone in that role, or Charlize Theron in that role, or Wesley Snipes in that role.) They didn't just get *anybody*, though. They got Denzel Washington, one of the greatest actors of all time. I still can't believe that they killed him off at the end of

---

1. That's what we're told anyway. We find out at the end of the movie that she's actually alive.
2. We basically got this with *The Foreigner*.

the movie. What a waste. We should've gotten at least three *Man on Fire* movies.

> **AN ACTION MOVIE KILLS HOF INDUCTEE:**
> When Maximus scissor-chops the one guy's head off during the "Are you not entertained?" scene in 2000's *Gladiator*.

This one checks off all the boxes. It has:

- **A great character.** Maximus Decimus Meridius, a battle-worn general in the Roman military who ends up being sold into combat slavery after a whole bunch of shit in his life goes extremely wrong.[3]
- **A great pre-fight moment.** By the time we get to the "Are you not entertained?" scene, Maximus, who is going by the name Spaniard, has proven himself a powerful gladiator and undeniable leader. So much so, in fact, he walks into the battle arena alone, allowing his men to stay in the holding cell so that they don't have to risk their lives in the fight. (I still remember watching this happen, realizing that Maximus was walking out there to fight everyone alone, then saying very loudly in the theater, "This motherfucker here.")
- **A great battle.** He takes on six fighters at once, each one armed and wearing battle armor. They all fall to his blade.
- **A great final kill.** He stabs the final guy in the chest with two swords, pulls them out, then swings them both at the guy's neck, scissor-chopping his head clean off his shoulders.
- **And a great ending.** Maximus, who hates that he has been forced into sport killing, takes measure of the carnage he's just caused, throws one of the swords into the gladiator viewing VIP boxes, shouts, "Are you not entertained?! Are you not entertained?! Is this not why you are here?!" and then throws his second sword down into the dirt and spits in disgust.

Top level.

> **AN ACTION MOVIE KILLS HOF INDUCTEE:**
> When Imperator Furiosa rips Immortan Joe's whole fucking face off his head at the end of 2015's *Mad Max: Fury Road*.

Four things here:

1. *Mad Max: Fury Road* is one of the three best movies we've gotten in the past twenty years.[4] (The top three are *Mad Max: Fury Road*, *The Social Network*, and *Get Out*, but not in that order.) I mention that because . . .
2. Charlize Theron is the best part of the movie. She plays Imperator Furiosa, a one-armed lieutenant in Immortan Joe's army. She's the person who eventually leads the revolt against him.
3. Imperator Furiosa is an all-timer of a movie character, and Charlize Theron is an all-timer of an

---

3. Commodus, the petulant emperor played pitch perfectly by Joaquin Phoenix, asks for Maximus's loyalty. Maximus, a man of honor and nobility, declines. Commodus orders his men to murder Maximus, as well as Maximus's wife and son. Maximus survives. His wife and son do not.
4. There's a blind guitarist in this movie. There's also a blind guitarist in *Road House* (Jeff Healey). There's also a blind guitarist in *Fargo* (Jose Feliciano). I don't know a lot about a lot, but I do know that if your movie has a blind guitarist in it, I'm going to watch it and I'm going to love it.

actress. She can play every kind of person and every kind of thing. She's had the strength of a god (*Hancock*) and drawn the ire of the devil (*The Devil's Advocate*). She's been a murderer with no eyebrows (*Monster*) and a debutante with perfect eyebrows (*That Thing You Do*). She's been an expert driver (*The Italian Job*) and also a person who gets driven (*Long Shot*). She's played a villain who kills a mother in front of her child (*Fate of the Furious*) and a hero who rescues a mother before her child is born (*Mad Max: Fury Road*). She can do it all.

4. Right before Furiosa kills Joe, she looks him right in the eyes and growls, "Remember me?" That's a cool thing to say before you kill someone because either (a) the person you killed does remember you, and they know exactly what they did to you in the past that made you come back and murder them; or (b) they don't remember you, in which case they have to spend all of eternity wandering around the afterlife saying stuff to themselves like, "Who the fuck was that who ripped my face off?!"

> **AN ACTION MOVIE KILLS HOF INDUCTEE:**
> When Rama and Prakoso fight to the death in the kitchen in 2014's *The Raid 2*.

Holy shit.[5]

> **AN ACTION MOVIE KILLS HOF INDUCTEE:**
> When Clive Owen kills a guy with a carrot during the opening of 2007's *Shoot 'Em Up*.

Clive Owen had a truly remarkable run during the middle stretch of the 2000s. Going in order, he was in the following movies from 2005 to 2007: *Closer* (a really great movie about really bad relationships), *Sin City* (a perfect vehicle for his obvious brand of coolness), *Derailed* (a thriller that manages to sweep your legs out from under you two times in a row), *Inside Man* (probably his best movie), *Children of Men* (really good), and *Shoot 'Em Up* (the movie that features the kill that gets him a surprise induction into the Action Movie Kills Hall of Fame).

The details that make up the plot of *Shoot 'Em Up* are of no real consequence. All that you need to know is that somebody in Hollywood was like, "Hey, don't you think it'd be cool if we just let Clive Owen kill a bunch of bad guys for an hour and a half?" And someone else was like, "Clive Owen is one of the four coolest people on the planet right now, so my answer is: Yes. You're goddamn right I do." And then together they wrote a check for nearly $40 million to get a movie where we got to see Clive Owen do exactly that, the first kill of which being one where Clive stops a guy from beating a woman, shoves a carrot into his mouth, then palm-strikes it out of the back of his head. And guess what he says to the guy's dead

---

5. Iko Uwais, the guy who plays Rama in *The Raid* and *The Raid 2*, is the greatest pure movie fighter we have ever had. He's fast, strong, gifted, and violent. He's so good at fighting in movies that I always feel like I have to whisper when I'm talking about him. That's why you and I are having this conversation in the footnotes rather than in the actual chapter text. It's the quietest I can be in print.

face immediately afterward? I'll tell you what he says: He says, "Eat your vegetables."

> **AN ACTION MOVIE KILLS HOF INDUCTEE:**
> When Danny Trejo uses a bad guy's intestines as a rope to escape out of an ambush in a hospital in 2010's *Machete*.

He really did that. Five guys were sent to a hospital to murder him and he snuck around behind them, killed two of them by slicing their faces to bits, then killed a third by cutting up his stomach, reaching inside, grabbing a hold of his small intestine, then running and jumping out of a window, using the intestines as a rope to swing down through a window on the floor below them.

> **AN ACTION MOVIE KILLS HOF INDUCTEE:**
> When John Rambo kills the guy in 1982's *Rambo: First Blood*.

There are three Rambo kills you need to know about. There's the one in *Rambo II* where he covers himself in mud to camouflage himself perfectly up against a river bank and then sneak attacks a guy who's hunting him (you need to know about this one because it's the coolest kill of Rambo's movie career). There's the one in *Rambo IV* where he literally shoots a guy in half using a mega machine gun (you need to know about this one because it's the most gruesome kill of Rambo's movie career). And there's the one in *Rambo: First*

Blood where he throws a rock at a helicopter and it hits the window and makes the pilot swerve the helicopter, which ends up making a guy fall out. That's the one that makes it into the Action Movie Kills Hall of Fame.

However, unlike most every other kill that's makes its way into the AMKHOF, the helicopter death scene isn't getting in because it's an especially memorable kill (best I can tell, it was an accident). No, it's getting in because of how important it was. Because consider this: The guy who falls out of the plane is the only person we see die in *Rambo: First Blood*. By the time we get to *Rambo IV* in 2008, 247 people die on screen.[6] Rambo catching that first post–Vietnam War body really sent him spiraling.

> **AN ACTION MOVIE KILLS HOF INDUCTEE:**
> When Coffy kills Brunswick at the end of 1973's *Coffy*.

Remember the footnote earlier about how I was going to break the Starting Point rule one time during the induction ceremony? That's this one right now. I'm breaking the rule for Pam Grier, because you should always break rules for Pam Grier.

Grier is the star of *Coffy*, a blaxploitation film about a fed up nurse who, in response to several tragedies and injustices, goes on a murdering spree. Her tour of punishment ends with her (a) running over a guy by crashing a car into the front of a house, (b) shotgun blasting a guy in the chest, (c) shotgun blasting a mafia boss while he doggie paddles in a pool, and then (d) killing her crooked politician boyfriend by shooting him in the groin in front of a white woman he either had just finished sleeping with or was about to sleep with. And it's the last one that makes it into the AMKHOF. And it does so for several reasons.

For one, *Coffy* is one of the most significant, most influential blaxploitation films ever made[7]. For two, if you imagine it so that all of everyone who ever starred in an action movie was invited to a giant dinner, Pam Grier is a part of a very small group of people who get a No Questions Asked seat at whatever table it is that the most distinguished actors and actress sit at. And for three, shooting a bad guy in the dick with a shotgun is a great move. If, for whatever reason, I one day get cast to star in an action movie, I promise you right now that that movie will lead the league in dicks shot with a shotgun. I'm gonna be like when Jordan led the NBA in scoring in '87, except but with dicks getting shot.

> **AN ACTION MOVIE KILLS HOF INDUCTEE:**
> When Roger Murtaugh revokes the diplomatic immunity of a crooked government employee in 1989's *Lethal Weapon 2*.

There are three parts of this kill that are important: (1) Murtaugh says a neat thing right before he kills the bad guy, and saying neat things right before or after you kill someone is always Action Movie Important.[8]

(2) The kill happens in *Lethal Weapon 2*, and that's important because the late eighties to mid-nineties is really when we started to see the emergence of the action movie franchise.[9] And (3) The evolution of Roger Murtaugh from *Lethal Weapon* to *Lethal Weapon 2* is symbolic. His whole bit in *Lethal Weapon* was that he was frustrated and annoyed that Riggs kept killing everyone. But by the end of *Lethal Weapon 2*, he was perfectly fine with shooting a guy in the head just because.

> **AN ACTION MOVIE KILLS HOF INDUCTEE:**
> When John McClane drops Hans Gruber to his death in 1988's *Die Hard* and when Neo kills Agent Smith by jumping inside of him in 1999's *The Matrix*.

I am going to take advantage of the fact that there is, at the moment, no governing body overseeing the Action Movie Kills Hall of Fame and squeeze two kills into one entry space here. And part of the reason I'm doing so is because these kills were the best in each of their movies, yes, but mostly I'm doing so because these movies were both watershed moments in action movie history. A very quick summary:

Before *Die Hard*, action movies were mostly seen as a genre for gigantor muscle men who maybe

---

7. Others include (but are not limited to) 1971's *Shaft*, 1972's *Super Fly*, 1973's *The Mack*, 1974's *Foxy Brown* (which also starred Pam Grier), and 1975's *Dolemite*.

8. The bad guy, a high-ranking government member from another country, shoots Murtaugh's partner in the back a few times. When he runs out of bullets he holds up a legal document so that Murtaugh can see it and says, "Diplomatic immunity," which is basically his way of saying to Murtaugh, "Yes, I am a criminal and you have witnessed me being a criminal, but fuck you. I get to go back to my home country." Murtaugh cranks his neck a bit, shoots a bullet into the bad guy's forehead, then says, "It's just been revoked."

9. *Beverly Hills Cop II* in 1987; *Lethal Weapon 2* in 1989; *Indiana Jones and the Last Crusade* in 1989; *Die Hard 2* in 1990; *Terminator 2: Judgement Day* in 1991; *Batman Returns* in 1992.

weren't so great at acting. After *Die Hard*, it was like, "Whoa. Wait. These movies might actually be better if we got real actors to play real humans in them." And that was a huge shift. And that's nothing to say of the way it narrowed the action down to a smaller space and conceit, which spun off in 100 different directions for 100 different knockoffs, starting almost immediately after it came out (examples: *Toy Soldiers* in 1991, *Under Siege* in 1992, *Speed* in 1994, *Sudden Death* in 1995, *The Rock* in 1996, *Air Force One* in 1997, etc.) and still happening today (*Skyscraper* in 2018).

The Matrix represented an equally big shift in the genre. Scott Tobias, a film critic buddy of mine, explained it as such in an email exchange we had one time: "When you [got] to *The Matrix* in 1999, you had a permanent shift away from physical action and practical stunts, and more of an emphasis on the plasticity of digital effects. The Wachowskis took all this incredible, stylized action that was happening in Hong Kong and added the technical innovation that was developing in Hollywood, so it's more of a transitional film."

AN ACTION MOVIE KILLS HOF INDUCTEE:
When Dalton rips out Jimmy's throat in 1989's *Road House.*

When I was putting the final version of the list of the kills that were going to make it into the Action Movie Kills Hall of Fame, I knew that the final spot was going to go to Patrick Swayze (who I have loved dearly for years). What I didn't know, though, was which kill was going to be picked. Because he had two during his beautiful time on Earth that stand taller than all the rest: There's the one that I settled on (the throat rip near the end of *Road House*), and there's the one at the end of *Point Break* where Swayze basically kills himself by swimming out into the sea during a super storm and trying to surf an unsurfable wave.

And honestly, the *Point Break* one is probably better (there's something really perfectly poetic and poignant about Bodhi, the most philosophical and earthy bank robber in cinema history, being swallowed up by the ocean; also, *Point Break* is a better overall movie than *Road House*; also, Bodhi is a more interesting examination of the life of a person who lives at the margins of the world). But it's just that, despite all the evidence to the contrary, I can't allow myself to believe that Bodhi is really dead. I just can't. There was no body ever found, and so he's not dead, is how I'm looking at it. That's what I'm choosing to believe. I'm choosing to believe that he was able to paddle his way to New Zealand. I'm choosing to believe he made it out. I'm choosing to believe that right now, as you sit there reading these words, he is sitting on the beach, staring out at the water and absorbing the cosmic energy of the galaxy.

JENNIFER LOPEZ IS NOT MEXICAN. I know that. Obviously, I know that.[1] But she played one in 1997. She was in a movie called *Selena*, and listen: The person she played—Selena Quintanilla, a Tejano singer from Texas who was on her way toward global stardom before she was murdered in a hotel room in Corpus Christi by the president of her fan club—was an iconic figure for Mexicans back then (and remains an iconic figure for Mexicans still, even more than two decades after her death). And so we attached ourselves to Lopez immediately, and absorbed her into our community, wholly and entirely, and it's been that way for nearly all of her career.[2]

When she starred in *Anaconda*, a movie about a documentary crew traveling down the Amazon River that ends up having to battle a giant snake, it was like, "Whoa! Look at that heroic Mexican battling that giant snake!" When she starred in *Enough*, a movie about a woman who plots a way to kill her physically abusive husband, it was like, "Whoa! Look at that brilliant and brave Mexican plotting a way to kill her physically abusive husband!" When she starred in *The Wedding Planner*, a movie about a wedding planner who Matthew McConaughey falls in love with, it was like, "Whoa! Look at that charming Mexican making Matthew McConaughey fall in love with her!"[3]

That's just how it's gone, and how it'll always go. Remember in *Goodfellas* how Henry and Jimmy could never officially get "made" because they had some Irish blood in them but they were still able to be a vital part of the crew?[4] It's like that here with Lopez and us, probably.

And so she's not Mexican.

I know that.

Obviously, I know that.

But she's in the gang.

———

There are two scenes in *Selena* that are first-ballot entries into the Movie Mexican Scene Hall of Fame (they're discussed in detail in the section that follows this one). Several other first-ballot entries:

- When the three guys have Jake Hoyt at the table playing cards in *Training Day*.
- When Pedro wins the student council election in *Napoleon Dynamite*.
- When Miguel sings to his grandmother at the end of *Coco*.
- The bar shootout in *Desperado*, and also that part in *Desperado* where El Mariachi's friends show up and they're all holding guitar cases, and also every other part of *Desperado*.
- When Richie sings "La Bamba" on stage in front of the big crowd in *La Bamba*.[5]

---

1. She's Puerto Rican. And this is going to come as quite a jolt for some of you, but: Mexicans and Puerto Ricans are not the same thing.
2. We closed our eyes during *Gigli*.
3. When she starred in *Maid in Manhattan*, a movie about a maid who works in a ritzy hotel where rich people are either rude to her or ignore that she is alive, it was like, "Oh, wait, I know this one."
4. "Jimmy and I could never be made because we had Irish blood. It didn't even matter that my mother was Sicilian. To become a member of a crew you've got to be 100 percent Italian so they can trace all your relatives back to the old country."—Henry Hill, *Goodfellas*
5. You can also include literally any scene from *La Bamba* that has Bob in it.

- Anytime Danny Trejo has done anything in a movie, forever, for all times past, present, and future.
- When Letty shoots Riley out of the plane with the harpoon gun in *Fast & Furious 6* and when Letty fights Ronda Rousey at the party in *Furious 7*.[6]
- When Alejandro interrupts the family dinner at the end of *Sicario*.
- When Benny "The Jet" hits the ball into Smalls's glove when Smalls is standing in the outfield with his eyes closed like an idiot in *The Sandlot*.
- When Mousie and Sad Girl have the "Burger King vs. McDonald's" back-and-forth conversation in *Mi Vida Loca*.
- Literally every part of *Stand and Deliver*, but especially the Finger Man scene.
- The "Get up, Chucky!" scene in *Blood In, Blood Out*, and the "Do your fucking job!" scene in *Blood In, Blood Out*, and also every other part of *Blood In, Blood Out*.
- The cruising scene in *La Mission*, and only the cruising scene in *La Mission*.
- When Officer Zavala fights Tre in the house in *End of Watch*.
- When Ana asks for her mother's blessing in *Real Women Have Curves*.

And, again, I know these people aren't all Mexican, or Mexican-American. But they're in the gang.

———

Selena is (mostly) a wonderful movie. But there are two scenes that stand taller than all the rest—one

of which is very cathartic, the other of which is very insightful.

The cathartic scene happens after Selena has fully found fame. She's at a mall shopping for dresses with a friend (Deborah, played by Seidy Lopez) and they come across one that Deborah would like to try on. Selena asks for one of the saleswomen to help them out. The saleswoman, a popsicle stick in a pantsuit who's been stalking around behind them to make sure they don't steal anything, quickly says, "Well, I don't think you'd be interested in that one." The implication is clear—"You're a Mexican, and so you must be poor," is what the saleswoman is saying—but Selena gives her the benefit of the doubt. "Why?" she asks, in an almost sheepish tone, rather than picking up one of the store's mannequins and throwing it at her, which is what she should've done there.

The saleswoman loads her Condescension Cannon to its max level and fires it at Selena's heart: "Well, because that dress is $800," she answers, her words slithering out of her mouth, each of them coated in the stink of bigotry and (likely) White Diamonds perfume. Selena, a saint, turns her tone just a tiny bit terse, asks her to remove the dress from the mannequin so Deborah can try it on, then walks away.

The next shot is of Selena standing outside of the dressing room, reaching through the curtain trying to help Deborah zip the dress up. As she fights with the zipper, a man carrying three boxes comes walking past. He sees Selena, stops moving, stares for a second, then says, "Selena?" She looks at him, smiles, waves, says hello, and then he completely freaks out. He starts stuttering; he drops his boxes; he starts

_____

6. Basically every Letty scene, really.

yelling in Spanish that Selena is in the store; it becomes this whole big thing.

Word spreads all throughout the mall that she's there. People pour into the store to see her, to get her autograph, to be near her. There are hundreds mushed in there. A different store employee asks what's going on. A girl tells her that Selena's there. She asks who Selena is. The girl tells her that she's in town for the Grammys.

Right at that moment, Deborah comes out of the fitting room. She says that she doesn't like the dress. Selena agrees. Then Selena turns to the original saleswoman and says, "Excuse me, miss." The saleswoman doesn't hear her because there are so many other people and noises packed into the store. Selena raises her voice. "Excuse me!" The saleswoman looks up at Selena. And Selena, in as nice a way as you can be while still telling someone to fuck off, says, "We don't need the dress. Thanks." Then she turns and winks at Deborah.

And yes, of course, for sure, definitely, no doubt, the whole scene is a play on the "You work on commission, right?" scene from *Pretty Woman*. But what's really great about it is the way they show how the words of that first guy who starts shouting about Selena being in the store echo through the mall. The first cut is to an old Mexican man cleaning up in an alley. A younger Mexican guy comes out and tells him in Spanish that Selena is nearby. Some other employees who are out there on their break overhear him and hustle inside. And it just goes on like that. There's cut after cut after cut of the message spreading, and each time it happens it's in the parts of the mall that the Mexicans are working in. They show the people working in the stockrooms, and cooking in the prep areas of the food court, and organizing products in a salon. It's like a peek behind the curtain, which, historically, both in real life and in film, is where the Mexicans have been allowed to exist uninterrupted. It's wonderful to watch the whole scene play out, and to see the care with which the director handles the situation.

The insightful scene happens earlier in the movie. Selena is riding around in a van with her father (Abraham Quintanilla, played by Edward James Olmos) and her brother (Abie Quintanilla, played by Jacob Vargas). Selena has found out that she and her band have been offered a big show in Mexico. She's very excited about playing there, but Abraham, who's experienced how turbulent it can be jumping from being identified as Mexican to being identified as Mexican-American, is far more cautious.

There's a whole back-and-forth between the three of them that's really good, but I'm going to splice up and stitch together Abraham's most salient points, because it remains the finest examination of being Mexican-American that's ever been recorded for film. He says:

"They don't accept us over there. They never have." Selena reminds him that he's Mexican, and that she's Mexican, and that her brother is Mexican, to which Abraham responds, "No, we are Mexican-American and they don't like Mexican-Americans. Listen, being Mexican-American is tough. Anglos jump all over you if you don't speak English perfectly. Mexicans jump all over you if you don't speak Spanish perfectly. We gotta be twice as perfect as anybody else."

Selena and Abie laugh to themselves about the notion. Abraham doesn't flinch. "I'm serious. Our family has been here for centuries and yet they treat us as if we just swam across the Rio Grande. I mean, we gotta know about John Wayne *and* Pedro Infante. We gotta know about Frank Sinatra *and* Agustín Lara. We gotta know about Oprah *and* Cristina. Japanese-Americans, Italian-Americans, German-Americans—their homeland is on the other side of the ocean. Ours is right next door; right over there. And we gotta prove to the Mexicans how Mexican we are, and we gotta prove to the Americans how American we are. We gotta be more Mexican than the Mexicans and more American than the Americans, both at the same time. It's exhausting."

It's a brilliant bit of writing and acting, really. And Olmos delivers the monologue perfectly, mixing together just the right amount of exasperation with just the right amount of beleaguered angst.

I would guess that every Mexican-American has had a moment where they've had to wrestle with that reality of not being Mexican enough for Mexicans and not being American enough for Americans, because it absolutely is a reality.

Probably my most obvious personal example is the time I had gotten a job at a Cicis Pizza while I was in college. I was hired to help cook the pizzas, and so I was just back there by the ovens for a few hours each of the two days I was working every week. Two of the other guys who worked there were also Mexican-American, except they were Mexican immigrants. They'd come to America a year or two earlier with their families and, as such, had lived the life that comes along with that.

I remember telling them I was in school just as a general piece of chitchat one day and then I remember them making fun of me, hand to God, for like a week straight about it. They'd say things about how I wasn't a real Mexican because I'd gone to college, and they'd say things about how I thought I was white because I'd gone to college; just a bunch of dumb shit like that.[7] And, I mean, I wish I could tell you that I was smart enough at the time to be able to explain to them how backward it was for them to think that only white people went to college, and that the heat from the pizza ovens bonded us in unexpected and very meaningful ways, and that they both ended up enrolling at the school where I was enrolled and that we all graduated together and advanced our family names. But that's not how that particular situation played out.

Instead, what ended up happening was—and let me tell you before I finish this story that it ends with me somehow morally the worst of the three of us— but what ended up happening was: My fourth week of working there, the manager accidentally issued a paycheck to me that was for about $400 more than I was supposed to get. Turned out, he mixed up my last name (Serrano) with the last name of one of the guys who was messing with me (Serna). I was working, at best, maybe ten hours each week. Serna was working, like, fifty or sixty hours a week because it was his full-time job. But so I got Serna's check and he got mine. And had it been a thing where we all got our checks at the same time, I'm sure we'd have all been able to

---

7. The opposite version of this is sometimes when I take meetings in Los Angeles to talk about TV stuff or movie stuff, the people on the opposite end of the table look at me like I walked into the room wearing a sombrero.

very quickly piece together the misunderstanding and get it fixed pretty easily. But it just so happened that I'd gone in early to pick up my check (it was my day off) and didn't bother opening it until I was in my car in the parking lot.

I saw how much it was for, tried not to have a heart attack from the shock of seeing a $470 check addressed to me, drove straight to the bank, cashed it, then drove home and called Cicis and quit.[8]

I found out from a friend who was working there that Serna got the correct check issued to him a few days later, and that definitely made me feel better about everything. But I oftentimes wonder what he said to his friend about the fake white Mexican college kid when he inevitably brought up the misprinted check while they were at work together.

——

Minus a small stretch when my dad was in the military and we lived elsewhere, I grew up in San Antonio. It's the only place that's in my head when I try and remember things from when I was a kid and preteen and teenager.

I don't remember a lot about the movies that were coming out during the mid-nineties, but I do remember when *Selena* came out.[9] I was fifteen years old. There was this whole big buzz for it. People—adults, moms, dads, tias, tios, fucking everyone, it felt like—

were excited about it in a way that I'd never seen, and in a way that I wouldn't understand until I was old enough to feel the tug of wanting to see someone who looked like me on a movie screen, or on a TV screen, or even on a billboard for something that wasn't an advertisement for a bail bondsman that was open twenty-four hours a day and accepted phone calls in Spanish.

People bought tickets and lined up to get into the first showing several days in advance. The week of the release, there were tents and chairs and all that set up outside of various theaters. It was on the news and everything. People slept there overnight. It was like our version of *Star Wars*. At the time, I dismissed the idea fully, in that baseless and blind way that teenagers do. I thought it was silly, dorky, lame that anybody could care about a movie that much. Boobs and basketball were far more interesting, I'd try telling everyone.

But it wasn't about the movie.

It was about what the movie meant.

And what it represented.

Or, better still: who it represented.

Because it represented us. And it did so in a way that rarely happened then, and, even more than two decades later, rarely happens now.

8. I recognize that this is a bad thing, but I still always laugh whenever I think about it. I'm laughing to myself literally right now again as I write this all out. Apologies to Cicis.

9. The only other one that I really and truly remember when it came out was *Congo*, a movie about special gorillas that start hunting humans in a jungle. Also, there's a gorilla in it who knows sign language and wears a special glove that speaks out loud the words that she's signing. Also, there's a part in it where hippos eat some people in a river. I don't know what the point of *Congo* was, but I know after I saw it I said to myself, "Well, I guess I'll just never go to the Congo then."

EVEN AFTER MORE THAN A DECADE I'm still not quite certain if I'm supposed to be embarrassed by this or not, but: The movie death that has affected me the most as an adult was when King Kong died in Peter Jackson's remake of *King Kong* in 2005. The way the scene happens is:

King Kong has already been captured and kidnapped and brought back to New York by Jack Black.[1] He gets forced into being part of a live show on Broadway. (He's basically chained on stage as they reenact the events that led up to his capture.[2]) He eventually freaks out, breaks out of his chains, then goes on a rampage. (He goes nuts because he thinks he sees Ann, the woman he's fallen in love with, except it turns out to just be an actress playing Ann.[3]) Somehow, he runs into Ann as he's tearing through the city streets, and so he picks her up and they escape into Central Park together.

While there, he comes across a frozen pond. And since King Kong is from a tropical island and has never seen (or felt) anything like ice, he becomes taken with it. He starts sliding around on it, crashing into snowbanks, gorilla-laughing at himself and with Ann. It's this really beautiful, gentle scene, and for a moment you forget that doom is inevitable. (This, I think, is the single finest achievement of the movie. It pulls you all the way in, and if you somehow weren't in King Kong's corner yet, it gets you there for sure. And that's what makes the following few minutes so heartbreaking.) As they play, and just as the chaos of everything that's happened prior is getting blurred into nothingness, a missile (!!!) comes blasting in from offscreen, exploding King Kong fifteen feet up into the air. The U.S. military has arrived, and the point is established immediately: They are there to kill King Kong.

The final few minutes of the movie play out like slow torture. You watch Kong get attacked and attacked and attacked, assaulted by all manner of bullets of machines. And I don't mind telling you: I cried watching it. I cried a great deal. And honestly, I'm still not entirely sure why. Perhaps it was because I found *King Kong* to be irresistibly charming (in that way that only animals can be) and hated that I had to sit there and watch him be killed by idiots? Perhaps it was because the movie's message had suddenly become obvious and loud and impossible to ignore (that humans always fuck everything up) and I knew that I was never going to forget it? Perhaps it was of some unexplainable connection that today, years and years later, I'm still not smart enough to fully understand or describe? I don't know. All that I know is, again: I cried watching it. I cried a great deal. I cried when I watched it with a friend during opening weekend, and I cried even more a week later when I dragged my wife to the movies to go watch it with me again.

I wish that I had a good way to end this section right now; maybe some grand lesson about life and about movies and maybe even about apes. I don't, though. All that I have is the truth. And an ache in my spirit.

---

1. You're the greatest and most powerful mega-animal that's ever been and you end up getting captured by Nacho Libre? Tough break.
2. A dick move, truly.
3. The most accidentally funny part of the movie is when King Kong breaks free, snatches up the actress, looks at her, roars a few times, then fucking chucks her sixty feet into the audience like a kid tossing a baseball in the backyard because he realizes it's not the real Ann.

—

Adults talking about times that they cried during a movie is something I am interested in. In part, it's because in almost all instances it becomes clear that there is a single unifying feeling, and thought, and urge, and connection in every story about death, which I find comforting. But also because it's always sweet to me to imagine someone sitting in a theater quietly crying to himself or herself because a pretend person on a screen has passed away. As such, the rest of this chapter will be that. I asked ten of my writer friends to tell me about a movie death that they experienced as an adult that has stuck with them.

—

MALLORY RUBIN ON WILSON FROM *CAST AWAY* (2000):

What is the nature of connection? What do any of us want from another being? Do we need to feel the warmth of their skin and the thrum of their heart, hear the sound of their voice, see the creases of their smile? Or do we just need to know that there's a constant in our lives, an ever-present promise that we're not alone?

When Chuck Noland crashes into the sea and maroons on a deserted island, he finds that promise in a volleyball. He names him Wilson (after the manufacturer), and as the hours turn to years, Wilson becomes as much of a lifeline for Chuck as fish or fire, providing the real sustenance of life: companionship. Wilson carries Chuck's blood, like a relation; listens to his sorrows, like a friend; comforts him, like a lover.

And then he's gone. Chuck wakes on the raft spiriting him back to civilization only to see his comrade drifting away. He dives in, screaming for Wilson as he would for his own child. "Wilson!" Chuck shouts as he recedes farther from view, peeking above and back below the horizon, oscillating between hope and desperation. "I'm sorry!" Chuck has to hold the rope, has to stay by the raft, has to stay alive. Otherwise, what was it all for? But doing so means sacrificing a love that kept him tethered not only to life, but to his own humanity. It's an agonizing portrait of grief and hopelessness, a reminder that if we don't drown in the sea, we might still succumb to our own despair.

—

JIA TOLENTINO ON MAMA COCO FROM *COCO* (2017):

I'll start off by admitting that I am not easily moved by cinematic sentiment—until the 2016 election turned my brain into mashed potatoes and my heart into a time bomb, I had cried at a movie death exactly twice in my life. (The first was when Roberto Benigni gets shot in *Life Is Beautiful*, and the second was when I watched *The Lord of the Rings* while very stoned and thought that Boromir and Aragorn were the same person.) After the election, I started crying more. But the whole game changed with *Coco*, the Day of the Dead Pixar movie that is, very possibly, the greatest mass-cultural achievement of our time.

In *Coco*, twelve-year-old Miguel goes to the Land of the Dead in search of a famous musician he believes to be his great-great-grandfather. He then discovers that the musician sucks, and that his real great-great-grandfather is a man named Hector—a shady ragtag trickster with an indomitable heart. For decades, Miguel's family has believed that this musically inclined ancestor cruelly abandoned his wife and daughter, the elderly Mama Coco. But actually, Hector was *murdered*! He never meant to leave the family! And he's been trying to get back to see Coco ever since!

Of course, this realization hits just as the sun is coming up after *Día de los Muertos*, and Coco's memories are fading—she's about to die, which means Hector's about to be forgotten and vanish forever. Miguel sprints back to the land of the living and plays Hector's old lullaby to Mama Coco, who remembers him, and smiles. Her almost-death, in a movie that is fully, gorgeously saturated in mortality, destroyed me. How awful, and how ordinary, now, to be separated from your family for no good reason. What a dream it would be to do right by the people we love.

—

SEAN FENNESSEY ON OBI-WAN KENOBI FROM *STAR WARS* (1977):

I still don't know if Obi-Wan is dead. He's gone, certainly; rendered apparitional after being struck down by Darth Vader. But the Jedi master's body, his corporeal form, just sort of . . . *disappeared*. It was a confusing sight for a young person watching *Star Wars* for the first time. The response wasn't *Why did the bad man kill him?* It was something closer to *Where'd that guy go???* If you saw it young enough, before the very concept of death had been awkwardly unpacked for you by your parents, it was downright confusing. Why do we lie to kids about beginnings and

endings? Babies are delivered by storks, Jedis vanish rather than decompose, and the Force is only to be used for good.

Obi-Wan, as portrayed by the great Alec Guinness, is a cool but tough uncle figure, a spiritual adviser, military leader, and style icon. When Vader's red blade slashes through him, just as Luke Skywalker arrives to witness his uncle's demise, Obi-Wan's robe and lightsaber collapse into a pile on the floor. As an adult, his death represents something else altogether—generational war, metaphysical acceptance, spiritual completion. It's death and rebirth all at once. "If you strike me down," he says to his former pupil Vader moments before the end, "I shall become more powerful than you can possibly imagine." They're his final words. Until he comes back.

—

MONICA CASTILLO ON VICTORIA PAGE FROM *THE RED SHOES* (1948):

I first watched *The Red Shoes* when I was a teenager, but the death at the end of this movie now means something different to me as a woman. Michael Powell and Emeric Pressburger's adaptation of the Hans Christian Andersen fairy tale of the same name follows Victoria Page (Moira Shearer), a ballerina caught in between her love for a composer and her demanding impresario who launched her career. Her real passion belongs to the ballet, and when forced to choose between the two men, she chooses to dance—to her detriment. The lines between make-believe and reality blur as the magically cursed ballet shoes of the show lead her to an untimely death in real life.

I once loved the movie for its exquisite cinematography and Shearer's grand performance, but now I also feel a pang of sadness watching it. In today's light, the narrative becomes a tragic allegory for the woman who wants to have both love and a profession. Her death was not caused by cursed dance shoes but by a man's intolerance to see his partner as an equal. While we can walk away from such situations now, I still think of the generations of women who had to sacrifice their passions for feelings, and how much we'll never know what became of them.

———

WESLEY MORRIS ON ANNIE WILKES FROM *MISERY* (1990):

I know, I know. The assignment was for a death that upsets you *as an adult*. So even though I saw Annie Wilkes die when I was fourteen and will never forget the twenty minutes of mucus that bungee-jumped into my lap, I just watched *Misery* again—as an adult. Film-wise, I'd always thought of this movie as a perfect contraption. How long until Paul, the bestselling novelist Annie kidnaps and tortures, finds a way to get out of her cabin? The pot boils and boils until the whistle goes off. But all the blubbering I did in 1990 came from the same realization I had watching *Misery* last week. It's a love story, about the romance we have with the people who make our culture and how the romance can corrupt and distort and pervert.

But *Misery* works too well. Annie might fall in love with Paul. But Kathy Bates made me fall in love with Annie. I can see as a grown-up what I could only sense as a kid, which was that Annie is unwell. The movie

needs her to be a psycho. It needs for her pot to whistle. But I now dread where this movie take us. I hate the pleasure it takes in getting Paul to the point where he doesn't just kill Annie, he pulverizes her. The sequence goes on and every time she's punched or tripped or bludgeoned, even now, starts me blubbering. Because you're never being asked to celebrate the thrashing of a lunatic, not really. You're being goaded to cheer the destruction of a woman who, basically, loved to read. I cry because I'm watching a character die a terrible death, a character who could have been my English teacher, my first editor, or my mom. Her death has never felt like justice. It's always felt like a crime.

———

AMANDA DOBBINS ON NOAH AND ALLIE FROM *THE NOTEBOOK* (2004):

A few years ago, my husband and I were back in our hotel room after a long day with various family members. We needed a little TV time to unwind, and since I was in possession of the remote, we chose to unwind with the 2004 masterpiece *The Notebook*. We turned the movie on somewhere around the boat scene—when Noah, played by Ryan Gosling, takes Allie, played by Rachel McAdams, on a canoe trip to see some very symbolic swans, and then it rains, and then they yell, "It still isn't over!" and then they have sex—and I planned to turn it off about twenty minutes later, before all the sad old people scenes started.

Fast-forward to: The old people peacefully dead in their bed together, the credits rolling, and me waking my husband up with the violence of my sobs. I have seen this movie upward of thirty times, and it basically has a happy ending. (Noah and Allie get back together! They live a long happy life in a mansion!) Still, I cannot watch it without weeping, in part because the dementia plotline is deeply heartbreaking and in part because the ending is a straight-up betrayal. Love like Ryan Gosling's and Rachel McAdams's should never die, not even of natural-ish causes at an advanced age. We were told it wasn't over.

—

DOREEN ST. FÉLIX ON MIA SULLIVAN FROM *THE BEST MAN HOLIDAY* (2013):

The Best Man Holiday is a case study in emotional manipulation. Its director, Malcolm D. Lee, simply cares not for our psychological state. He lulls us into a place of complacent nostalgia; in 2013, when it premiered, the Christmas vehicle looked like a handsome and formulaic sequel to the original ensemble movie *The Best Man*. We were expecting a little drama—a nearly foiled wedding, in the way of the comedy, or a betrayal of friendship—something *resolvable*. It was Christmas, after all. What we got instead was the agonizing loss of a mother, friend, and wife. I'm a grown-ass woman who is basically immune to movie clichés about unfair death, but there's something about the familial warmth of the Black ensemble that makes me a little irrational, a little helpless, more willing to be affected. Five years later, and I'm still crying.

Mia Sullivan, played elegantly by Monica Calhoun, is the platonic ideal of a hostess. Her voice never rises above a maternal whisper. She persuades the old crew of sexy and suave Black professionals (and a silk-robe-clad Terrence Howard) to get together again, for old times' sake, at her family mansion. Her husband, the NFL star Lance Sullivan, played by Morris Chestnut, is sulking the whole time. We learn why—the reunion is actually a prolonged farewell. First, it's a cough, then the bags under Mia's eyes deepen, and then her skin turns gray. Mia manages to stay on this wretched earth long enough to see her man win an impossible game. She wills him to win. She's gone before Christmas morning and Sullivan collapses at her grave. There's hope and a laugh and a baby at the end of the movie, but to be honest, I am always weeping too hard to watch the rest of it unfold.

—

JASON CONCEPCION ON PRIVATE STANLEY MELLISH FROM *SAVING PRIVATE RYAN* (1998):

The death of Private Stanley Mellish never fails to fuck me up. It's not the circumstances or the violence that affect me—though as a story set in World War II, those are substantial. No, what disturbs me about the scene is the way, in the moments before the knife goes in, Mellish cries, "Wait, wait."

In the scene, Mellish and another comrade are posted up in an apartment manning a machine gun. Germans are overrunning their position and they're out of ammunition. They send a guy off to get more, but before he can get back, the Germans storm the apartment. The other soldier is quickly killed, shot in the neck. Mellish takes out at least one German soldier. The last, though, charges him. They fight hand to hand. Mellish gains the advantage and pulls his combat knife. But the German manages to disarm him. He turns the knife on Mellish and, placing all his weight behind it, drives it into Mellish's chest.

I am, without fail, always disturbed when characters exhibit behavior that reminds me of myself. I find characters who are brave in the face of danger comforting. I have never fought a German to the death in a bombed-out French village in the middle of a firefight, but I'm certain I'd meet the challenge by vigorously shitting my pants; by remarking on the absurdity of the situation by attempting, like a kid playing tag, to call a time-out. "Wait, wait," I'd cry.

Just like Mellish.

I saw me in him.

———

DONNIE KWAK ON THE DEATH OF A RELATIONSHIP IN *MY SASSY GIRL* (2001):
To quote the great poet Omarion, "I got this icebox where my heart used to be." Well, for the most part, anyway. A movie death has never moved me to tears, but I have cried when two characters broke up in a film. Toward the end of the Korean rom-com *My Sassy Girl*, the girl and the guy have decided to part ways. They write each other letters and travel to the mountains to bury them in a time capsule in the mountains. (It is, to tell you again, a Korean rom-com.) After doing so, the girl asks the guy to walk to another mountaintop. When he arrives there, she screams out a tearful apology, which he can't hear because he's so far away.

Up until this point in the movie, the girl has been a bastion of strength and spunk—"sassy," as the title says. But in that moment, she couldn't be more vulnerable and fragile. I felt sad watching her emotional outburst

the first time I saw the movie; when I returned to the scene after a sad breakup of my own, the tears fell freely. It felt great, actually.

———

JASMINE SANDERS ON ROSIE FROM *FRESH* (1994):
Fresh, written and directed by Boaz Yakin, stars Sean Nelson as Fresh, a preteen drug courier in pyretic 1994 Brooklyn. He has a crush on Rosie, a girl at his school. One day, while out at a park, an older drug dealer gets upset that a young basketball player has shown him up and shoots him several times. The boy dies swiftly, his body crumpled over so that the camera misses his face, allowing him some dignity. A stray bullet hits Rosie in the throat. She dies slowly, her hands grasping her at her neck, which is now spurting blood, and Fresh places his hands atop her own.

As a child, it was this scene which stayed with me after viewing. Perhaps I'd thought it romantic, dying in the hands of a man who loved you, tragedy making the romance even sweeter. Or maybe I was rapt by this first rendering of a girl dying, having been taught via film and home that the primary (and therefore only) victims of urban violence were black boys. I think I counted Rosie's death as a triumphal testament to the vulnerability of black girls, whose frailties I had known but had never seen on screen. But even in *Fresh*, Rosie's death is metabolized via the male protagonist; he alone grieves her.

You see her neatly styled hair, the crisp jeans and manners, and you know that someone loves her. Someone is at home; likely some woman who'd looked after Rosie and will be left undone after she dies. I wonder who?

DO YOU WANNA read an essay ABOUT FRIDAY?

THE FIRST MOVIE THAT EVER ENTERED MY LIFE so thoroughly that it became unavoidable was *Friday*. It came out in April of 1995 and starred Ice Cube and Chris Tucker as Craig and Smokey, two friends who spend a day together outside of, inside of, and in the general proximity of Craig's house. I don't remember seeing a trailer for it on TV, or seeing a billboard for it on the side of the road, or seeing a poster at the theater for it, or even someone at school explaining the plot of the movie to me. But what I do remember is that one day everything in my life was normal and everyone I knew was talking the only way I'd ever known them to talk, and then suddenly, seemingly all at once and with great gusto, everyone was talking differently, saying the same five or six phrases again and again and again, in ways that made sense and also, because we were all early teenagers, in ways that did not.

Everyone was saying things like, "Every time I come in the kitchen, you're in the kitchen." And everyone was saying things like, "Don't nobody go in the bathroom for about thirty-five, forty-five minutes." And everyone was saying things like, "And you know this, *maaaaaaan*." And everyone was saying things like, "Playing with my money is like playing with my emotions." And everyone was saying things like, "You got knocked *the fuck* out!" And everyone was saying things like, "My neck! My back! My neck and my back!" *Friday* was so popular, so undeniable, so mesmerizing, so intoxicating, that it suddenly became okay to say to someone,

"You got to be a stupid motherfucker to get fired on your day off," even if the person you were saying it to had not been fired on their day off, or fired at all, or even had a job. It was a true zeitgeist shift, is what it was, which is probably the highest level of pop culture achievement a movie can reach.

——

The plot of *Friday* is as such: Craig Jones, a likable twenty-something-year-old living with his parents in South Central Los Angeles, has recently been fired from his job.[1] His friend, Smokey, an even more likable twenty-something-year-old who is bad at dealing drugs, finds out that Craig has been fired, and so he spends the day trying to get Craig to smoke weed with him. As they hang out, they watch the happenings of their neighborhood, which include, among other things: a pastor possibly sleeping with a married woman; a man getting his necklace taken by a bully; a woman lying about looking like Janet Jackson; and, of the most consequence, a drug dealer named Big Worm sending a handful of people to shoot at Smokey when he finds out that Smokey has smoked most of the weed he was supposed to sell.

And listen: I know that that sounds like the framework for a silly movie, and I suppose a big part of the point of *Friday* is to actually be a silly movie, but it's also a warm movie and a tender movie and a thoughtful movie.[2] Three examples:

---

1. He was fired for stealing boxes from his work. It's unclear whether or not he actually did it. I would guess no, but that's just a guess.
2. Prior to *Friday*, there were a string of movies set in Los Angeles that presented parts of the city as, in effect, war zones. There was 1988's *Colors*. There was 1991's *Boyz n the Hood*. There was 1993's *Menace II Society*. *Friday* sought to filter everything through a warmer lens. Even the part where there's a drive-by is funny, which I think is the first time a drive-by has ever been funny.

The friendship between Craig and Smokey. Outwardly, theirs is a friendship rooted in poking fun at each other. But the two care about each other a great deal. Because first, consider that Smokey shows up to visit Craig at around 8:30 in the morning and Craig does not respond by asking, "What the fuck are you doing here so early," which is what I suspect most people would say if even their very best friend showed up unannounced that early in the morning. Instead, Craig fusses at Smokey a bit for messing up his curtains, then tells him he'll meet him outside. And second, consider that, after making fun of Craig for a second for getting fired, Smokey decides to spend the rest of the day commiserating, and one of the defining characteristics of a close friendship is expressing empathy. And third, consider that, on multiple occasions, Craig walks Smokey home because he knows that Smokey is at risk of getting either jumped or shot at. (I like a lot of my friends, but I do not care about any of them enough to risk getting shot alongside them.) And fourth, consider how dejected and regretful Smokey is when he realizes that there's a very real chance that Craig might get hurt because of something Smokey's done. It's all very beautiful, really.

The relationship between Craig and his mother and sister. Same as with Smokey, Craig's sister and mother take turns lobbing soft jabs at Craig's chin (Dana, his sister, played by Regina Hall, pokes at him for not having a job; his mother, Betty, played by Anna Maria Horsford, pokes at him for not being able to find a girlfriend), but there are no points in the movie when it feels like the three genuinely do not love each other. (This is the most obvious when, after hearing what they suspect are gunshots, the first person that Dana asks about is Craig.[3]) It's all very beautiful, really.

The relationship between Craig and his father. A running joke in *Friday* is how uncool and in-the-way Craig's father, Willie, played by John Witherspoon, is supposed to be. But Willie is, by basically every measurement, a wonderful dad. He has no problem sharing personal space with Craig (the bathroom scene). And he has no problem leaning on Craig when Craig doesn't do what he's supposed to do (the scene in the beginning of the movie where he fusses at Craig for not having taken the trash out). But also he's there for Craig when he finds out that Craig has been fired (he has a possible job for him immediately). And also he delivers the movie's most touching scene (when he sees that Craig has a gun and talks to him about how big of a mistake that is[4]). And also he, in a last-ditch effort, kicks Smokey out of his house because he wants to try and prevent Craig from getting caught up in the blowback of Big Worm's attack on Smokey. And also he, while Craig and Deebo are fighting, has enough faith in his own wisdom to know that, win or lose, Craig will be a better person if he receives no help during the fight. It's all very beautiful, really.

---

3. A bonus: The only time in the movie we see Deebo show any sort of emotion that isn't menace is after the shooting when Dana asks him if he's seen Craig and Smokey. He hears the questions, thinks on it briefly, then, in a surprisingly earnest voice says, "Earlier." It's weird to hear him use that voice. It's like watching a great white shark hold a door open for a seal.
4. This scene is colossal. John Witherspoon, a fantastic comedic character, activates a serious side that he seldom showed in his movies. He's so smart, and so powerful, and so fatherly. It's like it's a scene from a whole different movie.

Separate from the ones I mentioned early, twelve other perfect lines from *Friday*:

- "**She's in school. She has all her teeth.**" That's a thing Betty says to Craig when she's talking to him about a girl who might make for a good girlfriend, and the only reason I want a *Friday* prequel is so that we can see the girls that Craig was dating before this moment that would necessitate his mom needing to point out that a girl has all of her teeth.
- "**What the fuck you doing stealing boxes for? Whatchu tryna build? A clubhouse?**" Smokey says that to Craig when he finds out that Craig was fired because supervisors said they had video of Craig stealing boxes at work. I laugh every time.
- "**I know you don't smoke weed. I know this. But I'ma get you high today. Cuz it's Friday, you ain't got no job, and you ain't got shit to do.**" —Smokey
- "**Yeah, it's just like it's both ours. We'll just keep it down at my house.**" That's what Red says after he asks Deebo for his bike back. Deebo says sure, and Red is happy, and then Deebo turns around and hits Red so hard that he nearly knocks his head off his shoulders. (A neat sidenote: The guy who plays Red is named DJ Pooh. He not only co-wrote the script with Ice Cube, but he was also originally supposed to play Smokey.)
- "**Bye, Felisha.**" —Craig
- "**Weed is from the earth. God put this here for me and you.**" —Smokey

- The whole back-and-forth exchange with the pastor. This was Bernie Mac and Chris Tucker going line for line with each other trying to see who could be the funniest. It's art.
- When Smokey makes up Spanish when he's smoking with the Mexicans. I remember rewatching this movie around 2017 and getting to this part and the person I was watching it with saying something like, "Wait. He's being racist right now." To which I responded with, "I don't care. It's fucking funny."
- "**Most people wanna borrow sugar. Or even ketchup. You wanna borrow my car? Hell no.**" —Smokey
- "**Remember it. Write it down. Take a picture. I don't give a fuck.**" —Smokey
- "**Y'all ain't never got two things that match. Y'all got Kool-aid, no sugar. Peanut butter, no jelly. Ham, no burger. Damn!**" —Smokey
- "**Why you bringing up old shit?**" —Smokey
- "**Man, I got mind control over Deebo. He be like, 'Shut the fuck up.' I be quiet. But when he leave. I be talking again.**" —Smokey
- "**He gon' cry in the car.**" This one, like many others on this list, was said by Smokey. Chris Tucker was so goddamn good as Smokey. It was, in the very truest sense, a breakout moment for him. You watched it and, same as people did with Julia Roberts in *Pretty Woman* or Sandra Bullock in *Speed* or Heath Ledger in *10 Things I Hate About You* or Laurence Fishburne in *Boyz n the Hood*, you said to yourself, "That person is a movie star."

—

A fun thing: In 2015, a movie called *Straight Outta Compton* came out. It was about the formation, rise, and subsequent deterioration of N.W.A., a controversial rap group from the late eighties and early nineties that helped popularize gangsta rap. Ice Cube was a member of the group,[5] and so a person played Ice Cube in the movie.[6] After we get to the part of the movie where the group has become very famous, there's a scene where a guy interrupts a party the group is having in a hotel room. "I'm looking for my girl Felisha," the guys says. "I heard she was up in one of these rooms," he continues, but in a way that lets you know he's not only there to find Felisha, he's also there to fuck up some people.

When Dr. Dre tries to run him off, the guy shows Dre that he's carrying a gun and asks, "Mind if I take a look?" Dre shoves him out of the entryway, slams the door closed, then walks through a door that connects his room to a separate hotel room, which is where the rest of the people at the party are. "Aye, where's Felisha at," Dre asks loudly, to no one and everyone. "Where's Felisha," he asks again when no one answers him. He points at naked girl after naked girl after naked girl, asking each if they happen to be Felisha. None of them are.

Eventually, Dre finds Felisha in a bathroom performing oral sex on Eazy-E.[7] Dre tells Eazy that Felisha's boyfriend is outside and that he's carrying a gun. Eazy gets up, goes to a stash of guns hidden under a bed, hands them to Cube, Dre, and MC Ren, then opens the door and chases off the angry boyfriend and his friends down the hall.

As Eazy, Cube, Dre, and Ren walk back toward the hotel room, they laugh and enjoy the victory they've just had. Cube, as he's walking back into the room, shoves a woman out into the hallway. And when he does it—and I promise to you when this happened in the theater where I was watching *Straight Outta Compton* turned all the way alive—but when he does it, he shouts, "Bye, Felisha." It was such a great payoff, and an entirely unexpected one at that, which is really surprising given that: (1) They say the name "Felisha" about a dozen times in the scene; (2) "Bye, Felisha" is an iconic line from *Friday*,[8] and has aged into an iconic line in pop culture, and if any movie was going to have a big and extremely satisfying callback to the line, it was going to be *Straight Outta Compton*; (3) Ice Cube starred in *Friday*, and it's Ice Cube's character in *Straight Outta Compton* who says the "Bye, Felisha" line;[9] and (4) F. Gary Gray, who directed *Friday*, also directed *Straight Outta Compton*.[10]

---

5. Some might say he was THE member of the group.
6. Ice Cube's son, O'Shea Jackson Jr., played Ice Cube in the movie. And I know that that sounds like the beginnings of a very bad situation, but O'Shea Jackson Jr. was incredible in the role.
7. This, I imagine, is exactly the place the guy who interrupted the party was hoping that she would not be.
8. Some might say THE iconic line from *Friday*.
9. Another nice little high-five is we get a quick glimpse of Ice Cube's character working on the script for *Friday* in *Straight Outta Compton*.
10. Separate of the *Friday* conversation: The "Bye, Felisha" line being able to sneak up on you the way that it does is a testament to how good of a movie *Straight Outta Compton* is. F. Gary Gray so completely immerses you into the N.W.A. world that you forget about basically everything else that isn't directly connected to it. And the hotel room scene where the "Bye, Felisha" line happens, which is shot in a way that, for most of it, is done as one take as you follow along through the chaos of the party, is remarkable.

—

When I was in the ninth grade, the girl that I was dating at the time cheated on me with a guy at the San Antonio Zoo. I will never forget it. I'd gotten in trouble at home because my mom found out that I'd been hiding my report card from her (I hid it because I had several Fs on there). She said I wasn't allowed to go outside for two weeks, and I wasn't allowed to watch TV for two weeks, and I wasn't allowed to listen to the radio for two weeks, and I wasn't allowed to use the phone for two weeks. The only thing I could do, she said, was go to school and come home. That's it. That was my life. And so the girl—I'm going to call her Andrea for the rest of this story—I guess Andrea decided she didn't want to stick out those two weeks. So she went on a date.

And listen, Andrea absolutely made the right decision there. The point of this story is not for me to imply otherwise. The guy she went out with was older than me (he was in the tenth grade), and taller than me, and more popular than me, and more handsome than me. And those are all of the most important things when you're fourteen years old. If you can get your hands on them, then you grab them. That's all there is to it. That's a call you make ten times out of ten. You always let a Harrison Barnes walk out of the door if there's a possibility you can end up with a Kevin Durant, you know what I'm saying?

But, man. At the zoo? At the *zoo*? That was tough for me to hear. I mean, do you know how excited you have to be about cheating on your boyfriend to cheat on him AT THE ZOO? That's not a place that's even a little bit romantic. I'd have swallowed it easier if he took her to Olive Garden or whatever.[11] But the *zoo*? With the monkeys and the ostriches and lions? Getting cheated on there really hurt my pride.[12] I remember I snuck on the phone and called her from my house and was really proud of myself for being such an outlaw and she cut me off real quick like, "Hey. I have something to tell you. I cheated on you with Mark." And I was like, "Hold on. What?" And she said it again. And I asked her how, and where, and why, and was doing that whole thing. And she was like, "We were at the zoo . . ." and that's all I heard. She kept talking, but that was the end of the answer in my head.

And the reason I'm mentioning it right now is because Mark, who actually lived just a couple of houses away from me and who I saw all the time and played basketball with occasionally, loved the movie *Friday*. He talked about it all the time and quoted it all the time. (If I'm remembering it correctly, the "Playing with my money is like playing with my emotions" line is the one he was most fond of saying, which is funny to think about now because just about everyone who lived in our neighborhood was right around the same level of poor.) In all likelihood, Mark was probably the first person I heard talking about *Friday*. And so now whenever I spend more than a few minutes thinking about the movie, I inevitably think about him, and about Andrea, and about the zoo. Such is life.[13]

---

11. Olive Garden is just about as fancy as it gets when you're a high school student in San Antonio. If you were a junior in high school and one of your friends said he was going to take his girlfriend out on a date to Olive Garden, you said something back to him like, "Whoa. Are you gonna propose to her?"

12. Get it? Pride. Because of lions.

13. If you and I were in the *Friday* universe and I was telling this story, I have to imagine Smokey would say something here like, "You got to be a stupid motherfucker to get cheated on at the zoo."

I'm certain that part of the reason that *Friday* was so beloved when I was growing up was because of *where* I was growing up.

The southwest side of San Antonio in the mid-nineties was, and remains today, a largely Hispanic population.[14] I cannot think of one single time I went to a place during my young life where basically everyone in whatever room I walked into did not look like a differently shaped version of me. And I guess because of that, there was always this weird disconnect between the stuff that I'd see in my daily life and the stuff that I would see on a movie screen or a TV screen.[15] It was like, "Okay, the world that I live in is one thing, and the world that I watch is a different thing." *Friday*, which featured an almost exclusively Black cast, was part of a group of movies that my friends and I saw during that very important stretch of your life when you start to discover things for yourself that made us feel like it didn't have to be that way. And of course there is a gigantic difference between being Mexican and being Black (or between any two races or ethnicities, really), but those two sides are occasionally connected by a Well, Neither Of Us Are White bridge.

To speak in very general terms, the Black population has always operated as kind of an unspoken big brother or big sister to the Mexican population. We, the Mexicans, sort of sit off in the background and watch the world spin around on its axis and when we see the Black population do a thing (or, also, the Asian population more recently), we're like, "Oh, hey. Wait. They let y'all do that? Cool. Maybe they'll let us try it too."

So when *Friday* came out, we didn't celebrate it as our own victory, but we definitely eventually celebrated it as *a* victory. (This, in a semi-joking way but also in a semi-serious way, is referred to as the Black-Mexican alliance. We root for them, they root for us. We, the Mexicans, have many alliances.) Which is why I was so pleased that Patricia Charbonnet, one of *Friday*'s producers, said the following of the film's difficulty in picking up early interest from studios: "It was right off of the heels of Robert Rodriguez doing *El Mariachi*, which was a super-low-budget independent film that took off so well. On the strength of the talent that Ice Cube possessed, I believed that certainly something like [*Friday*] could happen if we dedicated ourselves to moving mountains, even if we had not made a film before. There was a naive belief that if Rodriguez could do it, then for sure we could do it, too. If Cheech and Chong could make *Up in Smoke*, and the movies like that preceding it, certainly we could be part of a new paradigm."

It's neat to think about the production team for *Friday* sitting there looking at *El Mariachi* or a Cheech and Chong movie and saying something like, "Wait. They let y'all do that? Cool. Maybe they'll let us try it too." It's neat to think about the ways that people inspire other people. It's neat to think about how maybe all of everything really is connected. It's all very beautiful, really.

---

14. If this sentence is no longer true by the time you read this book, then something terrible has happened.
15. This was not something I actively thought about, but it was something I felt, same as how you don't ever really think about the ozone layer but you always feel its presence.

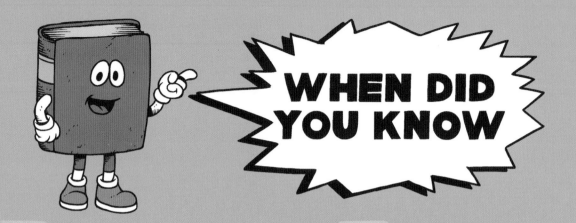

book-smart

WAS SPECIAL?

A MOVIE CAN BE CONSIDERED "GENER-ATION-DEFINING" FOR ANY NUMBER OF REASONS. It can be because of something obvious, like if its arrival becomes a tentpole moment for cinema (something like 1975's *Jaws* or 1991's *Terminator 2: Judgement Day*; movies of that kind). It can be because of something more nuanced but no less substantial, like if its success marks the beginning of something new, and if not explicitly "new" then certainly "refreshed" (something like 1985's *The Breakfast Club* or 1996's *Scream*; movies of that kind). It can be because of something acute and poignant, like if it grabs hold of a specific time period and its accompanying ideals (something like 1969's *Easy Rider* or 1999's *Fight Club*; movies of that kind).

Booksmart came out during the summer of 2019. It stars Beanie Feldstein and Kaitlyn Dever as Molly and Amy, two enthusiastically studious high school seniors who decide they want to spend their last night as high school students partying. Were I to guess, I would say *Booksmart* is going to age itself into that last category. It's a movie you watch and you say to yourself as you sit there, "This is clearly something that people will look back on in years and mark its arrival as an important thing." It's a movie you watch and say to yourself as you sit there, "Okay, this is special. *Booksmart* is special."[1]

———

The plot of *Booksmart*: Molly and Amy are smart kids in high school who find out that some of their classmates who worked less hard than they did also got into prestigious colleges. Upon learning this, Molly begins to regret that she's spent all of her time and energy focusing on being successful in school. She decides that she and Amy need to go a popular kid's end-of-year party so that they can say, even if only on a technicality, they also partied while in high school. That's the movie.

Oh, also: Molly has a crush on Nick, a tall, charming, handsome oaf with nice teeth. (It's his party that Molly and Amy want to go to.)

And also: Amy has a crush on Ryan, a girl who is good at skateboarding and has many tattoos. (She's going to be at the party as well, because everyone cool is going to be at the party.)

And lastly: Molly and Amy don't know where the party is, which is why the first 70 percent of their night is spent in different parts of the city, as they go spot to spot trying to find it.

———

Realizing a movie is special typically comes in stages. If it's a comedy (or something comedy-adjacent), the path is five levels long, and they are arranged thusly:

---

1. Critic Emily Yoshida had a great bit of insight into what made *Booksmart*, a small-budget indie, feel so immediately weighty. Writing for *Vulture*, she pointed out that high school movies have, since their inception, had a cast of common character archetypes, like The Jock and The Nerd and The Princess, etc. In the 2010s, we began seeing a new archetype, a character Yoshida described as "the socially conscious busybody, the walking #thread, Tracy Flicks with Netflix accounts, pre-THC Abbi and Ilanas, neither loser nor winner but Type A all the way." What *Booksmart* did is it offered up the two best, most complete, most fully fleshed-out versions of that character, meaning *Booksmart* served as "an official coronation of the type."

First, something will happen on-screen or be said on-screen and you'll see it and go, "Okay, so definitely the rest of this movie is going to be funny." After that, a second thing will happen on-screen or be said on-screen and you'll see it and go, "Okay, so definitely the rest of this movie is going to be very funny." After that, a third thing will happen on-screen or be said on-screen and you'll see it and go, "Okay, so this movie is definitely extremely funny." After that, a fourth thing will happen on-screen or be said on-screen and you'll see it and go, "Okay, we're all officially watching an upper-echelon movie right now." And then finally, a fifth thing will happen on-screen or be said on-screen and you'll see it and go, "Okay, this is special. This is going to be remembered as a special movie."

Let's go through each of the levels, eventually arriving at precisely when it is that you know that *Booksmart* is special.

LEVEL 1

"Okay, so definitely the rest of this movie is going to be funny."

For a movie to get to this level, something funny has to happen early on that establishes very quickly that the people (or person) at the center of it are naturally funny, and capable of taking an ordinary situation or line and turning it into something enjoyable. (Seth and Evan talking

about which porn site to subscribe to at the start of *Superbad* is a good example. You know as soon as that scene happens exactly what the movie is going to feel like and exactly the kind of humor you're going to be getting from each character.[2]) The earlier that kind of moment happens in a comedy, the better, and it happens almost immediately in *Booksmart*.

Molly is walking out of her second-story apartment to meet up with Amy so they can ride together to their last day of high school. As Molly heads down the stairs, she starts dancing. Amy sees her dancing, says, "Ohhhh shit," then opens the door, gets out of the car, and starts dancing too. It's a quick thing, but, same as the *Superbad* example, it sets in place three important pieces of information immediately:

1. **It lets us know that Molly and Amy are going to have great chemistry.** This is obviously important in a movie about two friends hanging out in different places, which is basically what *Booksmart* is.

2. **It lets us know that Molly is going to be the one to initiate most of the action in the film and that Amy is going to be the one who reacts to it.** This ends up being a big, big part of *Booksmart*. And, most crucially . . .

3. **It lets us know that Molly and Amy are innately funny.** Dancing in a movie is hard enough, but dancing in a movie so as to be funny is even harder. Too often, it feels unnatural and like

---

2. Pointing out *Superbad* here is not a coincidence. Philosophically, it's very similar to *Booksmart*, in that it's presented as a movie about two kind-of-awkward high school kids trying to make their way to a party, but really it's a movie about friendship, and how powerful a thing it can be when you're eighteen years old.

the person doing it is trying extremely hard to look like they're not trying at all. When Molly and Amy do it, though, it feels like the opposite of that. It feels like they've been doing that same bit together for years and we're all just finally getting to see them to do it on film. And beyond the dancing, there's a small exchange in the scene where Amy, after she and Molly have been dancing for a longer-than-expected amount of time, says in this half-serious, half-playful voice, "Are we gonna go to school, or . . . ?" Molly, still dancing, says, "Nope." It's perfectly timed, and perfectly delivered. And I know that just reading those two lines of dialogue together on this page right now makes it seem like it's not a very funny thing, but that's sort of the point I'm trying to make here. Molly and Amy are the kinds of characters who make ordinary things feel unexpected. And more than that, they can make expected things feel unexpected. (I watched the trailer for *Booksmart* three or four times before I got to see the actual movie in a theater. The "Are we gonna go to school, or . . . ?" line is in the trailer and so I was completely expecting it in the movie, but it didn't matter. I still laughed like it was the first time I'd heard it.)[3]

LEVEL 2

"Okay, so definitely the rest of this movie is going to be very funny."

So for a movie to get to that first level, really all it needs are a couple of people (or, in some instances, even one single person) who are funny enough that it doesn't really matter what they're asked to say, it's going to be interesting and charming. (Abbi Jacobson is someone like this, as is Mike Epps, as is Tig Notaro, as is Mindy Kaling, as is Eddie Murphy, as is Jason Bateman, as is Paul Rudd. There are a bunch. Those are a few.)

For a movie to get to this second level, though, it needs the funny people *and* it needs the funny writing. It needs jokes and lines that haven't happened yet in a movie. It doesn't matter if it's a big thing or a small thing, it just has to be a new thing. (The part in *This Is 40* when Melissa McCarthy comes unhinged while sitting with Paul Rudd and Leslie Mann in a school principal's office is a good example.[4])

It happens a bunch in *Booksmart*, but one of the best times is when Molly finds out that Amy has been using one of the items on a bookshelf in her room to masturbate. Molly starts going item by item through the shelf, trying to figure out what thing it is that Amy's been masturbating with, and it just gets funnier and funnier. Eventually, Amy tells Molly that it's the stuffed panda, and Molly, who's on the bottom section of a

---

3. A movie that makes it up to this level but not past it is 2007's *Blades of Glory*, which starred Will Ferrell and John Heder as feuding ice skaters who get forced to team up together.

4. The outtake of this is unbelievable. McCarthy gets Rudd and Mann both to crack early on, but rather than stop to let them collect themselves, she just keeps going after them, harder and harder, until someone off-screen yells for them to cut.

bunk bed, gets up and starts questioning Amy more about it. And they shoot the questioning from the top bunk down, so you get this funny angle on Molly, and Molly is just smiling and twisting the knife as Amy gets more and more uncomfortable. It's so much fun, and also so well shot.[5]

LEVEL 3
"Okay, so this movie is definitely extremely funny."

Getting this many levels up is where it starts to get tricky. Because for a comedy to get to this level it has to have a scene that toes up *riiiiiight* next to being completely unbelievable or far-fetched without ever actually feeling unbelievable or far-fetched. You need something like the food poisoning scene in *Brides-maids*, or the anchorman fight in *Anchorman: The Legend of Ron Burgundy*, or the four-on-four dance battle[6] in *Girls Trip*.[7]

In *Booksmart*, it's when Molly and Amy accidentally take drugs and end up hallucinating that they've turned into Barbie-like dolls. They're both freaked out at first, which is funny all by itself, but then they take off their clothes and start staring at their naked doll bodies in the mirror and that shit just gets wilder from there. Amy starts talking about how smooth every-

thing on her suddenly is, and the camera is cutting back and forth between her and Molly, and one of the times it cuts back to Amy she's holding both of her legs up over her head, and it's just so fucking funny, and so weird, and so great. It's a real moment.[8]

LEVEL 4
"Okay, we're all officially watching an upper-echelon movie right now."

For a funny movie to get to this level, it has to successfully introduce a non-comedy angle into its universe. More than that, though, it can't just be an empty gesture. It has to be a thing that makes the movie feel more robust, and more substantial, and like there's more at stake emotionally than some people just having a few laughs. (In most cases, two or more characters will get into a serious argument about something, similar to what happens about three-quarters of the way through every rom-com.) It's really hard to pull off, which is why so many modern comedies forgo legitimately trying to work it in.[9] Because if you try it and it doesn't work, then what happens is, rather than it taking the first 80 minutes of your movie and making them into a top-level thing, it takes the last 20 minutes of your movie and turns them into the part of your movie that everyone skips

---

5. A movie that makes it up to this level but not past it is 2000's *Best in Show*, which was a mockumentary about a group of people who compete with their dogs in a dog show.

6. You could go with the nightclub hallucination scene as well.

7. Regarding surprise dance battles in movies that aren't about dancing, this one is somewhere up near the top, along with the dance battle in *White Chicks*, the dance battle in *House Party,* and the dance battle in *American Pie: The Wedding.*

8. A movie that makes it up to this level but not past it is 1998's *There's Something About Mary.*

9. In most cases, they'll add it in, but mostly as a way to bridge together two separates part of a movie, like what they did with *21 Jump Street* when Jenko and Schmidt grow apart from each other while they're undercover.

whenever it's on cable. (*Wedding Crashers* is a good example of this. The first part of it—starting from the opening scene and going all the way up until Owen Wilson and Vince Vaughn get exposed as frauds—is undeniable. The last bit of it feels like a completely different movie.)

In *Booksmart*, they execute this perfectly. Molly and Amy have finally made their way to Nick's party and everything looks like it's going to work out. Molly has wiggled her way into some alone time with Nick and has begun charming him; Amy has worked up the courage to talk to Ryan and flirt with her and even jump into the pool in the backyard with her. And it's this really beautiful scene where Amy, proud of herself for having made the leap, is swimming underwater in slow motion and the light from the pool is shining in the water just perfectly and the music is playing softly and everything is idyllic and mesmerizing and you're just watching it all like, "Fuck yes! It's happening! She's really doing it! It's happening for her!" And then: heartbreak.

As Amy swims, she finds Ryan's legs, but she sees that they're entangled with another person's legs. She scrunches up her face in concern, comes out of the water, and sees Ryan, her potential girlfriend, making out with Nick, Molly's potential boyfriend. She scrambles out of the pool and everything that had just felt so peaceful and serene all of a sudden feels overwhelming and like someone is blowing a whistle directly into both of your ears.

Amy goes room to room in the party, finds Molly, and then tries to get Molly to leave the party with her. Molly, who doesn't know that Nick is making out with a different girl in the pool, bucks back at Amy for wanting to leave. They get into a gigantic argument about it. And it's worse than when they get into fights with other kids in the movie because these two know exactly what to say to hurt the other the most. And so they throw grenade after grenade after grenade, until they've set fire to their friendship. It's a tough stretch to get through because, I mean, by the time you get to it you've already spent 65 minutes with each of the characters, which is about 64 minutes longer than you need to realize how much you like them and care about them and are rooting for them.

LEVEL 5
"Okay, this is special. This is going to be remembered as a special movie."

You have to stick the landing here.[10] It's the only way a movie can get to this level. You have to have in place all of the things mentioned above—you have to have the funny people, and the good writing, and the very weird scene that makes total sense, and the emotional sledgehammer. You have to do all of that first, and then you have to stick the landing. You have to wrap everything up in a way that feels true, and feels substantial, and feels earned. It's happened in

---

10. I would like to mention here that so many great parts of *Booksmart* have gone unmentioned, not the least of which is the pizza guy robbery scene, which might be the line-for-line funniest two minutes of the whole movie. There's also the bathroom stall scene, and the scene where Molly makes Amy's parents uncomfortable, and the yacht party scene, and the murder mystery scene, and the rideshare scene, and the Alanis Morissette scene . . .

several comedies. They pulled it off in *Bridesmaids*. They pulled it off in *The 40-Year-Old Virgin*. They pulled it off in *The Hangover*. They pulled it off in *Coming to America*. Movies of that quality. And that's where *Booksmart* belongs. Because *Booksmart* pulls it off, too.

They figure out how to get Molly and Amy back together after their big fight (the cops show up to the party and Amy gets herself arrested so that everyone else can escape; Molly finds out about it the next morning and goes to visit her in jail and they reconcile[11]). They figure out how to give Molly her big moment at the graduation (she kisses a boy who has liked her for a long time and then she gives a wonderful graduation speech). They figure out how to give Amy her big moment after the graduation (a girl she'd begun hooking up with at the party before things went goofy shows up and gives Amy her phone number and tells her that she's good at sex things). They figure out how to have one last emotional, touching moment (Molly drops Amy off at the airport and they each pretend like they're okay until the other is out of sight, at which point they both start crying). And they figure out how to give you one last shot of joy (Amy sneaks around and jumps in front of Molly's car as Molly tearfully begins to drive away, and then the two of them decide to have a quick meal together).

They do it all.

And that's when you know.

That's when you know *Booksmart* is special.

After they've done it all.

---

11. When the cops are escorting Amy to the backseat of their squad car, she says, "Shotgun . . . just kidding." That's the first time I'd ever seen that in a movie. I laughed a lot.

WHO WINS WHAT

at the BRAND NEW

ACADEMY AWARDS?

PART 1

THE BIG SICK **WAS NOT NOMINATED FOR BEST PICTURE** at the 90th Academy Awards. That is something I consider to be unreasonable, given that it was not only the second-best movie of all of 2017, but also it's the best rom-com we've gotten since 2003's *Something's Gotta Give*. And so that's how we ended up with this chapter, as well as the two chapters that follow it. It's a three-part series rectifying some Academy Awards grievances. The way it came to be is as follows, and I'm going to use little arrows between each sentence because I feel like it helps best show the way a string of thoughts occur in someone's brain:

I was writing a part of the book late one night in September 2018. → It was about 2:30 a.m. when I finished what I was working on but I was not sleepy so I decided to turn on a movie and let it play while I stared through the television. → I went with *The Big Sick*, a movie I fell in love with in December 2017 and had watched about thirty times since. → Because I'd seen it so many times, I assumed my brain would turn itself off as I watched, which is what needs to happen for a person to fall asleep. → That didn't happen, though. → Instead, I got pulled into the movie again, and right at the end—right when Kumail and Emily share the look that lets you know they're going to get back together before the screen cuts to black and your heart is all full of love and hope and joy—I said out loud to myself, "I need a chapter in the book where I can talk about how good *The Big Sick* is and how happy *The Big Sick* makes me." → So, after a bit of brainstorming, I decided I was

going to write a thing where I was going to come up with a bunch of new Oscar categories and then hand out awards only to rom-coms. → I went with that idea because the Academy Awards have, by and large, historically ignored the rom-com genre.[1] → And so that's what I did. → But it turned out I didn't like it. → Because it felt too much like the Latin Grammys.

Do you know what the Latin Grammys are? The Latin Grammys have been around for about two decades now. They're exactly like the regular Grammys, except but it's an offshoot ceremony designed to honor music recorded in Spanish or Portuguese. It's always felt dumb to me that they existed. It's like the Recording Academy wanted to recognize Latin music, but not enough that they'd do it in a way that affected the already established Grammys even one single percent. In my head, I imagine that somebody (or a group of somebodies) complained that not enough Latin musicians were being recognized at the Grammys, and so someone in charge there was like, "Fine. Here. You can have your *own* Grammys. Just stay over there, okay?"

At any rate, it felt that same way to me when I built the special rom-com version of the Academy Awards for this book. By creating a rom-com-specific arm of the Academy Awards, it felt like I was indirectly delegitimizing rom-coms, which was the opposite of what I was trying to do. So I just deleted everything and settled on this new premise, which is:

The next three chapters here will be a thing where we go through the list of Oscar winners from 1995 forward and correct a bunch of mistakes. And,

---

1. The Oscar for Best Picture has not gone to a rom-com in over forty years. (*Annie Hall*, 1977)

again, I want to do that because I would like to weave some rom-com recognition into the Academy Awards ceremonies like it's always deserved to be, but also because the more I dug around in the archives of the Academy Awards, the more I realized how many movies that deserved Oscars didn't win any. And in part, I say that playfully, yes, as in, "Jean-Claude Van Damme should've gotten Oscar consideration for *Bloodsport*, lol." But also I say it seriously, as in, "*Do the Right Thing* not only didn't win the Oscar for Best Picture at the 1990 Academy Awards, it WASN'T EVEN NOMINATED."

So that's this.

———

A few housekeeping notes here meant to keep things tenable:

- We're only dealing with the big-ticket awards. That means it's Best Picture, Best Director, Best Actor, Best Actress, Best Supporting Actor, and Best Supporting Actress.
- Also: Just to make things a little more interesting, there will be no instances where all the category winners get replaced wholesale. At the very most, only up to three corrections can be made for each year.
- So as to prevent this from turning into 60,000 words of me just giving Best Actor or Best Actress awards to performances from characters like Kurt Russell's in *Big Trouble in Little China*[2] or Anna Faris's in *Scary Movie 2*,[3] the rule is this: For the

most part, the replacements offered up need to be serious suggestions based on legitimate arguments. But there are seven We'll Look the Other Way (WLTOW) exemptions available that can be used to pick a person or a movie as an Oscar winner that otherwise wouldn't have had a chance. So, for example, say I actually did want to give Jean-Claude Van Damme an Oscar for *Bloodsport* (I super fucking do), that's fine. But seeing as how that'd be a silly thing, it'd require me to spend one of the seven WLTOW exemptions.

- The reason 1995 is the cutoff date is there's a part in *The Big Sick* where Ray Romano's character, Terry, is sitting in the hospital with his wife, Beth, and Kumail. (Terry is the father of the girl who is big sick.) The three of them are looking at reviews of hospitals together. The hospital they're at has gotten several bad reviews. Upon learning this, Terry says, "This is why I don't want to go online 'cause it's never good. You go online, they hated *Forrest Gump*. Frickin' best movie ever." *Forrest Gump* won, among other things, Best Picture at the 1995 Academy Awards. So that's where we're starting.
- This one is less a rule and more of a heads-up, but: The Academy Awards take place the year after a movie comes out. So, with something like *Titanic*, that movie won Best Picture at the 1998 Academy Awards. It came out, however, in 1997. All the awards work like that, so that's how this will work as well.

---

2. "You know what ol' Jack Burton always says at a time like this?" has popped in my head at least once a day for the past thirty years.
3. SHE GETS IN A LITERAL FISTFIGHT WITH A HOUSECAT.

1995

Best Picture: *Forrest Gump*

Best Director: Robert Zemeckis for *Forrest Gump*

Best Actor: Tom Hanks in *Forrest Gump*

Best Actress: Jessica Lange in *Blue Sky*

Best Supporting Actor: Martin Landau in *Ed Wood*

Best Supporting Actress: Dianne Wiest in *Bullets over Broadway*

To be clear, I do not hate *Forrest Gump*. I don't even dislike it. It's a good-enough movie and an interesting movie and a clever movie and I have seen it many times, and I'm sure I will watch it many more times when it comes on television. BUT, I'm swiping the Best Picture award away from it and sending it elsewhere.

It's not going to *Pulp Fiction*, even though many people felt like it should've then and still feel like it should now. And it's not going to *The Lion King* (a legitimate Oscar contender that should've been nominated for Best Picture but wasn't). And it's not going to *Four Weddings and a Funeral* (a movie lifted up into greatness by Andie MacDowell). And it's not even going to *The Shawshank Redemption*, which is out and out the greatest prison movie that's ever been made and also regularly regarded as the best film

ever to not win Best Picture. Because here comes a curveball:

Your new Best Picture is *Speed*, a beautiful action movie starring Keanu Reeves (he is excellent in it as LAPD SWAT officer Jack Traven), Sandra Bullock (she's so good in *Speed* that halfway through the movie you're like, "Well, obviously this woman is headed toward the uppermost tiers of Hollywood stardom"), and a bus that couldn't go under fifty miles per hour or it'd explode. And the best part with this pick is I don't even have to use one of the seven WLTOW exemptions because it's a genuine Best Picture contender, and if that sounds ridiculous then let me remind you very quickly that Harrison Ford's *The Fugitive*, another great action movie similar in ethos to *Speed*, was nominated for two Oscars the year before, one of which was Best Picture (!).[4] So there you go.

Another change we're making here (and this one is likely more obvious than the *Speed* for Best Picture pick) is swapping out Robert Zemeckis as the Best Director winner and replacing him with Frank Darabont. He really directed the hell out of *The Shawshank Redemption* and deserves the statue.[5]

And the final change is: Jessica Lange is losing her Best Actress award because now it belongs to Andie MacDowell, who was flawless as Carrie in *Four Weddings and a Funeral*. (Hugh Grant has always been attached to Julia Roberts and Renée Zellweger and

---

4. Additionally, Tommy Lee Jones, who played the main U.S. marshal chasing after Harrison in *The Fugitive,* was not only nominated for Best Supporting Actor, he actually won it. (Tommy Lee Jones has played so many characters who were trying to catch someone. In addition to *The Fugitive,* he also did it in *Men in Black, U.S. Marshals, The Hunted, No Country for Old Men*, and *Jason Bourne*. I bet he's so fucking good at hide-and-seek in real life.)

5. The shot that he does as the camera swoops around to show the edge of the building as the guard holds Andy up at the edge of the roof is really something special.

Sandra Bullock in the rom-com conversation,[6] but please let's not forget that it was Andie MacDowell who first teased out of him the kind of awkward and stutter-stepped likability that he'd eventually center his career around.)

character and there will never be a time in your life where someone posts a fight video online and someone else doesn't come behind it and leave a version of the "You got knocked the fuck out!" line on there in the comment section.)

1996

Best Picture: *Braveheart*

Best Director: Mel Gibson for *Braveheart*

Best Actor: Nicolas Cage in *Leaving Las Vegas*

Best Actress: Susan Sarandon in *Dead Man Walking*

Best Supporting Actor: Kevin Spacey in *The Usual Suspects*

Best Supporting Actress: Mira Sorvino in *Mighty Aphrodite*

1997

Best Picture: *The English Patient*

Best Director: Anthony Minghella for *The English Patient*

Best Actor: Geoffrey Rush in *Shine*

Best Actress: Frances McDormand in *Fargo*

Best Supporting Actor: Cuba Gooding Jr. in *Jerry Maguire*

Best Supporting Actress: Juliette Binoche in *The English Patient*

Goodbye *Braveheart* for Best Picture, and goodbye Mel Gibson for Best Director, and goodbye Kevin Spacey for Best Supporting Actor. Hello *Seven* for Best Picture (HOW WAS THIS MOVIE NOT EVEN NOMINATED???????), and hello Robert Rodriguez for Best Director for *Desperado* (I'm going to use my first WLTOW exemption here, but it's important to me that you know that I honestly and sincerely love this movie and think that it is incredible and that Robert Rodriguez is deserving), and hello Chris Tucker for Best Supporting Actor for his role as Smokey in *Friday*. (The Smokey win is also going to cost me one of my WLTOW exemptions, but it shouldn't. He's an archetypal movie character and an influential movie

You know the thing that happens where an actor or actress plays a role in something and they do so with such vigor and gusto and believability that, for the rest of ever, each time you see that person you immediately think of the role before you think of the actual person? For example, every time I see Charlie Hunnam in something new I don't say to myself, "Hey, it's Charlie Hunnam in something new." Instead, I say something like, "Oh, wow. Jax Teller is the new King Arthur!" or "Oh, wow. Jax Teller is robbing a South American drug lord with Oscar Isaac and Ben Affleck!" That same thing happened for me with Ralph Fiennes after I watched him play a serial killer in *Red Dragon*. And since I didn't see

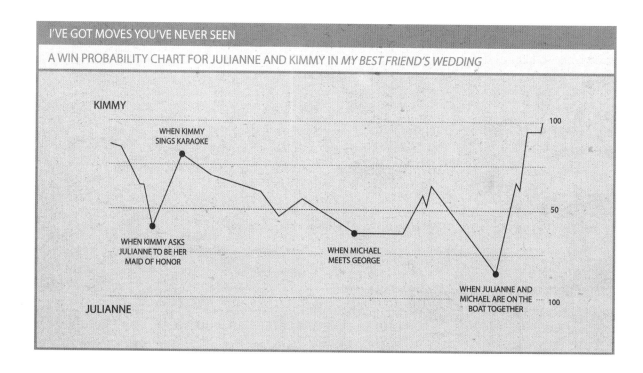

I'VE GOT MOVES YOU'VE NEVER SEEN

A WIN PROBABILITY CHART FOR JULIANNE AND KIMMY IN *MY BEST FRIEND'S WEDDING*

KIMMY

WHEN KIMMY
SINGS KARAOKE

100

WHEN KIMMY ASKS
JULIANNE TO BE HER
MAID OF HONOR

WHEN MICHAEL
MEETS GEORGE

50

WHEN JULIANNE AND
MICHAEL ARE ON THE
BOAT TOGETHER

100

JULIANNE

The English Patient until after I'd seen *Red Dragon*, it wasn't the brooding and mysterious László de Almásy I saw gliding around the dance floor with Katharine Clifton in *The English Patient*. No, it was the murderous Francis Dolarhyde I saw with her, and in that movie. That's why I'm taking away the three Oscars that *The English Patient* won in the big-ticket categories and giving them out to others. Your new Best Picture is *Scream* (responsible for resurrecting the horror genre), your new Best Director is Doug Liman for *Swingers* (it's less grand than *The English Patient*, but certainly no less impressive), and your new Best Supporting Actress is Liv Tyler in *That Thing You Do*.

1998

Best Picture: *Titanic*

Best Director: James Cameron for *Titanic*

Best Actor: Jack Nicholson in *As Good as It Gets*

Best Actress: Helen Hunt in *As Good as It Gets*

Best Supporting Actor: Robin Williams in *Good Will Hunting*

Best Supporting Actress: Kim Basinger in *L.A. Confidential*

What a year. Even if you ignore each of the movies that scored a win in one of our six big ticket categories here, you still have *Face/Off*, *G.I. Jane*, *The Fifth Element*, *Jackie Brown*, *Con Air*, *Boogie Nights*, *Men in Black*, *Event Horizon*, *The*

Game, Donnie Brasco, Spawn, Gattaca, Air Force One, The Devil's Advocate, The Edge, Cube, My Best Friend's Wedding, and Anaconda. That's EIGHTEEN really fun, really enjoyable movies (several of which are genuinely great). So let's do this: Let's go with Boogie Nights as our new Best Picture, because Boogie Nights is sublime and twenty years of distance between us and it means we can all look back and see that, after all is said and done, it never walks, it never runs, it's a winner.[7] And, despite the fact that Helen Hunt was flawless in As Good as It Gets, our new Best Actress is Julia Roberts because My Best Friend's Wedding is the single greatest rom-com that has ever been constructed. And to extend that point a little further, let's move the Best Supporting Actress away from Kim Basinger and over to Cameron Diaz, the bride-to-be (and secret archrival to Julia) in My Best Friend's Wedding.

1999

Best Picture: Shakespeare in Love

Best Director: Steven Spielberg for Saving Private Ryan

Best Actor: Roberto Benigni in Life Is Beautiful

Best Actress: Gwyneth Paltrow in Shakespeare in Love

Best Supporting Actor: James Coburn in Affliction

Best Supporting Actress: Judi Dench in Shakespeare in Love

Three things here: (1) This was a sneaky strong year for rom-coms and movies that are almost rom-coms but not really. There was You've Got Mail (Hanks! Ryan! Ephron!), Hope Floats (Bullock! Harry Connick Jr.!), How Stella Got Her Groove Back (Bassett! Whoopi! Shirtless Young Taye Diggs!), The Wedding Singer (the big gesture at the end when Adam Sandler sings to Drew Barrymore on the airplane!), There's Something About Mary (Ben Stiller's balls and dick trapped in a zipper!), and several others.

(2) All of the winner selections here are fairly airtight, so let me take this opportunity to cash in two more of the WLTOW exemptions.[8] I'm ditching Shakespeare in Love for Best Picture and replacing it with Armageddon (the scene where Ben Affleck cries and yells as his soon-to-be father-in-law Bruce Willis decides to stay on the asteroid has, for the past twenty years, leeched some real emotions out of me each viewing). And I'm ditching Roberto Benigni for Best Actor and replacing him with Blade from Blade because he deserves it for keeping us safe from the vampires.[9]

(3) Ben Affleck's character in Armageddon is named A. J. Frost. The main bad guy in Blade is named Deacon Frost. And I haven't quite figured out exactly what the Armageddon/Blade crossover is yet, but by God I promise you that I will figure it out before they bury my dead body in the earth.

---

7. It's important to me that you know that I was so excited to make this joke.

8. ONLY THREE LEFT.

9. This is a jokey answer, but Blade, which set the template for what a substantial comic book movie could be if it took itself more seriously, really does have an important legacy.

WHO WINS WHAT

at the BRAND NEW

ACADEMY AWARDS?

PART 2

2000

Best Picture: *American Beauty*

Best Director: Sam Mendes for *American Beauty*

Best Actor: Kevin Spacey in *American Beauty*

Best Actress: Hilary Swank in *Boys Don't Cry*

Best Supporting Actor: Michael Caine in *The Cider House Rules*

Best Supporting Actress: Angelina Jolie in *Girl, Interrupted*

Let's delete all three of the *American Beauty* awards. That means we need a new Best Picture, a new Best Director, and a new Best Actor. And this being such a mammoth year for movies, I think it'd be a little too disrespectful to use up one or more of the WLTOW exemptions, so let's treat the replacements here seriously.

For Best Picture, it'd be smart to pick something that has gone on to have, in one way or another, an ever-lasting effect on movies or moviemaking. That means we're picking between *The Matrix* (new technology), *Fight Club* (affirmation of David Fincher's directorial brilliance), *Being John Malkovich* (extremely weird), *The Blair Witch Project* (mainstreamed a clever film device), *The Sixth Sense* (zeitgeist moment), or *Office Space* (a cult classic moment). Of those, *The Matrix* today stands the tallest (we got the creation of Bullet Time; it was the first movie ever to sell a million copies of a DVD; it was an action movie but it worked very hard to exist as a philosophy movie; etc.). That's our new Best

Picture winner. Let's give Best Director to David Fincher for *Fight Club* because it's good and he should've probably won it for *Seven* anyway. And let's give Best Actor to Jim Carrey, who was positively brilliant as Andy Kaufman in *Man on the Moon*. That all feels right.

2001

Best Picture: *Gladiator*

Best Director: Steven Soderbergh for *Traffic*

Best Actor: Russell Crowe in *Gladiator*

Best Actress: Julia Roberts in *Erin Brockovich*

Best Supporting Actor: Benicio del Toro in *Traffic*

Best Supporting Actress: Marcia Gay Harden in *Pollock*

I do not dislike any of these picks. They're all strong. If anything, there's maaaaaaaaybe an argument to be made that you can take the Best Actress award from Julia Roberts and give it to Ellen Burstyn in *Requiem for a Dream*, but I'd jump in front of a bus being driven by an even bigger bus before I ever did anything like that to Julia Roberts, so no thank you.

How about this: Since Russell Crowe won Best Actor for his role as Maximus in *Gladiator*, let's swipe the Best Picture award from that movie[1] and go with a dark horse pick instead. Let's give it to *Memento*, a movie filmed in reverse about a man who loses the ability to form new memories that I have seen at least ten times and still don't all the way quite understand. And I guess let me go ahead and also grab Marcia Gay

---

1. This is a mistake. I love *Gladiator*.

Harden's Best Supporting Actress award that she won for her part in *Pollock* (which to me always felt more like a stage play than a movie) and cash in one of the WLTOW exemptions so I can give the award to Eartha Kitt for her role as Yzma in *The Emperor's New Groove*. She was so fucking funny in that.

2002
Best Picture: *A Beautiful Mind*
Best Director: Ron Howard for *A Beautiful Mind*
Best Actor: Denzel Washington in *Training Day*
Best Actress: Halle Berry in *Monster's Ball*
Best Supporting Actor: Jim Broadbent in *Iris*
Best Supporting Actress: Jennifer Connelly in *A Beautiful Mind*

Two things here: (1) give Ethan Hawke his oscar for his role as Jake Hoyt in *Training Day*. Everyone else is safe. That's the only change that needs to be made. (2) There was a larger conversation going into this year's Oscars about how Black actors and actresses are so infrequently honored at the Academy Awards. (This is a conversation that is still happening today, as it were.) When Halle Berry won the Oscar for Best Actress (making her the first ever Black woman to win the award), she gave this really touching, really tearful, really beautiful speech. When Denzel Washington won Best Actor a little later in the evening (his first ever win in the category, because I guess nobody at the Academy watched him in 1992's *Malcolm X*), he glided up the stairs, then glided to the microphone, then accepted

his award, then hugged Julia Roberts (she was presenting the award), then stood at the mic and waited for everyone to sit down. When they did, he laughed a little, then said, "Two birds in one night, huh?" It was incredible, and a perfect Denzel Washington moment.

2003
Best Picture: *Chicago*
Best Director: Roman Polanski for *The Pianist*
Best Actor: Adrien Brody in *The Pianist*
Best Actress: Nicole Kidman in *The Hours*
Best Supporting Actor: Chris Cooper in *Adaptation*
Best Supporting Actress: Catherine Zeta-Jones in *Chicago*

I would very much like to replace all of these, but since we're capped at three replacements let's go with: (1) Take the Best Picture award away from *Chicago* and give it *City of God*, which has aged itself into a truly remarkable piece of art. (2) Take the Best Director award away from Roman Polanski and give it to Fernando Meirelles for *City of God*. (3) And take the Best Actor award away from Adrien Brody[2] and give it to Robin Williams for his role in *One Hour Photo* as Sy Parrish, an extremely lonely photo lab employee who becomes obsessed with a family whose photos he develops over a long period. Williams is incredible as Parrish. Watching him toggle back and forth between a kind-eyed old man and a mentally unstable loon is really unsettling. (His 2002 is such an interesting slice of his career. He played Sy in *One Hour Photo*, a maniacal former children's show

---

2. Apologies to Adrien, who I have always liked. Did you watch him in *Predators*? He was wonderful in it.

host gone mad in *Death to Smoochy*, and a killer in *Insomnia*.[3]) (I care a great deal about Robin Williams.[4]) (I think part of that might be because he kind of looks like my dad.) (I don't know.) (It's complicated stuff.) (And I'd rather not try and parse it out in the pages of this book.)

2004

Best Picture: *The Lord of the Rings: The Return of the King*

Best Director: Peter Jackson for *The Lord of the Rings: The Return of the King*

Best Actor: Sean Penn in *Mystic River*

Best Actress: Charlize Theron in *Monster*

Best Supporting Actor: Tim Robbins in *Mystic River*

Best Supporting Actress: Renée Zellweger in *Cold Mountain*

There's a scene in *Cold Mountain* where Renée Zellweger, who plays a no-nonsense molasses-mouthed mountain girl, auditions for a job as a laborer by tearing the head off a rooster that's been bothering Nicole Kidman. And the reason I mention it here is because when that scene happened, my wife, who was watching the movie with me one night, saw it and said to me, "If it's not too much of a problem, would you mind doing that to me? Because I don't think I can watch too much

more of this." *Cold Mountain* is bad. And Zellweger's accent is a full-on C-A-T-A-S-T-R-O-P-H-E. Let's take her Best Supporting Actress award and give it to Marcia Gay Harden for her spot in *Mystic River* because (a) she was perfect in *Mystic River*, and (b) we took her Best Supporting Actress earlier so this is retribution for that.[5]

Also, as wonderful as Charlize Theron is in *Monster*, let's grab the Best Actress award from her and give it to my beloved Diane Keaton for *Something's Gotta Give* because that was one of the five or six best ever performances in a rom-com.

And I don't want to replace the Best Picture award outright, but what I would like to do is go ahead and slide in a Best Picture nomination for *Love Actually*. So now that's a thing, too.

2005

Best Picture: *Million Dollar Baby*

Best Director: Clint Eastwood for *Million Dollar Baby*

Best Actor: Jamie Foxx in *Ray*

Best Actress: Hilary Swank in *Million Dollar Baby*

Best Supporting Actor: Morgan Freeman in *Million Dollar Baby*

Best Supporting Actress: Cate Blanchett in *The Aviator*

---

3. I still remember watching the trailer for *Insomnia* the first time in a movie theater. I had, to that point in my life, only known Robin Williams as a sweetheart and good guy actor. When they showed him in the trailer right as they're revealing he's a killer, I very loudly said to my girl-friend-who-became-my-wife, "HOLY FUCKING SHIT!"

4. So much so, actually, that I asked Arturo to draw a picture of Robin Williams as Patch Adams treating Robin Williams as Jack, his character from *Jack* who aged four times faster than everyone else. It's the art on the next page.

5. To be clear, I am very high on Renée Zellweger. She has been in several of my favorite movies.

It's time to cash in the sixth of the WLTOW exemptions, because we're taking Best Picture away from *Million Dollar Baby* and Hail Mary-ing it down the field to *Man on Fire*, a movie where Denzel Washington spends a fair amount of time killing participants in a kidnapping ring in ways that are both impressive and innovative (you can read about them in the Action Movie Kills Hall of Fame chapter). Let's also take the Best Actress award from Hilary Swank and slide it over to Lindsay Lohan for her role as Cady Heron in *Mean Girls* (THIS IS NOT A WLTOW EXEMPTION BECAUSE SHE WAS LEGITIMATELY GREAT IN THE MOVIE). Those are the only two changes for this year. Apologies, Hilary. You're great.

2006

Best Picture: *Crash*

Best Director: Ang Lee for *Brokeback Mountain*

Best Actor: Philip Seymour Hoffman in *Capote*

Best Actress: Reese Witherspoon in *Walk the Line*

Best Supporting Actor: George Clooney in *Syriana*

Best Supporting Actress: Rachel Weisz in *The Constant Gardener*

So if we get to replace up to three award winners each year, let's use the first one to replace *Crash* for Best Picture with *Brokeback Mountain* for Best Picture. Then let's use the second pick to replace *Crash* for Best Picture with *Brokeback Mountain* for Best Picture again. And then let's use the last pick to replace *Crash* for Best Picture with *Brokeback Mountain* for Best Pic-

ture one final time. Hopefully one of those three times will stick, and hopefully *Crash* will stay good and buried for the next thousand years, all the way until some archeologists accidentally dig it up and release an evil spirit into the world to take over the body of a little girl like what happened in *The Exorcist*.

2007

Best Picture: *The Departed*

Best Director: Martin Scorsese for *The Departed*

Best Actor: Forest Whitaker in *The Last King of Scotland*

Best Actress: Helen Mirren in *The Queen*

Best Supporting Actor: Alan Arkin in *Little Miss Sunshine*

Best Supporting Actress: Jennifer Hudson in *Dreamgirls*

I feel a tiny part of me wanting to sneak Best Actor away from Forest Whitaker to give it to Ryan Gosling for his drug-addicted teacher Dan Dunne in *Half Nelson*, but Whitaker gave too commanding of a performance to be overtaken. So he's safe. So are *The Departed* and Scorsese and Helen Mirren and Jennifer Hudson and Alan Arkin. No changes this year. I will, however, throw in some new nominations. Let's get Christian Bale and Hugh Jackman nominations for their roles in *The Prestige* (pick whoever you want to get the Best Actor nom and give the Best Supporting Actor to the other). Let's also get a Best Director nomination for Spike Lee for *Inside Man*. Let's get Meryl Streep a Best Supporting Actress nomination for *The Devil Wears Prada*. Let's get Vince Vaughn and Jennifer Aniston Best Actor and Best Actress nominations for *The Break-Up*.[6] And let's get Will Smith a Best Actor nomination for *The Pursuit of Happyness*, which would've cleaned up at the Oscars if Will had been less active in his own salvation and let a white man or woman save him instead.

2008

Best Picture: *No Country for Old Men*

Best Director: Joel and Ethan Coen for *No Country for Old Men*

Best Actor: Daniel Day-Lewis in *There Will Be Blood*

Best Actress: Marion Cotillard in *La Vie en Rose*

Best Supporting Actor: Javier Bardem in *No Country for Old Men*

Best Supporting Actress: Tilda Swinton in *Michael Clayton*

Another benchmark year in movies. Consider: *There Will Be Blood*, *Zodiac*, *Juno*, *Superbad*, *Michael Clayton*, *Ratatouille*, *Shooter* (a gold star Good Bad Movie), *3:10 to Yuma*, *Grindhouse*, *Gone Baby Gone*, *American Gangster*, *The Bourne Ultimatum*, and *Eastern Promises*. Regarding awards, I think it makes the most sense to swap out *No Country for Old Men* with *There Will Be Blood* for Best Picture because *There Will Be Blood* is a perfect movie, so that's one change. And also let's move the Best Actress trophy from Marion

Cotillard's bookshelf and set it down on Ellen Page's bookshelf (*Juno*). Beyond that, Russell Crowe (*3:10 to Yuma*) deserves a nomination for Best Supporting Actor but he doesn't get to steal it from Javier Bardem, who was phenomenal as the villainous Anton Chigurh in *No Country for Old Men*. Likewise, Will Smith deserves a nomination for Best Actor for *I Am Legend* (the most underrated performance of his career) but he doesn't get to steal it from Daniel Day-Lewis. And that's basically it. Everything else feels fine.

2009

Best Picture: *Slumdog Millionaire*

Best Director: Danny Boyle for *Slumdog Millionaire*

Best Actor: Sean Penn in *Milk*

Best Actress: Kate Winslet in *The Reader*

Best Supporting Actor: Heath Ledger in *The Dark Knight*

Best Supporting Actress: Penélope Cruz in *Vicky Cristina Barcelona*

Just two award-winner replacements here: We're losing Sean Penn for Best Actor and replacing him with Mickey Rourke in *The Wrestler* (Rourke was nominated but didn't win, even though he should've). And we're losing Kate Winslet for Best Actress and replacing her with Liv Tyler because she was great in *The Strangers* and *The Strangers* is great and I don't understand why more people don't talk about *The Strangers* more

---

6. Jennifer Aniston is quietly an elite-level performer in rom-coms. A sampling: *She's the One*, *Picture Perfect*, *The Object of My Affection*, *The Switch*, *The Break-Up*, *Just Go with It*, *All I Need Is Pizza*, *Second Chance*, *The Getaway*, and *Three-Day Weekend*. (Those last four are made up.) (Sorry.)

often.[7] For some surprise nominations, let's throw Best Supporting Actor to Cam Gigandet because he was very scary and hateable as the villain in *Never Back Down*. Let's throw a Best Supporting Actress nom to Kristen Bell because she was aces as Sarah Marshall in *Forgetting Sarah Marshall*. And let's throw a Best Actor nomination to Will Smith for *Hancock*, less because of the movie and more just because I am fucking going to keep trying to give Will Smith an Oscar somewhere even if it kills me.

2010

Best Picture: *The Hurt Locker*

Best Director: Kathryn Bigelow for *The Hurt Locker*

Best Actor: Jeff Bridges in *Crazy Heart*

Best Actress: Sandra Bullock in *The Blind Side*

Best Supporting Actor: Christoph Waltz in *Inglourious Basterds*

Best Supporting Actress: Mo'Nique in *Precious: Based on the Novel 'Push' by Sapphire*

Best Picture and Best Director are safe because *The Hurt Locker* is airtight and even if it wasn't it wouldn't matter because Kathryn Bigelow is one of my very favorite directors so I would never take an Oscar out of her hands.[8] Two categories that are not safe, though, are Best Actor and Best Actress. Jeff Bridges loses his Oscar to Jeremy Renner in *The Hurt Locker*

(and let me also add in a Best Actor nomination for Joseph Gordon-Levitt in *(500) Days of Summer* while we're here) and Sandra Bullock loses her Oscar to Vera Farmiga, who I am moving out of the Best Supporting Actress category (she was nominated for her part in *Up in the Air*) and dropping her now into the Best Actress category. If that's not allowed,[9] then Sandra Bullock's Oscar for Best Actor in *The Blind Side* goes to Sandra Bullock in *The Proposal*, a far more enjoyable movie and also we should probably at least mention in passing that Sandra Bullock has really put up some impressive rom-com career numbers.

---

7. This is the second Oscar Liv Tyler has picked up, and it literally was not until this very moment that I realized how much I've enjoyed Liv Tyler's career. (*Empire Records*, *That Thing You Do*, *Armageddon*, *The Lord of the Rings* trilogy, *The Strangers*.)

8. Her four best movies: 1991's *Point Break*, 2008's *The Hurt Locker*, 2012's *Zero Dark Thirty*, and 2002's *K-19: The Widowmaker*.

9. I don't know why it wouldn't be allowed, given that I am kind of just making all of this up as I go.

PART 3

2011

Best Picture: *The King's Speech*

Best Director: Tom Hooper for *The King's Speech*

Best Actor: Colin Firth in *The King's Speech*

Best Actress: Natalie Portman in *Black Swan*

Best Supporting Actor: Christian Bale in *The Fighter*

Best Supporting Actress: Melissa Leo in *The Fighter*

It seems so obvious now, and it should've been obvious at the time, but: The new Best Picture winner is *The Social Network*, and the new Best Director winner is David Fincher for *The Social Network*, and the new Best Actor winner is Jesse Eisenberg for his Mark Zuckerberg in *The Social Network*. And this will be the only time I do this, but I'm going to break the No More Than Three Replacements rule here and also give Andrew Garfield the Best Supporting Actor award for his Eduardo Saverin in *The Social Network*, as well as the Best Supporting Actress award to Rooney Mara for her Erica Albright in *The Social Network*. Thank you.

2012

Best Picture: *The Artist*

Best Director: Michel Hazanavicius for *The Artist*

Best Actor: Jean Dujardin in *The Artist*

Best Actress: Meryl Streep in *The Iron Lady*

Best Supporting Actor: Christopher Plummer in *Beginners*

Best Supporting Actress: Octavia Spencer in *The Help*

I didn't know anything about *The Artist* (a black-and-white silent film) before my wife and I sat down to watch it, which is why I remember getting, like, maybe twenty minutes into it before I turned to her and whispered, "What the fuck is happening right now?" (I am not above admitting that the scene where the guy finally starts hearing things is kind of cool. I am also not above admitting that the scene where the woman makes the suit come alive was great.) As such, I'm using all three replacements here for three wins *The Artist* scored in our big-ticket categories. The new Best Picture winner is *Drive* (it's not a silent movie, but Ryan Gosling treats it like it is), the new Best Director is Gavin O'Connor for *Warrior* (a movie so inspiring that I briefly tried my hand at mixed martial arts[1]), and the new Best Actor winner is Vin Diesel as Dominic Toretto in *Fast Five* (the last of WLTOW exemptions, but absolutely it was worth it).

2013

Best Picture: *Argo*

Best Director: Ang Lee for *Life of Pi*

Best Actor: Daniel Day-Lewis in *Lincoln*

Best Actress: Jennifer Lawrence in *Silver Linings Playbook*

Best Supporting Actor: Christoph Waltz in *Django Unchained*

Best Supporting Actress: Anne Hathaway in *Les Misérables*

Someone please call Ben Affleck and let him know that he's just lost the Oscar for Best Picture to *Magic*

1. It was a disaster, I am sad to report.

Mike and that if he wants it back he's going to have to turn on Ginuwine's "Pony" and grind his way across a stripper stage just like Channing Tatum had to. While you're making phone calls, please also call Daniel Day-Lewis (the second greatest living actor, behind only Denzel Washington) and let him know that he's just lost the Oscar for Best Actor to Jake Gyllenhaal in *End of Watch*, and since you're talking to Jake on the phone you can let him know that his partner in *End of Watch*, Michael Peña, swiped the Oscar for Best Supporting Actor away from Christoph Waltz.

(A story that I will never forget about *End of Watch* is: I watched it one night back when I was still a teacher. I was totally blown away by it. I'd been lying down while it was on but by the time we got to the end and they were having that big shootout and chase scene I was—and I swear this is true—I was standing up in front of the TV like I was watching a very close and very important sporting event. I went to work the next day really excited to talk about it. I asked the teacher in the room next to me if he'd seen it. He said yes, and that he'd loved it. I said that the ending really got to me. And this is what I'll never forget. He said, "Me too. It was the first time I'd cried since my mom died." I was like, "Holy shit. We're having a real moment here, me and you." And he was like, "We are." And I say all of that to say this: What is the point of the Oscars if not to recognize and award movies that help eighth-grade science teachers better understand one another?)

2014

Best Picture: *12 Years a Slave*

Best Director: Alfonso Cuarón for *Gravity*

Best Actor: Matthew McConaughey in *Dallas Buyers Club*

Best Actress: Cate Blanchett in *Blue Jasmine*

Best Supporting Actor: Jared Leto in *Dallas Buyers Club*

Best Supporting Actress: Lupita Nyong'o in *12 Years a Slave*

This will sound like an exaggeration, but I promise to you that it is not: Seeing *Gravity* in a theater when it came out for real felt like a religious experience to me. I've never been able to fully explain why it felt that way or how it felt that way,[2] but that's the feeling I had in my heart afterward. We were walking out of the theater and my brain and body were exhausted from the movie and as we walked through the parking lot toward my car I very seriously said to my wife, "That must be what it feels like when people go to church." She said, "What?" I repeated myself. And she said, "I fell asleep for part of it." And then I said, "So it's exactly like church then?" And then a laugh track came on and our 1990s family sitcom went to commercial break. Anyway, Best Picture goes to *Gravity*, Best Actress goes to Sandra Bullock in *Gravity*, and let's go ahead and give Alfonso Cuarón a second Best

---

2. This is a thing that is somewhat troubling for me, what with it being my job to explain exactly these sorts of things and situations. I think maybe the best way to describe it is to say that I felt like I'd experienced something that reached me in an existential way. I've never been religious, but I have always been fascinated with outer space, and I'm referring to both the vastness of space and also the way that any conversation of outer space always seems to wordlessly confirm how tiny and unimportant everything is.

Director trophy since he won it outright the first time around but deserves to have won two because of how good it was.

A sidebar: A movie called *Prisoners* came out in 2013. It starred Hugh Jackman as a dad whose kid gets kidnapped and Jake Gyllenhaal as a detective who tries to find the kid. It was a just okay movie, but it will always be important to me because I went and watched it with that same science teacher I mentioned earlier. We were attending some conference in downtown Houston and we were supposed to stick around the whole day but we didn't. Instead, we walked through the conference, grabbed the stuff we needed, then left and went on a date together. We went to go eat brunch and then somehow ended up at a theater watching *Prisoners*. I had a good time. We never told anyone about it. He was a good work friend.

2015

Best Picture: *Birdman*

Best Director: Alejandro G. Iñárritu for *Birdman*

Best Actor: Eddie Redmayne in *The Theory of Everything*

Best Actress: Julianne Moore in *Still Alice*

Best Supporting Actor: J. K. Simmons in *Whiplash*

Best Supporting Actress: Patricia Arquette in *Boyhood*

Rosamund Pike gave what has to be considered the best villain performance since Heath Ledger's Joker in *The Dark Knight* when she allowed herself to lean into the empty-eyed insanity of Amy Dunne in *Gone Girl*. She should've won the Oscar for Best Actress, and so, with an all-caps and bolded apology to Julianne Moore, we're sending the Best Actress award to Pike now. (*Gone Girl* somehow was not even nominated for Best Picture, which is a real tragedy. Let's give them a nomination here.) We can also go ahead and grab that Best Actor trophy from Eddie Redmayne and send it to Jake Gyllenhaal. He gave an insta-Hall of Fame performance in *Nightcrawler* and it should be celebrated as such. (HE WASN'T EVEN NOMINATED!) And just because it's sitting right there, let's eagle claw the Best Picture win away from *Birdman* and get it over to *Whiplash* where it truly belongs.

A sidebar: Miles Teller is the star of *Whiplash*. He's very good in it, as he tends to be, because he is a strong actor. I can say with great certainty that I like him, and that I seek out his movies when they're released. But I mention him right now because back in 2016 I received an email from a guy I'd never spoken to before named Sean Freidlin who'd written an article about Teller that highlighted all of the times he'd been in a movie where a car crash happened. It happens in *Whiplash* (he's driving and gets hit), and it happens in *Rabbit Hole* (he accidentally hits a small child with his car), and it happens in the *Footloose* remake (he's not involved in the crash, but it affects his life), and it happens in *That Awkward Moment* (he gets hit by a car as he crosses a street), and it happens in *Bleed for This* (he's the passenger in a car that crashes head-on into another), and that's not even all of them. And so ever since reading that article I've watched every Miles Teller movie waiting for the car crash and I want you to do it too.

2016

Best Picture: *Spotlight*

Best Director: Alejandro G. Iñárritu for *The Revenant*

Best Actor: Leonardo DiCaprio in *The Revenant*

Best Actress: Brie Larson in *Room*

Best Supporting Actor: Mark Rylance in *Bridge of Spies*

Best Supporting Actress: Alicia Vikander in *The Danish Girl*

One of my personal favorite years for movies. We got *Straight Outta Compton* (far better than anyone was expecting), *The Big Short* (five star performances across the board), *Trainwreck* (an excellent romantic comedy), *The Intern* (Robert De Niro and Anne Hathaway are wonderful together), *Southpaw* (it's not that good but I'm a big Gyllenhaal fan and also Rachel McAdams has a scene in it where she dies and she is a powerhouse in that moment), *The Martian* (fun), *Mad Max: Fury Road* (legit incredible), *The Revenant* (LEONARDO DICAPRIO FIGHTS A GODDAMN BEAR), *Jurassic World* (magnificent), *Sicario* (Emily Blunt is the best and Benicio Del Toro is the best and Josh Brolin is the best), *Furious 7* (the most heartrending entry in the *Fast and the Furious* franchise), *San Andreas* (The Rock vs. a natural disaster), *Room* (I can barely breathe), *Creed* (perfect in literally every way), *The Hateful Eight* (either very good or very bad, depending on how you feel about Quentin Tarantino), and *Mission: Impossible—Rogue Nation* (strong).

We could hand out awards in a bunch of different directions, for a bunch of different reasons. But the three that absolutely cannot be ignored: Ryan Coogler gets Best Director for *Creed*, Charlize Theron gets Best Supporting Actress for her Imperator Furiosa in *Mad Max: Fury Road*, and O'Shea Jackson Jr. gets Best Supporting Actor for his Ice Cube in *Straight Outta Compton*. (The only reason I'm not taking Leo's Best Actor from him and giving it to Michael B. Jordan for *Creed* is because that was basically a career recognition win for Leo. But we can at least give Michael B. Jordan a Best Actor nomination.)

2017

Best Picture: *Moonlight*

Best Director: Damien Chazelle for *La La Land*

Best Actor: Casey Affleck in *Manchester by the Sea*

Best Actress: Emma Stone in *La La Land*

Best Supporting Actor: Mahershala Ali in *Moonlight*

Best Supporting Actress: Viola Davis in *Fences*

The first thing that needs to happen is Viola Davis needs to be moved from Best Supporting Actress over to Best Actress. She wasn't a supplemental piece in *Fences*. She was central to the entire movie. So there's that. She's your new Best Actress winner. (And this doesn't count as one of the three replacements because she was already a winner.)

And moving Viola over means that Naomie Harris, who was legit special in *Moonlight*, gets the suddenly freed-up Best Supporting Actress trophy. (This can count as the first of the three replacements, I suppose, even though it shouldn't because it should've been this way in the first place.)

For the other two replacements, let's go with *Moonlight* and Barry Jenkins as the new Best Director (HOW DID HE LOSE THIS????????), and *Fences* and Denzel Washington as the new Best Actor (HOW DID HE LOSE THIS TO CASEY AFFLECK????????), and right here seems like a good time to point out that if things had broken the way they were supposed to at the 2017 awards it'd have been the first time ever that Black actors, actresses, and director would've swept the major categories, which would have been massive.

Additionally, let's toss some nominations out there: Best Picture nomination for *Hell or High Water*; Best Supporting Actor nominations for Jeff Bridges and Ben Foster in *Hell or High Water*; Best Actress nomination for Amy Adams in *Arrival*; and a surprise Best Actor nomination for Ryan Reynolds in *Deadpool*, if you can even believe that. I remember reading this interview one time where either the director of *Ray* said that Jamie Foxx was born to play Ray Charles or Jamie Foxx said that Jamie Foxx was born to play Ray Charles in a movie. I feel the same way about Ryan Reynolds with *Deadpool*.

2018

Best Picture: *The Shape of Water*

Best Director: Guillermo del Toro for *The Shape of Water*

Best Actor: Gary Oldman in *Darkest Hour*

Best Actress: Frances McDormand in *Three Billboards Outside Ebbing, Missouri*

Best Supporting Actor: Sam Rockwell in *Three Billboards Outside Ebbing, Missouri*

Best Supporting Actress: Allison Janney in *I, Tonya*

I lied earlier. The whole No More Than Three Replacements rule is being broken again here.

BEST PICTURE TO *GET OUT*, obviously. BEST DIRECTOR TO JORDAN PEELE FOR *GET OUT*, obviously.

BEST ACTOR TO DANIEL KALUUYA IN *GET OUT*, obviously. BEST ACTRESS TO ALLISON WILLIAMS IN *GET OUT*, obviously. BEST SUPPORTING ACTOR TO BRADLEY WHITFORD IN *GET OUT*, obviously. BEST SUPPORTING ACTRESS TO CATHERINE KEENER IN *GET OUT*, obviously. I DON'T CARE ANYTHING ABOUT THE RULE SAYING YOU CAN ONLY REPLACE THREE AWARDS, obviously. BECAUSE *GET OUT* IS A PERFECT MOVIE, obviously.

And of course let's give a Best Picture nomination to *The Big Sick*, of course. And a Best Director nomination to Michael Showalter for *The Big Sick*, of course. And a Best Actor nomination to Kumail Nanjiani in *The Big Sick*, of course. And a Best Actress nomination to Zoe Kazan in *The Big Sick*, of course. And a Best Supporting Actor nomination to Ray Romano in *The Big Sick*, of course. And a Best Supporting Actress nomination to Holly Hunter in *The Big Sick*, of course.[3]

2019

Best Picture: *Green Book*

Best Director: Alfonso Cuarón for *Roma*

Best Actor: Rami Malek in *Bohemian Rhapsody*

Best Actress: Olivia Colman in *The Favourite*

Best Supporting Actor: Mahershala Ali in *Green Book*

Best Supporting Actress: Regina King in *If Beale Street Could Talk*

The 2019 Oscars were both exhilarating (Alfonso won Best Director! Regina King won Best Supporting Actress! Olivia Colman's speech after she won Best Actress!) and sucky (*Green Book* won Best Picture,

---

3. I wish that I'd have written this book exactly one year earlier because right here would've made for such a perfect ending to this chapter. I could've written a final sentence at the end of this *The Big Sick* section like, "That's how all of this started, so that's how all of this has to end." It would've been so great.

and Bradley Cooper lost Best Actor, and Lady Gaga lost Best Actress). And so this is easy: Give *A Star Is Born* the Oscar for Best Picture because it was auspicious and trenchant and crushing. (It put its elbows into the most tender parts of your psyche. *Green Book* did not. Watching *Green Book* felt like someone calling your name and then when you turned around they tossed a big piece of ham at you, and I'm not sure exactly how that makes sense but I know that it does.) And give Bradley Cooper the Oscar for Best Actor because he gave one of those performances where an actor or actress disappears completely into the role that they're playing, and, insofar as I understand it, that is the entire point of acting. (Rami Malek was good as Freddie Mercury in *Bohemian Rhapsody*, but Bradley Cooper was sublime.) And give Lady Gaga the Oscar for Best Actress because she pinned down every single part of that movie that she was supposed to have pinned down. (If you want to put up a big fight for Olivia Colman keeping her Oscar, then that's fine. She was very good in *The Favourite*.)

Some other nominations: a Best Picture nomination to *Mission: Impossible—Fallout*; a Best Actress nomination to Elsie Fisher in *Eighth Grade* and Best Picture nomination to *Eighth Grade* and Best Director to Bo Burnham for *Eighth Grade*; Best Picture nomination to *Widows*; Best Picture nomination to *If Beale Street Could Talk*; Best Actor nomination to Jason Statham in *The Meg*;[4] and Best Picture nomination to *Annihilation*.

---

4. I'm fucking serious.

WHO'S IN THE

PERFECT

POLICE
P02190

SWAT

HEIST MOVIE CREW?

"WHO'S IN THE PERFECT HEIST MOVIE CREW?" is hard to answer quickly because it's one of those questions that's actually several questions rolled up into one.

What I mean is, think on it the same as you would if somebody asked you, "Hey, what should I wear tomorrow?" That seems like a regular question and a simple one to answer, right? But it's only regular and simple assuming you already have several other pieces of information. You have to know what the weather is going to be, for one, because you can't be like, "You should wear a parka," and then you find out when you open the door that it's ninety degrees outside. And you have to know what the day's activities entail, for two, because you can't be like, "A bathing suit and some flip-flops will be fine," and then you get in the car and it turns out you're headed to a funeral.[1] And you have to know what mostly everyone else is going to be wearing, for three, because then otherwise you might end up in a *Bridget Jones's Diary* bunny costume situation.

If you have all that information, then yes, answering "Hey, what should I wear tomorrow?" is easy. If you don't, then it becomes way trickier. It's the same way with "Who's in the perfect heist movie crew?" question. You can't go into it blind. You need to gather some information first. You need to know three things. You need to know:

1. **Where is the thing that you need your crew to steal?** Different locations require different tools, and different tools require different skill sets, and different skill sets require different people. The crew in 2017's *Baby Driver*, for example, was very lo-fi, because their plans were very lo-fi. Each of their robberies mostly consisted of (a) having some people run into a bank or whatever, (b) waving some guns around, (c) stuffing some money into bags, then (d) running out to the car and hoping that Baby, the driver, could outmaneuver the police during the inevitable chase. They were a Driver Dependent Crew, if you'd like to put a term on it. But take them and measure them up against the crew in 2010's *Inception*. That crew's robbery plans were far more nuanced and intricate. They weren't breaking into banks. They were, quite literally, breaking into people's brains. It was a whole different thing, so they were a whole different thing.[2]

2. **What is it that you need your crew to steal?** Are we stealing gold (like in, say, 2003's *The Italian Job*)? Are we stealing information (like in, say, 1996's *Mission: Impossible*)? Are we stealing diamonds (like in, say, 2007's *Flawless*)? Are we stealing a Fabergé egg (like in, say, 2004's *Ocean's Twelve*)? Are we stealing proof of wartime atrocities (like in, say, 2006's *Inside Man*)? Are we stealing the necklace right off someone's neck (like in, say, 2008's *Ocean's 8*)? Are we stealing an entire fucking bank vault (like in, say, 2011's *Fast Five*)? Are we stealing money to fund our summer fun dreams (like in, say, 1991's *Point Break*)? On and on and

---

1. I guess if you were going to a funeral for a sea creature then this might be fine, but I don't know that sea creature funerals happen nearly often enough to take that kind of risk.
2. They were a Technology Dependent Crew, as it were.

on and on. The item being stolen, same as above, dictates what kind of crew you're going to need.

3. **What is the ultimate objective of your specific crew?** This one, unlike the two above, has less to do with the technical side of the actual heist and more to do with your own personal preference. Because do you like heist movies where it becomes clear that everyone is headed for doom? If so, you're going to need to make sure you include no less than one (but preferably two) characters who can send everything sideways.[3] Do you like heist movies where the characters you're rooting for are able to escape free and happy and you get to feel good about everything? If so, you're going to need to make sure you have a leader whose first instinct is not to shoot everything the fuck up as soon as there's any kind of hiccup.[4] Do you like heist movies where someone in the crew betrays the crew and gets away with it? Heist movies where someone in the crew tries to betray the crew but ends up burning themselves? Heist movies where the crew is inexperienced?[5] Heist movies where the crew is veteran and unflappable?[6] Heist movies where the crew isn't even really a crew, it's just one or two people?[7] Heist movies where . . . etc.

Same as the first two questions above, the way you want your heist to end will determine whom you choose to be in your heist.

———

FIVE QUICK HEIST MOVIE LISTS LISTS:

ELEVEN THINGS THAT HAPPEN IN HEIST MOVIES, ARRANGED BY HOW FUN THEY ARE

1. The montage where the team gets together.
2. The scene where the participants sit in a diner and use condiments and whatnot to map out the robbery. (I really like when they argue over who is going to be what condiment.)
3. The thing where someone has to be pulled in for "one last job."
4. When someone slowly realizes that they've been duped.
5. The part where someone explains to the group why the heist is impossible.
6. When someone who legitimately works at the place being robbed gets knocked out so his uniform can be stolen.
7. When the big misdirect gets explained at the end.
8. When someone shoots a guard and everyone gets mad at him and he says, "He was going for his gun! I had to do it!"

---

3. A good one would be Cleon from 1995's *Dead Presidents*. He was not only fiery, but also he made the classic mistake of flashing money around shortly after the heist.

4. A good one would be Jimmy Logan from 2017's *Logan Lucky*, a delightful movie where Channing Tatum and Adam Driver play brothers who appear to be dumb but actually end up being very smart.

5. Like the crew in 2018's *Widows*, a truly great heist movie that was, as film critic Adam Nayman explained, "genre pleasures framed by deeper social and political themes."

6. Like the crew in 1995's indelible *Heat*.

7. Like 1975's iconic *Dog Day Afternoon*, or 2012's underappreciated *The Place Beyond the Pines*.

9. When they show a quick shot of a small thing and you realize it's going to cause a giant fuck-up later in the movie.

10. When some piece of technology screws up.

11. The thing where a tech guy gives some fancy explanation for a thing and someone annoyedly says, "In English please."

BEST HEIST MOVIES THAT INVOLVE MARK RUFFALO DOING MAGIC

1. *Now You See Me*
2. *Now You See Me 2*

HEIST MOVIES TITLES, ARRANGED BY HOW MUCH THEY SOUND LIKE MOVIES ABOUT HEISTS

1. 2001's *Heist*. This one isn't a good movie but it's still a little bit fun to watch because it's like every person in it is competing in a Best One Liner in a Heist Movie competition.

2. 2015's *Heist*. One of those movies that sounds incredible on paper (De Niro! Dave Bautista! A heist! People trapped on a bus! A twist ending!) but then when you watch it you're like, "Ah. Okay. That's why I never heard of this."

3. 2011's *Tower Heist*. My beloved Michael Pena is in this, which means I love it.

4. 1981's *Thief*. As far as thieves go, a jewel thief has got to be the most glamorous kind of thief.

5. 2010's *The Robber*.

6. 2001's *Bandits*. Nope.

7. 2001's *The Score*. De Niro! Norton! Brando! A twist ending! Great movie!

8. 2002's *The Good Thief*. Nick Nolte's voice in this movie sounds like an old tractor engine.

9. 2003's *The Italian Job*. I mentioned earlier the thing about heist movies having a scene where someone gets the gang together. The one in this movie, while dorky, is very good.[8]

10. 2009's *Thick as Thieves*. This one isn't a very good movie, but it at least has Morgan Freeman saying this very good line: "Some people were born to compose music. Others to split the atom. I was born to steal shit."

11. 2001's *Snatch*. This title either sounds a little bit like a heist or a lot like a very adult movie.

12. 1996's *Mission: Impossible*. I'm not sure if this is technically a heist movie, but its biggest set piece—when Ethan Hunt and crew break into CIA headquarters—is incredibly heist-y so I'm including it here.

THE BEST LINES IN 2001'S *HEIST*

1. Joe: "I wouldn't tie my shoes without a backup plan."

2. Jimmy, after telling a story about how a Bible that a guy was holding in his pocket prevented a bullet from hitting him right in the heart: "And had he had another bible in front of his face, that man would be alive today."

3. Mickey, talking about money: "Everybody needs money! That's why they call it 'money'!"

4. Joe, when the main bad guy asks him if he wants to hear his final words: "I just did." (Then he shoots him in the face.)

---

8. Here's one of the lines delivered Mark Wahlberg, the leader of the group: "That's Left Ear. Demolitions and explosions. When he was ten he put one too many M80s in a toilet bowl. Lost the hearing in his right ear. He's been blowing stuff up ever since."

5. Pinky, when asked if a guy is going to be cool: "My motherfucker is so cool, when he goes to bed, sheep count him."[9]

6. Joe, when he tells a guy about how you could steal Ebbets Field if you plan a good enough getaway and the guy reminds him that Ebbets Field is gone: "What'd I tell you?"[10]

7. Joe, discussing the importance of being quiet: "I don't want you as quiet as an ant pissing on cotton. I want you as an ant not even thinking about pissing on cotton."[11]

HEIST MOVIE MASKS, ARRANGED BY HOW MUCH TIME I'VE SPENT ON THE INTERNET TRYING TO FIND AND BUY EXACT REPLICAS

1. The ex-presidents masks from *Point Break* (specifically the Ronald Reagan one)
2. The clear masks from *Set It Off*
3. The hockey masks in *Heat*
4. The clown masks in *The Dark Knight* (specifically The Joker's, and I know this isn't a heist movie but I don't care)
5. The nun masks in *The Town*
6. The little girl masks in *Sugar and Spice*

—

I am a basic man of simple tastes. As such, these are the answers to the three questions that I asked earlier:

1. **Where is the thing that you need your crew to steal?** It's in a bank vault, of course. There's just something so appealing, so undeniable, so intoxicating about the idea of robbing a bank. Maybe it's because we've all been inside of one before? Or maybe it's because we all understand that banks hold money and money is good? Or maybe it's because we've all, at this point, seen enough bank robbery movies to feel like we'd be able to avoid the traps that trip up so many robbers? (Avoid the dye packs! Never go for the vault! Make sure nobody sets off the silent alarms! But also have a plan in place for what to do when someone sets off the silent alarms because they somehow always do that shit! Watch out for the off-duty cop who just so happens to be in the bank depositing a check during the robbery! Don't accidentally say anyone's real name! Don't let any identifying marks or items get revealed!) If I'm planning a heist, it's happening in a bank. I want to honor that tradition.

And if I can be very, very specific here, it's happening in a Bank of America. Remember in 2016's *Hell or High Water* how the brothers were robbing Texas Midlands Bank branches because Texas Midlands Bank was trying to foreclose on the land that their deceased mother had owned? That's how I'm going to be with my Bank of America robbery, except it's not because they tried to foreclose on some Serrano family land, it's because one time I'd overdrawn on my account and didn't get an email alert from them about it until, like, 4 a.m. the next day, which resulted in me getting hit with three overdraft

---

9. This one is cool in that way that an older uncle who thinks he's still young tries to be cool.
10. This one is cool in a Dad Joke kind of way.
11. This one probably isn't cool at all, but I appreciate how hard he worked at the imagery.

charges of $35 apiece. I bought lunch at Taco Bell and it cost me less than $7 in real life, but because I'd unknowingly gone into the red in my account it actually ended up costing me almost $42. Nobody on the planet has ever spent $42 at Taco Bell before. Spending $42 at Taco Bell is like spending $300,000,000 at Target.

2. **What is it that you need your crew to steal?** Seeing as how we're setting this heist up in a bank, let's keep everything tidy and neat: The thing that I need for my crew to steal is money. Real money. Cash money. Literal dollars. Not something money-adjacent (like bearer bonds), and not something that's worth money but isn't actual money (like jewelry in a safety-deposit box or something). Only true, for real, no question about it, no tricky loopholes, green paper money.

3. **What is the ultimate objective of your specific crew?** While I will freely acknowledge that 2001's *Ocean's 11* is, in all likelihood, the part-for-part, beat-for-beat, second-for-second, most purely entertaining heist movie of all time, I don't want a 2001 *Ocean's 11*-y kind of heist. I want something a little more rugged. I want one of those heists where you slowly fall in love with each of the characters and then you have to watch several of them get killed during the final robbery; one of those heists where there's a chase scene but you know that it's not ending in any way other than with hundreds of thousands of dollars worth of damage to public property and a firefight; one of those heists where the person chasing the robbers is just as astute and formidable (and morally ambiguous) as the robbers themselves; one of those heists where an innocent bystander gets shot; one of those heists where, if someone is able to make it out, you feel good about it, but also you feel a little bit bad about it.

So given the answers to the three questions, that means we have six roles to fill in. We need: the Leader; the Nameless Member of the Crew Who You Know for Sure Is Going to Die Because They Didn't Get Very Many Lines in the Movie Before the Final Heist; the Driver; the Ill-Tempered Muscle; the Member of the Crew Who Tries to Double-Cross Everyone; and the Law Enforcement Officer Chasing the Team.

———

THE LEADER: Danny Ocean from the aforementioned *Ocean's* franchise is cosmically cool, for sure, and also an ace Leader in general. But since we know that our heist is likely going to involve a scenario where a guard has to be killed, Danny isn't a good a pick here.[12] To that point, none of the *Ocean's* people are going to be good for us, really. They can do a lot of impressive robbery things, absolutely, but I can't talk myself into believing they'd be able to shoot their way out of a tight spot if they needed to. So they're all out.[13] Except Don Cheadle. He gets to stay. For obvious reasons.

---

12. A better Clooney pick would be Jack Foley, his character from *Out of Sight*. He checks off all the same boxes that Danny Ocean does, except he's also a killer.

13. AND LET ME SAY AGAIN: I love the *Ocean's* movies. And I love the characters in the *Ocean's* movies. And I understand that barring them all from selection here ends up with losing a lot of good people and hurting a lot of feelings. But when you're robbing banks, you don't have time to worry about feelings, because worrying about feelings is how you end up dead.

I'm also going to eliminate Dalton Russell from *Inside Man* (a gifted tactician but, same as Ocean, I just can't trust that he'd put a bullet in someone so that his team could escape[14]); Terry Leather from *The Bank Job* (mostly I'm eliminating him because his last name is "Leather," which is ridiculous); Scott Lang from *Ant-Man* (Luis is eligible); Jackie Brown from *Jackie Brown* (I'd like for my leader to have a few more robberies on their résumé); Neil McCauley from *Heat* (I need someone who'd at least pretend like they were interested in helping me get out alive[15]); Anthony Curtis from *Dead Presidents* (he's too short, and, as a five-foot-seven man myself, it hurts to write that as the reason for his dismissal); and Dominick Cobb from *Inception* (he's cool, but a little too off center). You know who I want? You know who I'm taking as the Leader of my crew here? Give me Bodhi from 1991's *Point Break*. He cares about his team, and he's guided by a code, but also he clearly has a powerhouse of a presence, and he has no qualms with shooting a person or kidnapping someone's girlfriend and turning a murdering psycho loose on her whenever the need arises.

THE NAMELESS MEMBER OF THE CREW WHO YOU KNOW FOR SURE IS GOING TO DIE BECAUSE THEY DIDN'T GET VERY MANY LINES IN THE MOVIE BEFORE THE FINAL HEIST: Pick anyone from 2014's *American Heist* or 2010's *Takers*, two movies that I have passively watched several times and still can't remember the name of literally one single charac-ter from either of them. (I guess it has to be one of Hayden Christensen's characters by default, given that he's in both of these.) (He's got a great face.) (And he looks good in hats.) (I'm not exactly sure how that's helpful here, but I know that it definitely is.)

THE DRIVER: Baby from *Baby Driver* is a talented driver, sure, but still a little too unproven for me. And Ryan Gosling's Driver from *Drive* is out because technically it is not a heist movie.[16] You know who I want? I'll give you two picks here. Give me Letty from *The Fast and the Furious* series (there's more on her driving ability in the last chapter of this book), and if you say that she's not allowable as a pick because all the movies in *The Fast and the Furious* franchise are a few steps outside of being considered heist movies then first let me say, "Fuck you," and second let me say, "Then give me Deirdre from 1998's *Ronin*, seeing as how she's responsible for one-half of the single best car chase scene in any heist movie ever." Other possibles: Handsome Rob from 2003's *The Italian Job* and Randall Raines from 2000's *Gone in 60 Seconds*. Last place is Tyrone from 2000's *Snatch*.

THE ILL-TEMPERED MUSCLE: Separate of the Leader, this is almost always my favorite character in the heist movie. I like how uncontrollable they are, and how they either (a) give in to their impulses entirely and end up fucking up the heist totally, or (b) go riiiiiiiight up to the edge of giving in to their impulses, then someone talks them back at the last possible second, making for a few extremely tense seconds.

---

14. They pretend to shoot someone in *Inside Man,* but only so the cops will take them more seriously. We find out later that it was all a setup.
15. Same reason that Joker from *The Dark Knight* is getting cut.
16. I don't like that his name is Driver. I mean, I get what they're going for with it—that whole Mysterious Man angle—but mostly it just makes me think he has a very dorky name in real life that he knows doesn't fit his persona, or his neon cool aesthetic. It's probably something like "Melvin Dorkman."

Ostensibly, there are a bunch to choose from here, but really there are only five legit contenders. Fifth place is James "Jem" Coughlin from 2010's *The Town*. Fourth place is Waingro from *Heat*. Third place is Tanner Howard from 2016's *Hell or High Water*.[17] Second place is Mr. Blonde from 1992's *Reservoir Dogs*. And first place is Cleo from 1996's *Set It Off*, which was a monstrous and unforgettable performance in a movie that, even more than twenty years later, still feels alive and vital. She's the pick here. Cleo is the move.

THE MEMBER OF THE CREW WHO TRIES TO DOUBLE-CROSS EVERYONE: An interesting take on this was Ty Hackett in 2009's *Armored*. He worked at a security service and several of the guards decided they were going to rob an armored truck for $21 million. They eventually talked him into participating, but after one of the other guards shoots a homeless man who's a potential witness, Ty backs out, barricading himself inside of the armored car they've just stolen. He doesn't keep the money for himself, and also he was the good guy in the movie, so I'm not sure if he'd even be eligible for this pick or not. Either way, I don't figure he's the way to go. You need someone slimier. You need someone slipperier. You need someone charming enough to disarm you in the beginning, but who also has an innate sinister vibe to their essence, so that when they double-cross you, you go, "Oh. Duh. I should've seen that coming." I think I have to go here with Edward Norton, because he has spent a large amount of his movie time being exactly that kind of person. (His two most applicable roles: when he was Steve in *The Italian Job*, and when he was Jack/Brian in 2001's *The Score*.)

THE LAW ENFORCEMENT OFFICER CHASING THE TEAM: Since this is a gnarly crew, I need a gnarly person chasing them. I want someone who's coming in off the top rope in every scene. I want a guy with a bad beard and some tattoos he regrets and whose personal life is falling apart because his job has turned him into an angry box full of broken glass. I want a guy who looks like he always has liquor on his breath and a knife somewhere on his person. I want a guy who's willing to get a little illegal during the chase, and who's got his own team of mercenaries behind him who also aren't afraid to get a little illegal during the chase. I want a guy who, when he wants to interrogate someone, he sneaks up on him, knocks him out, drags him to a hotel room, then says stuff like, "Do we look like the types who'll arrest you? Put you in handcuffs, drag you down to the station? We just shoot you. It's less paperwork." I need Gerard Butler's Big Nick O'Brien from 2018's *Den of Thieves*. He's the only one with a shot at chasing down my team. He's my guy.

And that's the crew. Bodhi from *Point Break* as the Leader, Hayden Christensen's character from *Takers* as the Nameless Member of the Crew Who You Know for Sure Is Going to Die Because He Didn't Get Very Many Lines in the Movie Before the Final Heist, Letty from *Furious 7* as the Driver, Cleo from *Set It Off* as the Ill-Tempered Muscle, Edward Norton's character from *The Score* as the Member of the Crew Who Tries to Double-Cross Everyone, and Big Nick from *Den of Thieves* as the Law Enforcement Officer Chasing The Team.

---

17. Curiously enough, he's the enforcer in this movie but it's his quiet brother, Toby, who has the movie's most turbulent moment. (When he beats up the guy at the gas station who pulls a gun on Tanner.)

DID THE

ROCKFORD
PEACHES

MAKE THE
RIGHT
DECISION
TRADING **KIT?**

A LEAGUE OF THEIR OWN IS A FICTION-ALIZED RETELLING of the formation of the All-American Girls Professional Baseball League, which, as the name implies, was a professional baseball league for women.[1] It's one of the three best baseball movies that have ever been made,[2] and so I would like to talk about it for a bit. However, the stuff that gets discussed in this chapter will not make any sense to anyone who does not have a strong familiarity with the movie's plot, so let's run through that first.

In *A League of Their Own*, we follow Dottie Hinson and Kit Keller, sisters from Oregon who get the call-up to try out for the AAGPBL. Dottie is tall and fearless and heroic and a baseball genius (she plays catcher), and so of course she's the one everyone fawns over. Kit is short and kind of a whiner and very ordinary (at least she is when measured up against Dottie, anyway), and so of course she's underappreciated (she plays pitcher). They end up both making the league, and also they both make the same team (the Rockford Peaches).

The Peaches are coached by Jimmy Dugan, a former professional player and current alcoholic. He mostly ignores the team at first, but then he realizes his team is very good and decides he doesn't want to ignore them anymore. Separate of Dottie and Kit, the other main players on the team are:

- **Mae Mordabito:** She plays center field. She's the lead-off batter. She's very good. Were there no Dottie, she'd probably be the leader of the team.
- **Doris Murphy:** She plays third base. She's loud and obnoxious, but in the most charming way possible. She's the movie's comic relief.
- **Marla Hooch:** She plays second base. She's the best hitter on the team, and likely the best hitter in the entire league. The running gag with her is that she's unattractive.
- **Ellen Sue Gotlander:** She plays shortstop and pitcher.
- **Betty "Spaghetti" Horn:** She plays left field and relief pitcher.
- **Evelyn Gardner:** She plays right field. (She's the one in that "There's no crying in baseball!" clip that everyone knows.) She seems nice enough, but she screws up things a bunch.

Nearing the end of a game that could send the Peaches to the playoffs, Kit begins to struggle as pitcher. Jimmy and Dottie meet with her at the mound. She asks to finish the game, but Dottie, after a moment of hesitation, says that Jimmy should replace her. Jimmy does, and the Peaches win the game. Dottie and Kit get into a big fight in the locker room, and Kit (basically) tells Dottie that being her sister sucks because no matter what she does she knows that she'll never be able to keep pace with Dottie.

Dottie, very hurt by what Kit says, asks to be traded from the team. The team decides to trade Kit instead. This (duh) sends Kit into a rage, which she ends by saying she can't wait to play Rockford in the World Series. And guess what? It fucking happens, is what.

---

1. It operated from 1943 to 1954. It was started by several professional baseball executives as a response to World War II drawing hundreds of MLB players away from their teams and into conflict.
2. The other two are *The Sandlot* and *Major League*. No matter what order you arrange those three into, you will be both correct and wrong.

Rockford and Kit's new team, the Racine Belles, meet in the World Series. Only here's the thing: Shortly after Kit is traded, Dottie's husband comes home from the war. Dottie cuts out on the team before the World Series starts, opting instead to go back home. She misses the first six games of the series, then returns for game seven. And here's a big thing, and what sets up the movie's biggest moment: Kit is the starting pitcher for that game.

Rockford and Racine play to a standstill to the ninth inning, but then Kit gives up two hits in a row, putting two base runners on with Dottie coming up to bat. She pitches it, and Dottie crushes a line drive at her head, scoring two runs. Kit has a mini-breakdown between the top of the ninth and the bottom of the ninth, but ultimately gets a chance to redeem herself. She comes up to bat with her team down one, a runner on base, and a chance to either lose the game, tie the game, or win the game. Dottie calls time, then tells her pitcher to throw high fastballs because it's the one pitch that Kit can't hit and also can't lay off of. The pitcher does so, and Kit gets two quick strikes. Kit and Dottie share a look before the third pitch, and it's another high fastball, but this time Kit blasts it into the outfield.

The runner scores and as Kit is rounding second, her third-base coach signals for her to stop. Kit, fully possessed, ignores the call, and speeds around the corner toward home. Dottie realizes what's happening, and so she catches the ball from Doris and braces for impact. Kit crashes into Dottie like a goddamn F-150 crashing into the side of a building, and both players go tumbling through the air. To everyone's surprise, Dottie—who, again, is bigger and stronger and more everything than Kit—loses her grip on the ball as she hits the ground. Kit touches home plate, scores, Racine wins, and the stadium goes 100 percent bonkers. Kit gets carried off the field as the Peaches slink into their locker room, heartbroken and miserable.

That's the movie, and I would think that the four big questions that come out of it are at least a little bit obvious:

1. Who gets the most blame for Rockford losing the World Series?
2. Did Dottie drop the ball on purpose so that Kit could finally have her big moment?
3. Did the team make the right decision in trading Kit away after she and Dottie got into that fight?
4. What's the single funniest thing that Doris Murphy says in the movie? (This one, I will admit, is decidedly less obvious than the other three.)

Let's answer those, but in the opposite order.

———

WHAT'S THE SINGLE FUNNIEST THING THAT DORIS MURPHY SAYS IN THE MOVIE?

Short of Dottie, Doris is my favorite Rockford Peach. You know the characters in a movie who, even when they're saying something ordinary, it's still just so funny? That's the kind of character Doris is. The eight funniest things she says in *A League of Their Own*:

8th Place: On the first day of tryouts, Doris tries to psych out Dottie and Kit by throwing a baseball at them. Dottie catches it barehanded without even flinching. Doris, completely shook, says to Mae, "Jeez, let's go practice."

7th Place: Doris and Mae are dancing with a few men at a bar. Doris takes one of the men and flips him feet over head. Someone asks her how she did it. She says that Mae taught her, that the two worked at a strip club. "She was one of the dancers. I was a bouncer."

6th Place: Dottie sees Marla Hooch, drunk and up on stage at the bar, singing to a man in the audience. She asks Doris what they did to her. Doris says, "Nothing. We just gave her a dress."

5th Place: A teammate sees a picture of Doris's boyfriend and is taken aback by how ugly he is. After a second, she tries to comfort Doris by saying that looks aren't important. Doris, without missing a beat, says back, "That's right. The important thing is he's stupid, he's out of work, and he treats me bad."

4th Place: The league is struggling to generate fan interest and so Mae, a former dancer, suggests that maybe she can arrange it so that her breasts pop out while she's fielding a ball. Doris asks, "You think there are men in this country who ain't seen your bosoms?"

3rd Place: A woman named Brenda gets out during a game. As she walks past Doris to get to her dugout, Doris shouts, "You're out, Brenda." (This is the second-best example of her saying a regular thing in an extremely funny way.)

2nd Place: Ellen Sue throws a pitch that hits the dirt. It's called a ball by the umpire. Doris, ever vigilant in her support of her teammates, shouts, "Ellen Sue! Ellen Sue! Ellen Sue! That looked good to me, Ellen Sue! That looked good to me."

1st Place: The thing earlier about Doris's boyfriend being ugly: When the teammate first sees the picture, she asks if it's out of focus. Doris pinches her lips together a little and then says, "No. That's how he looks." (This is the first best example of her saying a regular thing in a funny way.)

———

DID THE TEAM MAKE THE RIGHT DECISION IN TRADING KIT AWAY AFTER SHE AND DOTTIE GOT INTO THAT FIGHT?

I mean, it's easy to look at the result of the World Series and say that it was a mistake, but that's a bad way to approach things for two reasons:

(1) Measuring decisions based solely on what ends up happening later is oftentimes the easiest way to convince yourself that a bad thing was actually good, or that a good thing was actually bad. For example, if you one day said to yourself, "You know what I'm going to do today? Rather than putting my infant daughter in her crib at bedtime in a normal way, I'm going to see if I can jump shoot her into it from across the room like a basketball," and then you did it and it worked out fine and so you were like, "I knew it. I knew that would be a good idea." It wasn't a good idea. You just got lucky, is all.

(2) Dottie was, hands down and no question, the very best player in the league. She literally bats 1.000 in the movie. She also dives into a dugout to catch a foul ball. She also makes a catch while doing the splits (the photo of which ends up on the cover of *Time*, very likely saving the league from withering away into nothingness). There's no way Rockford was ever going to trade her away before they traded Kit away, because there's no way anyone was going to be able to make an argument that trading away the

league MVP to keep a barely All-Star pitcher happy would make any kind of sense. Kit had to go. It was the only call to make.

So: Yes. Rockford made the right decision in trading Kit.[3]

DID DOTTIE DROP THE BALL ON PURPOSE SO THAT KIT COULD FINALLY HAVE HER BIG MOMENT?

Yes. I wish it weren't the case, but it is. The movie gives us just enough clues to let us know that it's happening. To wit:

Dottie says on multiple occasions that she doesn't love baseball, that it's just something she does.[4] It's why she has to be coerced into even trying out for the league. It's why she abandons her team right before the World Series starts when her husband comes home from the war. It's why she only plays the one season. Dottie *liked* baseball, yes, absolutely. She probably liked it a lot. But she didn't *love* it—at least, not the way that Kit did. Baseball was everything to Kit. And Dottie understood that. It's why she wanted Kit to win. She knew that, even beyond just the personal and athletic glory, winning that World Series would mean a different kind of life would lie ahead of Kit than if she'd lost it.[5]

"There's a lot of reasons I can't go." That's what an elderly Dottie tells her daughter at the beginning of the movie. Dottie's daughter is trying to convince Dottie to go to the AAGPBL reunion and Hall of Fame induction ceremony. Dottie pretends like she doesn't want to go because she doesn't think anyone will remember her, but really it's because even all those years later she still feels guilty about throwing Game Seven.

"Now remember: No matter what your brother does, he's littler than you are so give him a chance to shoot." That's what an elderly Dottie says to one of her grandsons as she's on her way out of the house to the reunion. The grandson she's talking to has a younger brother. They're playing basketball together. This, I think, is the most obvious signal that Dottie dropped the ball on purpose.

"Why you gotta be so good, huh?" That's a line that Kit says to Dottie during a fight they have in the locker room after that game where Dottie has Kit benched. Kit goes into this whole speech about how whenever Dottie is around she feels like she barely even exists. And when she's done, Dottie is very visibly shaken. It's right here, I would guess, where Dottie decides she's going to sacrifice baseball for Kit's own well-being. (Which is why she tells the person running the league that if they don't trade her then she's quitting and going home.) (Bonus: Kit makes a similar argument earlier in the movie when she talks Dottie into trying out for the league. It's the one card she

---

3. A technical note: The trade happens right before the playoffs start. No professional sports league allows trades to happen that late in the season. I think about that every time I watch this movie. Also: We never find out what player(s) Rockford picked up in exchange for Kit. I feel like the AAGPBL's trade guidelines were far too sketchy.

4. There's literally a line where, well after her career is over, she says, "It was never that important to me. It was just something that I did. That's all."

5. There's this movie called *Mr. Destiny* that came out in 1990 that deals with almost this exact thing. A guy strikes out in a big at bat in high school and then goes on to live what he feels like is a regular, boring, bad life. A magic bartender (lol) goes back in time and makes it so that he actually hit a game-winning home run in the at bat, and his whole life changes; he's rich, and successful, and so on and such and such.

can play against Dottie that Dottie never has a good enough answer for.)

A precedent. There's a play earlier in the season when Dottie gets trucked by an opponent's catcher at home plate in a play similar to the one between Dottie and Kit. The catcher is much bigger than Kit, and Dottie takes the collision like it's nothing. Getting smashed by the catcher and not dropping the ball and then getting smashed by a significantly smaller Kit and not dropping the ball is like bench pressing 180 pounds easily but for some reason not being able to bench press 115 pounds.

After she gets the big hit off Kit to put Rockford up 2–1 in the ninth inning of game seven, she sees Kit having a breakdown in the dugout. It's clear that watching her sister go through it affects Dottie. And I have to assume that Dottie knew Kit was going to be batting third that inning, which is when she started on plotting setting up Kit for her shot at heroism. And that leads us to the three things people who argue that Dottie did not drop the ball on purpose like to point out . . .

EVIDENCE THAT APPEARS TO BE AGAINST THE CASE THAT DOTTIE DROPPED THE BALL ON PURPOSE

She had Kit pulled out of that game. This would seem to be proof that Dottie values winning over her sister's feelings, which, if extrapolated outward, means of course Dottie would never give up a World Series just to make her sister feel better. But the Getting Pulled from the Game situation and the Dropping the Ball situation are two very different things. In the former, Kit still gets to be part of the winning side.[6] In the latter, Kit is haunted by the three hits that she gave up in the top of the ninth to lose the World Series for her team for literally the rest of her life.

The ninth inning hit I mentioned a moment ago. You might say, "If Dottie wanted Kit to win, why not just go down swinging in her at bat in the top of the ninth? If she would've done that, Kit's team would've won and Kit would've still gotten to be the hero." And to that I say, "Because Dottie wasn't sure right then that she wanted to let Kit win. It wasn't until after the hit when Dottie saw Kit falling apart in the dugout that knew she had to save Kit."

Telling the pitcher about Kit's weak spot as a batter. Right before Kit's at bat in the bottom of the ninth, Dottie calls time and then goes and tells her pitcher to throw high fastballs, that Kit "can't hit 'em, can't lay off 'em." This would seem to be a clear sign that she wants to win, and that she's willing to sacrifice Kit to do so. Except here's the thing: She wasn't sacrificing Kit. She was setting Kit up for the biggest hit of her life. Kit, we're told (and shown) for the entire movie that the high fastball is her favorite pitch. Kit also knows that Dottie knows she likes the pitch (and that she has trouble with them). After the pitcher throws two straight high fastballs, Kit and Dottie stare at each other. It's right here where Kit sniffs out that another high fastball is coming, and why she's prepared to hit it. Dottie knew that Kit was going to figure it out, which is pretty much the most she could do for Kit in that moment.

Kit was smart, and capable, and clever. Had Dottie played her hand in any kind of other way, Kit would've been able to tell that Dottie had tipped things in her favor, which would've ruined it for Kit. Dottie had to set all those

---

6. Also: Who would really be upset about a starting pitcher making it through *only* eight and two-thirds innings? If anything, Kit was being a tad bit selfish and unreasonable here.

pieces up in exactly the right way, which is exactly what she did.[7]

—

WHO GETS THE MOST BLAME FOR ROCKFORD LOSING THE WORLD SERIES?

The first pick you have to go with is Dottie, seeing as how she orchestrated the ending. But I don't figure that's right. She was mostly just reacting to the situation she'd found herself in. (You can give her 25 percent of the blame, if you like.) (Also, let's consider for a second how insane it was that the best player in the league decided she'd just skip out on the World Series the day before it started.) (And I'd also like to ask her a few questions about her alibi.[8])

The second pick is you have to go with Jimmy Dugan, seeing as how (a) he let Dottie play in game seven, and (b) he never replaced Evelyn, their right fielder, despite the fact that Evelyn screwed up more times than nearly everyone else in the movie. But I don't figure that's right either, because he proved himself to be a very good manager. Rockford went into the World Series missing their best player (Dottie), a starting pitcher (Kit, who'd gotten traded a week or two earlier), their starting left fielder and relief pitcher (Betty "Spaghetti" Horn, who left the team after she received news that her husband had been killed in the war), and their best hitter (Marla Hooch, who left the team after she got married to the guy she was singing to in the bar). Getting Rockford to a game seven is an impressive enough achievement to save Jimmy from absorbing too much blame here. Give him 15 percent of the blame.

Marla has to get a ton of blame for cutting out on the team after getting married. (Give her 20 percent of the blame.) Betty gets a pass because of the dead husband thing. (Give her 0 percent of the blame and 100 percent of the condolences.) And Kit has to get a pass because Dottie probably overreacted to the fight she had with Kit that led to Kit being traded. (Give her 10 percent of the blame.)

All of those people are out. You know who the answer is? You know who gets the most blame for Rockford losing the World Series? Evelyn. She was the one who had her son hanging around the dugout telling everyone they were going to lose before game seven. She was the one who made the error early in game seven that allowed Racine to score their first run (she missed the cutoff throw, which is the same mistake she'd made in a game earlier in the season that cost Rockford a lead). And she was the one who was playing way too far up in the infield when Kit got her hit in the bottom of the ninth. (The ball sailed clean over her head, a good thirty yards behind her. She should've known that Kit was taking big swings. Any contact Kit made was going to result in the ball sailing.) She's 30 percent responsible for Rockford losing the World Series.

---

7. Another thing to point out is that the score was 2–1 when Kit went up to bat. She drove in the tying run (which Dottie anticipated) before making a break for home to try and win the game (which Dottie was somewhat surprised by). You can make the argument that Dottie being somewhat surprised by Kit going for home is a good piece of evidence that she didn't drop the ball on purpose, but I'd counter with Dottie was happy that Kit went for it all because it provided Dottie with the most perfect and natural way to gift the victory to Kit.

8. She says that she and her husband got "as far as Yellowstone Park" when she cut out on the team before deciding to come back. If that's the case, and if they were leaving from anywhere near Illinois (the general area most of the games took place), things still don't really match up. That's a round trip of about thirty-eight hours. She gets back in time for game seven. Even if Racine and Rockford played doubleheaders in three straight games (which definitely they didn't do), she should've still made it back before games five and six.

THIS WILL BE PREPOSTEROUS, but please treat it seriously: It's sometime between 7:30 p.m. and 8:30 p.m. on a Friday night. And it's raining outside. And it's been a long week of work for you. And if you're married or dating in your real life, you're single and live alone in this pretend life I am constructing for you right now. Additionally, you have enough money in your bank account that you don't feel even one single percent of the constant pressure in the back of your brain that's always there when you're worried about how you're going to pay upcoming bills. And the thing that was supposed to be happening later in the evening that you'd promised you'd attend has just been unexpectedly canceled. And so, with great freedom and even greater joy, you decide that your plans for the evening now are as such: You're going to order some takeout to be delivered to your place for dinner and you're going to eat it and watch things on television and just be a mostly happy, mostly relaxed, mostly normal person.

But you decide you don't want to hang out by yourself. So you pick up your phone to buzz someone to come over and hang out with you. Only except here's the thing, because here's the twist: Your phone in this scenario is not the normal phone you likely have in your pocket or sitting next to you somewhere right now. It's a special phone, unique in one extremely specific, extremely odd regard: It only has three numbers in it, and the three numbers it has in it are (1) the telephone number to reach Jack Nicholson's version of the Joker from 1989's *Batman*; (2) the telephone number to reach Heath Ledger's version of

the Joker from 2008's *The Dark Knight*; and (3) the telephone number to reach Jared Leto's version of the Joker from 2016's *Suicide Squad*. Those are the only three people you can reach. (And, to be clear, it's the characters from the movies that you can call, not the actors who played them.) So, who do you call? What number are you dialing first? Which one of those three seems like he'd be the most fun to spend your evening with?

———

Per a 2017 report from the United States Department of Agriculture, it costs, on average, a little over $233,000 to raise a child in America from birth to the age of seventeen. And if you decide you want to pay for your kid to attend college, now you're talking about upward of a lifetime total of something like $380,000 to $433,000, assuming your kid doesn't get any scholarships. And I tell you that to tell you this:

It was my youngest son who (inadvertently) came up with the premise of this chapter. The way it happened is my wife was out at lunch with two of her friends and so I was supposed to be watching our sons, which means (a) the two older ones were playing video games; (b) I was getting some work done on my laptop; and (c) the smallest kid was running around doing whatever it is he does when nobody is looking. (Oftentimes it's something innocuous and cute, like playing with Lego blocks or reading a book to a stuffed animal, but occasionally it's something irksome but funny, like one time he went into the refrigerator, took out the container of strawberries, then bit the tips off all of them just because he felt like it.[1]

Anyway, I was sitting there working and the little one came running over. He said, "Daddy, what are you doing? Working?" I said, "Yes, sir." He said, "What are you working on? Basketball?" I said, "No, sir. Not this time. I'm actually reading about a guy named Hannibal Lecter. He's a real bad guy. In fact, sometimes he eats people."[2] He thought about what I'd said to him, allowing his tiny brain to process the idea of cannibalism for the first time. Then he said, "I would *not* wanna be friends with him." Then he ran off to go back to playing.

I sat there for a second, then said to myself, "Hmmm. That's a fun idea. I'm gonna do a thing in the movie book where I write an entire chapter about which movie villains would make for good hangs." And so that's what this is. I just straight up stole his idea. He can take it off that $400,000 or so that I'm going to spend on him.

———

A Bunch of Movie Villains, but Certainly Not All the Movie Villains, or Even a Substantial Number of Them, for That Matter

Hannibal Lecter from *Silence of the Lambs*: In almost all instances, the default answer to "Would a cannibal make for a good hang?" should be "Fuck that." (*Texas Chainsaw Massacre*, *Bone Tomahawk*, *Ravenous*, *Parents*, *Raw*, etc.) Hannibal is the one exception, though, in part because he's just so alluring and so intriguing, but also because he has a clear and definite code. Consider the part in 2001's *Hannibal* where Clarice interviews Barney, one of the guards at the asylum where Hannibal lived before he escaped in *Silence of the Lambs*. Clarice says, "Barney, back when you turned Lecter over to the Tennessee State Police—" Barney interrupts her, saying, "They weren't civil to him. And they're all dead now." Clarice says back, "Yeah. They only managed to survive his company three days. You survived him six years at the asylum. How'd you do that? It wasn't just being civil." To which Barney responds, "Yes, it was." If you want to hang out with Hannibal, the only real rule is don't be a dick. If you're a dick, you die. If you're not a dick, then you probably get to go to an opera or a museum or something very culture-y like what Hannibal enjoys.[3] Good hang.

Miranda Priestly from *The Devil Wears Prada*: A very good hang, assuming you are dressed appropriately. (Or, actually, I don't know. Because Stanley Tucci was dressed impeccably for all of *The Devil Wears Prada* and she still screwed him over. This one's on you. You have to decide for yourself.)

---

1. When I asked him why he did this, I was expecting him to shrug his shoulders and run away, given that that's how he had answered basically every question I asked him from the time he was three up until the time he was five. He didn't do that, though. In fact, he was quite adamant in his answer. I held up a strawberry and said, "Hey. Why'd you do this?" And he looked at the strawberry and then he looked at me. Then his face got real mad. Then he said, "I don't like pointy fruit." He was so confident about it that in my head I was like, "Yeah, man. *Fuck* pointy fruit. Get the bananas. We got work to do!"

2. If I were 20 percent more clever, I'd have come up with an impromptu joke here for him about pointy people.

3. I suspect using the word "culture-y" would not go over so great with Hannibal. It'd be like when the one guy in the symphony kept fucking up so Hannibal killed him and then fed him to some people at a dinner party.

Tyler Durden from *Fight Club*: A very good hang, assuming you like fistfights and general anarchy.

Anton Chigurh from *No Country for Old Men*: This is going to be the dumbest explanation here but also it will be true and insightful: Anton would be a bad hang and the way that I know that is because of his haircut. It is entirely unreasonable. It looks like he walked into a barbershop and said, "Hey, can you just make me look as fucking insane as you can? Thanks."

Patrick Bateman from *American Psycho*: He's the opposite of a Hannibal Lecter type. There are times when he kills for a reason, sure, like when he chopped Jared Leto to bits with the ax. But mostly he's just wilding out. Bad hang. (*American Psycho* is a great example of a movie that I like a lot but only for a little bit of time. I really enjoy the beginning of *American Psycho*. It's enjoyable to watch all the way up until he starts killing people. Once he starts killing people I'm like, "Okay, that's good for me. I'll see y'all later.")

Scar from *The Lion King*: Four things here: (1) Scar is the second most vile and villainous animated movie villain that's ever been. Among other things, he killed Mufasa; tried to kill Simba on two separate occasions; blamed Mufasa's death on Simba; and spearheaded a union between the hyenas and the lions that ultimately led to everyone's ruin. The only character he loses out to is Ernesto de la Cruz from *Coco*.[4] That being said, I think they'd both be fun to hang out with. They're both very charming and also they can sing and also they're both very handsome. Good hang(s).

(2) Why did Scar have an accent? What was going on there? (3) People don't talk about this enough, but it was pretty crummy luck for Scar that a drought hit the Pride Lands after he took over. That's beyond his control, I'd argue. Tough break for him there. (4) How much blame needs to fall to Mufasa for not sniffing out that Scar had grown into a full-on bad guy? He should've picked up on that.

Chong Li from *Bloodsport*: A bad hang, unless you're super into the gym, in which case he might be a great hang. (I do not like the gym. Asking me to go to the gym is no different than asking me to jump into a volcano.)

Commodus from *Gladiator*: A very bad hang, assuming you do not enjoy incest. (If you do enjoy incest, then you and Commodus could hang out and watch *Game of Thrones* and have a grand ol' time, I imagine.)

Simon Phoenix from *Demolition Man*: Two things here: (1) SIMON PHOENIX SPEAKS SPANISH. He does it right after they wake him up for his parole hearing. It's part of the reason that Wesley Snipes has been beloved within the Mexican community for years and years. (2) Simon Phoenix is a very good hang, assuming he does not need your eyeball to unlock a retina scanner.[5]

Alex Forrest from *Fatal Attraction* (and also a bunch of other angry ex-lovers): Regarding upset ex-girlfriends or ex-wives in movies, Glenn Close as Alex in *Fatal Attraction* is as good as it's ever gotten.

---

4. Ernesto also tried to kill a child twice in his movie.
5. Simon Phoenix definitely overreacted here. He needed the prison warden's eyeball to open up the doors to the cryo-prison because it was locked with a retina scanner. But rather than just forcing the much weaker, much softer warden to put his head up to the scanner so it could scan his eyeball, Simon cut out his whole eye and held it up there himself.

Behind her it's Amy from *Gone Girl*, then Julie from *Vanilla Sky*, then Brandi from *A Thin Line Between Love and Hate*, then Asami from *Audition*, then Lisa from *Obsessed*. That's the starting lineup plus one player coming in off the bench. On the upset ex-boyfriends or ex-husbands side of things, it's Bill from *Kill Bill*, Charlie from the 2011 version of *Straw Dogs*,[6] Noah from *The Boy Next Door*, David from *Fear*, Carter from *The Perfect Guy*, and Martin Burney from *Sleeping with the Enemy*. That's their starting lineup plus one player coming in off the bench. At any rate, all of these people are good hangs, until one tiny thing goes wrong and then all of a sudden they extremely are not good hangs.

Santanico Pandemonium from *From Dusk Till Dawn*: She would be a good hang, but only up until she turns into the vampire monster thing, at which point she would become an extremely bad hang, and possibly even the worst hang. (If you hate snakes, then she'd probably never be a good hang, what with her having the ability to summon a gigantic anaconda out of nothingness like she does at the beginning of her dance routine in the movie.)

Bishop from *Juice*: Bishop killed one of his best friends and then tried to kill his other two best friends after that. So I *KNOW* that he should be categorized here as a bad hang. BUT, Tupac was just so magnetic as Bishop, and so charming as Bishop, and so radiant as Bishop that even though I know hanging out with Bishop is, in effect, a death sentence, I'm still answer-ing the phone when he calls me. Good hang, right up until he shoots me.

Thanos from *Avengers: Infinity War* (and all the other villains from movies based on comic books, excepting Nomak from *Blade II*, the Vulture from *Spider-Man: Homecoming*, Catwoman from *Batman Returns*, and Loki from *The Avengers*): Bad hangs. Sorry.

Every marquee movie monster (Jason Voorhees, Leatherface, Michael Myers, Pennywise, the little girl from *The Ring*, Pinhead, the guy in *Pan's Labyrinth* with the eyes in his hands, Brundlefly, etc.) that is not Freddy Krueger: Bad hangs, obviously. Freddy gets listed as a good hang because he's funny and also because it feels like you could talk your way into him not killing you for an evening. Leatherface and Michael Myers and all the rest of them aren't offering you any sort of mercy. Any night of hanging out with them ends with some of the insides of your body suddenly on the outside of your body. (The worst hang of all of these is a tie between Brundlefly on account of the acid vomit and the little girl from *The Ring* on account of her being soaking wet all the time. I really just hate the idea of a wet person sitting on my couch.)

Gollum from *The Lord of the Rings*: Ewww. Bad hang. And gross hang.

Sho'nuff from *The Last Dragon*: I can't think of a person that has ever been more maligned in a movie where people fight than Sho'nuff from *The Last Dragon*. Because when you really and

---

6. I'm not sure if there will be another spot later in this book for me to say this or not so I'm just going to drop it in right here: James Marsden, who plays the hero David in *Straw Dogs*, has an all-time great Movie Star Face. He has the kind of face where if you got bonked on the head and forgot everything about everything, you'd still be able to look at him and go, "Oh, duh, that's a movie star. He's a movie star."

truly and actually think about it, all he wanted was to be seen as the best martial artist alive. That's why he spent the whole movie trying to fight Leroy. He knew that people believed Leroy was the best fighter around, and so he chased that fight with Leroy. He wanted to beat him in combat so that he could be seen as the king. That's all. I mean, he could've very easily killed Leroy and just gotten him out of the way if he wanted to. (Remember when he went to Leroy's dojo with his cronies? It'd have been super easy for him to just put a bullet in Leroy right then.) But Sho'nuff didn't want that. He didn't want to cheat his way to the top. He knew there was no honor in winning that way. So he just goaded Leroy and goaded Leroy and goaded Leroy until finally he figured out exactly what he needed to do to get Leroy to fight him. And then they fought and Leroy beat him and that was that. That was the end of things. Good hang.

The Xenomorph from *Alien* (and a bunch of other aliens): Nope. Bad hang. There are only, like, six or seven movie aliens that would make for good hangs.[7] E.T. from *E.T.* would be a good hang. So would Mac from *Mac and Me*. Paul from *Paul* would be a good hang (and maybe even the best hang, depending on how you feel about eating birds while they're still alive). Ford from *The Hitchhiker's Guide to the Galaxy* would be good. Bumblebee from *Bumblebee* would be good. Starman from *Starman* would be good. And maaaaaaaybe Superman would be a good hang, though I suspect that'd be a lot like hanging out with a youth pastor. All the other movie aliens would be bad hangs. The aliens from *Fire in the Sky*, the alien from *The Thing*, the aliens from *Critters*, the aliens from *Attack the Block*, the aliens from *Signs*, the aliens from *Killer Klowns from Outer Space*, the aliens from *War of the Worlds*, the aliens from the *Predator* franchise,[8] Sil from *Species* and the Female from *Under the Skin*, and more and more and more: all bad.

Alonzo from *Training Day*: A good hang. He's a very nefarious villain in *Training Day*, sure, but he tries hard not to be, and what I mean is: Everybody remembers that Alonzo sets up Jake and kills Roger and then tries to kill Jake later on a few different times. But Alonzo didn't want it to be that way. Because think back on Alonzo's mission in the movie: Alonzo had this really intricate, really involved plan in place to hustle his way into the money he needed to pay off the Russians. I mean, it was a masterful plan; the kind of planning only the most gifted of tacticians can put together. And so he very easily could've orchestrated it so that the plan included Jake dying. But that wasn't Alonzo's first option. Alonzo's first option was to include Jake in everything. He didn't plot Jake's death until Jake became a threat. Had Alonzo's first instinct been to kill Jake, then fine, he'd be labeled a bad hang here. But that wasn't his first instinct. Alonzo's first instinct was to get Jake drunk, get Jake high, then give Jake $250,000. That's a superb hang.

———

---

7. For this part, I'm only talking about aliens in movies where people are surprised to learn that aliens exist. Mostly all of the aliens in movies where people know aliens exist seem like they'd be fun hangs. The only real exception would be Jabba the Hutt. He seems like the pits.
8. There's a chance that the one Predator that helps Adrien Brody in *Predators* might be a good hang, but it'd probably be smart to just go ahead and avoid all the Predators.

REGARDING THE EARLIER HYPOTHETICAL ABOUT THE JOKERS

Working backward to frontward, I think it's pretty clear that Heath Ledger's Joker is the last place finisher here, right? Mind you, Ledger's performance as the Joker was obviously the most exquisite of those three.[9] But his whole Agent of Chaos existence would make for a hangout night that was far too unpredictable and kinetic to be enjoyable. You'd say something like, "Hey, you wanna get some Chinese and watch a few episodes of *The Office*?" And he'd respond with something like, "What about if instead of that we blow up a hospital and steal a police car?" And you'd respond with something like, "No, that definitely seems like less fun. Perhaps as a compromise we can watch *Scrubs*? It's at least *set* in a hospital." And he'd respond with something like,[10] "How about this: Let's cut open a man's gut and sew a cell phone into him?"

Jared Leto's Joker is the second-place finisher, if for no other reason than because he seems a little less likely to kill you than Ledger's Joker. (I don't have a lot to say about Jared Leto's Joker, only that I imagine hanging out with him would probably be like hanging out with a young André 3000, in that weird, sexually charged kind of way that hanging out with a young André 3000 looked to be like.)

And that means Jack Nicholson's Joker is the first-place finisher. He's the one Joker who seemed to actively be having the most amount of fun, and so that's one key part here, because fun is good. But more important than that, is he's the one who seems the most reasonable. And I know that's a weird thing to say about a guy who barbecued a man's flesh off his bones with a hand buzzer, but considering the company I think it makes sense.

---

9. I want to make sure that this is stated as plainly and authoritatively as possible at least once in this book: Heath Ledger as the Joker is the single greatest acting performance that has ever happened in a superhero movie, and one of the all-time great performances across all genres. There are no holes in it. Everything about it is perfect.

10. A thing that I didn't realize about Heath Ledger's Joker until I rewatched *The Dark Knight* the fourth or fifth time is that his most famous and everlasting monologue in the movie—the part where he talks Harvey Dent into becoming a villain—is a brilliant bit of maneuvering. He spends the entirety of *The Dark Knight* putting a highly elaborate plan in place to tear Gotham apart forever, and then he somehow in the matter of a few seconds convinces Harvey that he never had a plan at all EVEN THOUGH HE'S LITERALLY IN THE MIDDLE OF EXPLAINING TO HIM EXACTLY WHAT HIS PLAN IS. And so I say for a second time: Heath Ledger as the Joker is the single greatest acting performance that has ever happened in a superhero movie, and one of the all-time great performances across all genres.

WHICH WAS BETTER:

get out

OR

THE SOCIAL NETWORK?

THERE IS A LOT OF INFORMATION that needs to be worked through over the next 3,000 words of this chapter so, rather than dance through a showy introduction, let me state the following as directly and efficiently as possible:

Line up all of the movies that have come out since 2007. All of them. Every one of them. Grab *There Will Be Blood*[1] and *Mad Max: Fury Road*.[2] Grab *Slumdog Millionaire*[3] and *Zero Dark Thirty*.[4] Grab *Ex Machina*[5] and *Moonlight*.[6] Grab *Interstellar*[7] and *Boyhood*.[8] Grab *Arrival*[9] and *The Big Short*.[10] Grab *Whiplash*[11] and *No Country for Old Men*.[12] Grab *Inside Out*[13] and *Toy Story 3*.[14] Grab *Gravity*[15] and *Lady Bird*.[16] Grab *The Hurt Locker*[17] and *The Favourite*.[18] Grab more, and more, and more, and more. Grab literally every single one. And know this about them: They are all in a footrace for the third spot on the podium. Because the best movie of the past twelve years is either *The Social Network*, a fictionalized retelling of the founding of Facebook, the biggest and most massive modern addition to human history, or it's *Get Out*, a horror movie about a black man who visits his white girl-friend's parents for a weekend in upstate New York and finds out that the family is harvesting the bodies of black men and women and inserting the brains of rich and ailing white men and women into them.

So which one is better? Pick one. That's what this chapter is. You can only pick one. *Get Out* or *The Social Network*?

———

Pick One: Better Leading Actor? Jesse Eisenberg was nominated for an Oscar for his portrayal of Mark Zuckerberg in *The Social Network*. Daniel Kaluuya was nominated for an Oscar for his portrayal of Chris Washington in *Get Out*. Neither of them won.[19] Both

---

1. Daniel Day-Lewis is supernatural here.
2. A testament to the unending genius of George Miller.
3. Remember how exhilarating it was when you realized the narrative device that had been written into place here.
4. Kathryn Bigelow shows everyone how you take Jessica Chastain and turn her into one of the most captivating performers on the planet for 157 minutes.
5. Oscar Isaac, will you marry me?
6. Barry Jenkins announces himself as a master.
7. If Matt Damon plays an astronaut in a movie he's only either going to be the most likable person or the most hateable person.
8. Ethan Hawke and Patricia Arquette and Ellar Coltrane... [pretend like I'm doing that thing where a person pulls their glasses down their nose a little bit and then looks over the top of them at you].
9. All-caps AMY ADAMS.
10. Adam McKay was so great here that he somehow made a movie about the housing market feel electric.
11. Definitely my tempo.
12. If Oscar Isaac says no to marrying me, then Javier Bardem will do.
13. I'm going to cry.
14. Okay, now I'm crying.
15. I wrote about this one in chapter 20.
16. Welcome Saoirse Ronan to the pantheon.
17. The best moment of Jeremy Renner's career.
18. Unquestionable.
19. Eisenberg lost to Colin Firth for his role in *A King's Speech*. Kaluuya lost to Gary Oldman for his role in *Darkest Hour*.

of them should have. They gave career-defining performances; legacy-defining performances; the kinds of performances that are so mesmerizing and so acute that they immediately were recognized as canon.[20] A measure of each:

For his role as Zuckerberg, Eisenberg leaned all the way into what appears to be his natural state of annoyed superiority. And I hope that doesn't sound like an insult, because I absolutely mean it as a compliment. Perhaps a better way to say what I'm meaning here is: Eisenberg has a powerful face. Everything on it—his eyes, his nose, his chin, his brow—seems angled and aggressive. He has one of those gazes where you desperately want him to zoom in on you, and then as soon as he does you immediately want him to stop. He is an unmistakable movie star, and possesses a rare kind of "I'm smarter than you" sophistication that makes every character he plays feel like he's always at least 40 percent bothered that you even exist. And so Eisenberg took all of those things and turned the volume up as high as he could get it when he played Zuckerberg. And he started in on you as soon as the movie opened, and didn't quit pressing down on your forehead until the final scene.

For his role as Chris, Kaluuya slow-played his hand. He gave you pieces of his skillset one by one, and he did so at his own pace and with a discernible amount of confidence. He just built and built and built and built, and everything felt so tense and measured, and then when he got to the hypnosis scene and finally showed you how nakedly emotional he was able to get, it was just like,

"Umm . . . Holy fucking shit." You were totally drawn in, and totally at his mercy. You felt exactly what he wanted you to feel, exactly when he wanted you to feel it. It was masterful, and immediately clear after the movie was over that he was something special.

So really what you have to ask yourself here is: (a) Do you more enjoy a performance where you are immediately greeted with overwhelming greatness, which is what Eisenberg did in *The Social Network* because he knew that the responsibility of making it work as a movie was, before anything else, going to sit on his shoulders. Or (b) do you more enjoy a performance where the overwhelming greatness is teased out, which is what Kaluuya did because he knew how delicately all of even the tiniest pieces of *Get Out* needed to be handled in order for the movie to land as profoundly as possible? I think I like the second. I like the experience of watching the stakes grow higher and higher, and watching a movie grow weirder and weirder, all the while its centerpiece grows bigger and more spellbinding. I think Kaluuya gets this. That's a point for *Get Out*.

Pick One: Better Leading Actress? There is no leading actress in *The Social Network* to contend with Allison Williams as Rose Armitage in *Get Out*, so Williams is the winner here by default. (Another point for *Get Out*.) But just so we're all of the same understanding here: Even if there was a leading actress in *The Social Network*, this category would still to go to Williams, who tightrope walked across the script in an

---

20. The same can be said of Jordan Peele, who wrote and directed *Get Out*. (Aaron Sorkin and David Fincher, the writer and director of *The Social Network*, were already recognized as upper level elite.)

unforgettable way.[21] She's so good and convincing as Rose, the evil girlfriend who's responsible for luring black bodies to the Armitage residence, that every time I rewatch *Get Out* I see her sitting on that bench with Chris as he talks about his mother's death and she's just so empathetic and tender that I'm always like, "Oh shit. She's actually really gonna help him get home this time."

Pick One: Better Supporting Actor? This is Lil Rel Howery as Rod Williams versus Andrew Garfield as Eduardo Saverin. And Lil Rel is funny and sweet as Rod, sure, but Andrew as Eduardo wins this one going away. He's marvelous as Eduardo. He's slick and firm and warm and measured; he balances out Jesse Eisenberg's Mark Zuckerberg perfectly.[22] Every single pointy elbow and dead-eye stare that Zuckerberg offers up into the universe has an Eduardo moment that helps cushion its landing some, helps balance it out some. You see Zuckerberg on one side of the galaxy pulling the legs off of an attorney during a deposition (the "You have part of my attention. You have the minimum amount" scene), and then you see Eduardo on the other side of the galaxy politely asking an attorney for permission to repeat a question so he can better answer it. You see Eduardo actively participating in (and excited to be attending) a Caribbean-themed party in col-

lege, and then you see Zuckerberg show up to the same party, and not only is he not excited about it, he hates it so much that he asks Eduardo to step outside into a twenty-degree evening just to have a conversation. You see Zuckerberg attend a meeting in his pajamas just to be a dick, and you see Eduardo make it a point to dress appropriately for two different events at once (a party and a business meeting) because he's not sure which one he's flying across the country to attend. Garfield nails every single line, every single beat, every single look while doing all of it. He wins here. This is a point for *The Social Network*.[23]

Pick One: Better Supporting Actress? What you're looking at here is Rooney Mara as Erica Albright in *The Social Network* versus Betty Gabriel as Georgina in *Get Out*. Both are dazzling performances.

Rooney has two really wonderful moments. The first is during the opening scene of the movie when she's out on a date with Mark. He is being very curt and very short and very laser-like, and she is being a polite and pleasant and considerate human who is trying to tend to all of his idiosyncrasies at once. He fires missile after missile at her, and she just keeps on plucking them out of the air, over and over again, until she decides she's had enough.

---

21. Remember the way she drops all of the emotion out of her face when she goes from frantically looking for the keys to revealing that she's actually in on the scam? That was such a suffocating moment. She really makes you believe all the way up until the very last possible instant that she's on Chris's side. Watching her face change as she shows Chris she's been holding the keys the whole time makes you feel like you've just been hit in the chest with a baseball bat.

22. So, too, does Rod's goofiness balance out Chris's self-seriousness, but it's a different level.

23. If you want to put Andrew Garfield as Eduardo Saverin up against Bradley Whitford as Dean Armitage, the dad in *Get Out*, that might be a slightly more even matchup. But Garfield still wins there. The only way this becomes a toss-up is if you plug in Catherine Keener. She plays the mom in *Get Out*. And she uses every bit of her innate warmness to turn her character into something terrifying.

The best part of the exchange is when Mark, who spends the entire conversation trying to outsmart Erica, believes he's backed her into a corner after she tells him that she's never met anyone who rows crew shortly after she says she likes guys who row crew. Speaking of how he could never physically keep up with them, Zuckerberg says, "Okay, well, they're bigger than me, they're world class athletes, and a second ago you said you liked guys who row crew so I assumed you had met one." Without even giving the thought more than half a second to go unchecked, she very casually says, "I guess I just meant I liked the idea of it, you know, the way a girl likes cowboys." He squints his eyes a little bit, allows his brain to compute her answer, finds it satisfactory, lets two full seconds pass,[24] then he says back to her, "Okay," and changes his track. It's a quick thing, but it's enough to let you know that she's able to outpace him even when he is in full-on attack mode.[25]

Erica's second wonderful moment is even quicker. She's broken up with Mark after their disaster date, and so Mark goes home and starts blogging about her as he gets drunk. Erica's roommate sees the posts, mentions to her that Mark is blogging about her, and then Erica walks over to see what he's written. In one of the posts, he made a comment about her using padded bras, and as she's looking over her roommate's shoulder to see what he's written, two guys interrupt them. One of them is holding up a bra and making an insensitive joke. The camera cuts to Erica, and she doesn't say a word. She just stares forward, her eyes fully wet but not yet crying. It's a great shot, and one that, despite being less a second or two long, sits down heavy in the back of your throat.

Georgina is on screen longer in *Get Out* than Erica is in *The Social Network*, and she's great for all of it, but there's one part where she is uniquely brilliant.

Chris has just told Rose that he believes Georgina has been unplugging his phone from its charger because she's mad that he's dating a white woman. Rose (we're led to believe) mentions it to Georgina, who then approaches Chris to talk about it. She says that it was an accident, and they have this whole back and forth that ends with Chris explaining how anxious and jumpy he gets when he's surrounded by white people. And that's where we get the full power of Betty Gabriel as an actress.

Because what we find out later on is that Georgina isn't a regular person. She's a person who has had her body hijacked by an elderly white woman (her real identity is she's Rose's grandmother). Fake Georgina, confronted with the idea that white people are possibly evil, begins to wrestle with her Real Georgina's subconscious as Fake Georgina talks to Chris. And rather than let the Real Georgina come back to the surface, Fake Georgina pushes her back down, hiding her behind a teary-eyed smile and uncomfortable laugh. It's wildly unsettling the first time you watch *Get Out*. And it's wildly impressive during subsequent rewatches, because that's when you realize that what Betty Gabriel is doing right there is pretending to be an old white woman who is pretending to be a younger

---

24. This doesn't sound like a long time, but two seconds of silence in this script is like forty-five minutes of silence in basically any other script.
25. This part, if you squint, can be used as a metaphor for how Mark might be brilliant at understanding computers, yes, but he's terrible at understanding humans.

black woman while somehow simultaneously showing the emotions of each for a few seconds.

Rooney Mara is 100 percent great as Erica Albright. But Betty Gabriel is 200 percent great as Georgina, what with her successfully playing two warring characters at once. She wins here. That's another point for *Get Out*. (It's three points to one point right now, by the way.)

Pick One: Better Soundtrack? There are some truly magnificent musical cues in *Get Out*. Some come via songs that help better situate you in the world that you're being dropped down into (like when Chris is listening to "Redbone" by Childish Gambino as he's getting ready in the morning at the beginning of the movie[26]). Others come via songs that make you feel utterly lost and completely helpless (like when the big strings come on as Chris is falling in slow motion toward nothingness the first time he gets pushed down into The Sunken Place). And other-others come via songs that let you know exactly how dire a situation is about to become (like when Rose's unbelievably unsettling brother, Jeremy, stands on the porch and plays the ukulele as Chris and Rose walk back into the house a couple of minutes before the family tries to attack Chris). As a collection of music and sounds,

the whole thing is wonderful and perfectly snapped together.

That said, the soundtrack for *The Social Network*, built nearly from the ground up by Trent Reznor and Atticus Ross, is a masterpiece. It's urgent, and unnerving, and it feels just as important to the movie as the script because it is, essentially, a part of the script. It works in tandem with the dialogue to help make it feel like the movie's characters are either (a) speeding around corners on tiny roads on the edges of giant mountains,[27] (b) building toward something gargantuan,[28] (c) getting ready to tear something down in an extremely beautiful way,[29] or (c) measuring the profundity of a situation.[30] It's top level work that is relentlessly crucial. It wins here. Mark down another point for *The Social Network*.

Pick One: Better Clever Small Thing? This category would seem to be tilted way far in *Get Out*'s direction, given that the entire movie is set up a bunch of clever small things that build their way into one clever gigantic thing. (People wearing hats and wigs to cover their surgery scars! Everyone at the auction wearing a small piece of red! Chris using a buck's antlers to kill Rose's dad! Walter running sprints at night! The way Rose eats the milk and Fruit Loops separate of one another! etc.) But *The Social Network* has several

---

26. Jordan Peele explained in an interview with HipHopDX that in addition to simply being a wonderful song, it also matched up nicely with the general theme and tone of *Get Out*. "That's what this movie's about," he said, talking about the "Now stay woke" line that he chose to open up the shot into Chris's apartment. "I wanted to make sure that this movie satisfied the black horror movie audience need for characters to be smart and do things that intelligent, observant people would do."

27. Like when Sean Parker is talking to Mark about how it's their time in the nightclub.

28. Like when Mark is narrating his evening's actions as he blogs his way through heartbreak.

29. Like when they use "In the Hall of the Mountain King" during the Henley Royal Regatta boat race.

30. Like when "Baby, You're a Rich Man" plays during the movie's final scene as Mark sits alone at his computer refreshing his Erica Albright's Facebook page after he sends her a friend request as we get updates on all the key players in the movie.

of them, too. The best, and one I didn't notice until I'd seen it probably about ten or eleven times: Remember the scene I mentioned earlier where Erica and Mark are on that terrible date? Okay, there's a part in there where Mark, because he is a social idiot, makes a remark about how Erica should be nicer to him because if he gets into a very exclusive organization he's trying to get the attention of, he'll take her with him to the parties, and that if she goes to the parties with him she'll be able to meet people she otherwise wouldn't. His comments hit her ear as an insult, and so she sarcastically says, "You would do that for me?" He misreads it as sincerity, and when he does she pulls the carpet out from under his feet.

Later in the movie, after Mark has drawn the ire of a bunch of student organizations on campus for creating a website that allows people to rank the attractiveness of female students, he's approached by three guys who want him to work on their website. As a way to try and talk him into it, they tell him that working with them would help him rehabilitate his image at Harvard. Same as how Erica sniffed out the condescension in his remark about taking her to parties she wouldn't be able to attend otherwise, Mark receives their words as an insult. And same as how Erica responded, he says to them, "You would do that for me?" It's a neat little trick. It's like he's a robot who's learning human emotions as he experiences them from other people.

At any rate, *Get Out* still runs away with this category. *Get Out* wins here. Which means *Get Out* wins the whole thing, four categories to two.

Pick One: *Get Out* or *The Social Network*? It's *Get Out*. *Get Out* wins. It's very close, but *Get Out* is the best movie to have come out since 2007.

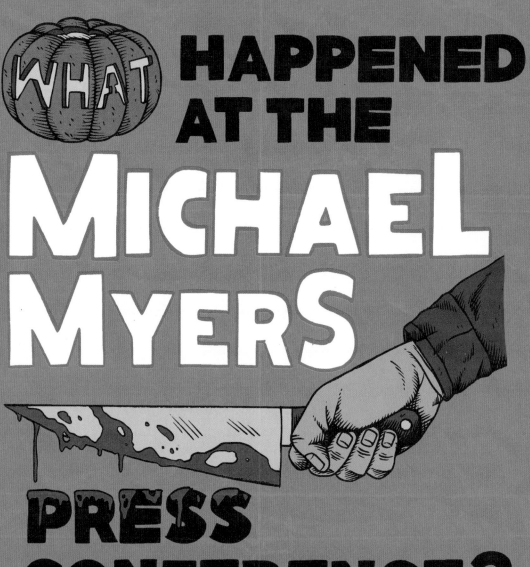

WHAT HAPPENED AT THE MICHAEL MYERS PRESS CONFERENCE?

THIS IS THE THING WHERE AN NBA PLAYER sits at a table on a tiny stage in a room full of sports reporters after a big game and answers their questions, except it's not an NBA player, it's Michael Myers, famed killer from ten of the eleven *Halloween* movies. And it's not after a big game, it's after a night of killing.[1]

———

Michael walks in and sits down heavily into a seat. A reporter raises his hand, moving it back and forth, hoping to catch Michael's eye. "Michael, Michael! Over here," he shouts. Michael sees him. "Yeah, go ahead," he says, taking a drink of a Gatorade sitting on his table, then putting the top back on.

REPORTER 1: Michael, great performance. Can you talk a little about what your strategy was going into the evening? What was the game plan?

MICHAEL: I mean, I was just hoping to stab as many people as I could, you know? That's what you hope for every night. You always go out there hoping you're gonna have a good night. Sometimes you do, sometimes you don't. When you do, you just try to keep it in your mind that this is a marathon, not a sprint. A win is just a win. And when you don't, you just tip your hat to your opponent and get ready to suit up again. At the end of the day, I try to not get too caught up in the stats. I just try to play my game, take what the defense gives me.

REPORTER 2: Defense?

MICHAEL: Sorry. The victims. I take what the victims give me.

REPORTER 3: What is it that you're looking for the victims to give you?

MICHAEL: Their necks, mostly. Big fan of necks. Choking them, snapping them, cutting them open.

REPORTER 2, jumping in: That's actually kind of what I wanted to ask about, Mike. There's been a lot of talk recently about how your attack is a little . . . I don't know . . . *one-dimensional*. Almost all of your kills come by stabbing, oftentimes with a butcher knife. Do you ever think about that? You ever consider switching it

---

1. I came up with this chapter at, like, 3 a.m. one night/morning in October 2018. I'd gone to see what was then the newest *Halloween* movie and really enjoyed it and so I was spending a lot of time thinking about Michael Myers and considering Michael Myers and reading about Michael Myers and reading about the *Halloween* franchise. He is, without question, the greatest movie monster that's ever been, and also the most important movie monster that's ever been. The movie DNA that John Carpenter and Debra Hill stuffed into him and into the movie when they created it can be found in virtually every horror movie that's come out since 1978. It was truly and unquestionably a shifting point in American cinema. That's not why I wrote this chapter, though. I wrote it because I was lying there one night thinking about how Michael Myers never talks in his movies and then I started imagining him at a press conference like NBA players do and I couldn't stop laughing. I rolled over to my wife's side of the bed and tapped her on the shoulder and then said in a very 3 a.m. voice, "Hey. Hey. Wake up. It's an emergency." After she realized she'd been woken up, she said, "What's going on? Is everything okay? Are the boys okay?" I said back, "What do you think of this: Michael Myers at a press conference." To which she responded, "...Boy."

up. Maybe getting a gun? Be a little more efficient. You've never done the gun thing before.

MICHAEL: First of all, that's not true. I used a gun one time on that one woman in *Halloween 4*. Kelly. That was her name.

REPORTER 3: Well, sure, but you didn't shoot her with it. You jammed it through her chest, which, I'm not sure if you're aware of this or not, but that's not how guns work.

Michael grabs the Gatorade again. Opens it. Takes a drink. Then puts the cap back.

MICHAEL: Worked pretty good for me, I think.

REPORTER 1: That's not what he's asking you, Mike. He's saying that guns are for shooting, not stabbing.

MICHAEL, annoyed: I've been shot like fifty times. I know how guns work.

REPORTER 5: So then why did you stab her with it?

MICHAEL: What are you asking me here? I mean, what are you *really* asking me here? You're asking me why I kill in the way that I'm the best at killing? That's dumb. Nobody ever asks Steph Curry why he doesn't play in the post. He shoots threes. He's the best shooter of all time. That's what he does. Just like me. I stab. That's what I do. I'm the best stabber of all time. My job is to try to win. It's the defense's job to figure out how to stop it.

REPORTER 2: Defense?

MICHAEL, annoyed: Victims. Come on.

REPORTER 4: There was a part in *Halloween: Resurrection* where you killed a guy by crushing his head in your hands.

Michael takes another quick sip of Gatorade, then puts the cap back on.

MICHAEL: Yeah. That was Jim. That was a good one.

REPORTER 4: Why'd you do it that way? You were holding a knife and you could've easily stabbed him to death but you didn't. You jammed the knife into the wall, then grabbed him and squeezed his head until his eyeballs nearly popped out.

MICHAEL: You all have to make up your mind. First you're mad that I'm stabbing too much. Now you're mad that I'm not stabbing enough?

REPORTER 4: Well, not entirely. I guess really what I'm asking is if you'd like to respond to the notion that you can be, at times, a bit of a show-off? Because you were showing off there when you killed Jim that way. And there are a bunch of kills like that where you're doing a little more than necessary. Like, remember in the 2018 *Halloween* when you pulled that guy's teeth out and then gave them to that one woman?

MICHAEL: I can't give a woman a gift?

REPORTER 4: Is that what you were doing? Giving her a present?

MICHAEL: Yes. She'd come to see me at the sanitarium. I thought we had a connection. I wanted to impress her. I thought: "Hmmm. What's a romantic gesture?"

REPORTER 4: And bloody teeth is what you came up with?

MICHAEL: Yes.

REPORTER 4: Did she like them?

MICHAEL: She did not.

REPORTER 4: Okay. Well, even if we ignore that one, there are other times where you were showing off. Any time you stabbed someone into a wall and left them hanging there like terrible art, that was showing off. The time in the 1978 *Halloween* when you killed the one guy, then got dressed up like a ghost and walked into the girl's room and killed her: That was showing off.[2] The time you used that fuse box to explode that guy's head in *Halloween 6*: showing off. The time you picked up the one guy and threw him twenty feet threw the air onto a transformer and electrocuted him: showing off. The time you tore that cop's head off and then stuffed a flashlight up into his skull through his neck like he was a jack-o'-lantern: showing off. The time you scratched up that guy's car with the garden claw and then jammed it into his forehead: showing off. I can keep going.

MICHAEL: Man, look. You call that showing off. I think that's just my love of the game showing.

REPORTER 2: Game?

MICHAEL: Game. Killing. Whatever. I just love it. Remember when Jordan did "The Shrug" in the Finals after he hit all them threes against Portland? Or when Iverson stepped over Lue in the Finals? It's kind of like that. I love the game. Sometimes it shows itself in ways that maybe a lot of people aren't expecting.

REPORTER 3: I definitely was not expecting you to stick the syringe in that one woman's eyeball,[3] so I guess this tracks.

REPORTER 1, jumping in: You mentioned how much you love killing. So let me ask you this: There have been a few different theories thrown out there about why it is that you kill. One says that it's because you're real and actual pure evil. Another one says that your rocky home life as a child is what sent you off on this path. A third one says that the reason you kill is because it's the effects of a curse and there's a cult involved. Is one of those true? Is it something dif-

---

2. This is my favorite moment of the entire franchise. Two people, Lynda and her boyfriend Bob, have just had sex. Bob goes downstairs to get a beer. Michael attacks him, chokes him, the stabs a knife through his chest, pinning him to a wall. Michael decides he's also going to kill Lynda, but rather than just walking in there and stabbing her, he gets a sheet and puts it over his head like he's a ghost. And that by itself is already hilarious, but also, as I guess a way to really sell to Lynda that he's Bob, Michael takes Bob's glasses off his dead face and puts them on over the ghost sheet. So when he walks into the doorway of the room he's standing there with a sheet over his head and wearing Bob's glasses. He's in a mask, under a sheet, wearing glasses over both. I love it.

3. *Halloween II.*

ferent entirely? What's going on here, Michael? Why do you kill?

MICHAEL: Man, I don't get into all that. I just wanna go out there and play my game. That's all.

REPORTER 4: Mike, you're the greatest horror movie monster of all time. You've got the kills, you've got the staying power, you've got the iconic mask and the iconic weapon, you've got the perpetual nemesis, you've got the music. Your shadow is now truly extra, extra big in Hollywood's horror hallway. Is there anyone else out there that you see as real competition?

MICHAEL: I don't want to sound dismissive or disrespectful here, but I don't think so.

REPORTER 5: *Nobody?*

MICHAEL: I can't think of anyone, no. It's like you all said: I've been at this for over forty years. I was the template for a lot of these other killers out here. You can't be better than the person you're copying, you know what I'm saying?

REPORTER 1: So Jason Voorhees and Freddy from the *A Nightmare on Elm Street* series aren't up there with you?

MICHAEL: I mean, if you're asking me if they're hall of famers, then obviously the answer is yes. We can all be in the hall of fame together, sure. But if you're asking me if either of those guys are sitting at the head of the table during our hall of fame dinner, then no. It's me.

REPORTER 2: What about . . . and this is a longshot here, but what about the monster from the *Jeepers Creepers* franchise? Is he up there?

MICHAEL: I like his hat, I guess. But he's several levels back.

REPORTER 4: How about Chucky from *Child's Play*?

MICHAEL: The doll? [*laughs*] Any movie monster you can hold in a Yorkshire terrier's travel kennel isn't getting a seat at the table. Sorry.

REPORTER 6: The Ghostface killer from *Scream*?

MICHAEL: You've gotta be kidding me. You're talking about high school kids. They were actual high school kids.

REPORTER 2: Laurie Strode was a high school student the first time you saw her.

MICHAEL: [*staring*]

ALL THE REPORTERS: [*staring*]

MICHAEL: [*staring*]

ALL THE REPORTERS: [*staring*]

MICHAEL: I guess you got me there. But the point remains.

REPORTER 5: The little girl from *The Ring*? Regan from *The Exorcist*? The shark from *Jaws*? *The Thing*? The Xenomorph from *Alien*? Jigsaw from *Saw*? Leatherface? The Babadook? Pumpkinhead? Pinhead? That thing that had eyeballs in his hands in *Pan's Labyrinth*?

MICHAEL: Listen, those monsters are all great, but when it comes down to it, I'm putting 'em all in the dirt. For what it's worth, though, I got to spend some time with the Babadook one time. Great guy. Shows a lot of potential. Weird teeth, but all in all a great guy.

REPORTER 6: Mike, but what's going on with Laurie?

MICHAEL: What do you mean?

REPORTER 6: She's still alive.

MICHAEL: I mean, what do you want me to say? She's fast. And smart. I thought I'd finally gotten her in *Halloween: Resurrection*, but I guess not. I guess she walked off that knife wound and being dropped off a building. She's resilient. You gotta respect it. You know, I don't think I've ever really talked about this, but I think a lot about that time in '78 when I could've had her. It was like I was up seventeen in the fourth quarter and still lost. That's the one game that still haunts me.

REPORTER 3: Yeah, that was a tough break. You had her trapped right there in the closet and she still managed to wiggle away.

MICHAEL: I know, man. I'd like to have that one back. But, you know, it is what it is. And I was young in my career. I guess that's why they call rookie mistakes "rookie mistakes." But I'll get her eventually. That's a promise.

Michael takes another drink of Gatorade.

REPORTER 1: If I can go back to something you said earlier, do you think there's going to be a time when you ha—

Someone's phone buzzes loudly. Everyone checks their phones. REPORTER 4 realizes it's his phone. He reaches for it to silence it.

MICHAEL, to the room: I guess we're all just gonna leave our phones on then, huh?

REPORTER 4: Sorry. It was a text. It's from Laurie. She's watching the press conference on TV, I guess. She must've just heard you say you were gonna get her eventually.

MICHAEL: Oh yeah? What'd she text you?

REPORTER 4: I don't want to say.

MICHAEL, with a little more force in his voice and moving the knife he's holding just enough to remind everyone that he's still holding it: What'd she text you?

REPORTER 4, reluctantly: She said . . . and this is her saying it, not me. I'm just reading it. But she says, and I quote, "lol bitch no u'r not."

MICHAEL: [*stares*]

A moderator off to the side of the stage tells everyone Michael is only going to be answering questions for a few more minutes.

REPORTER 1: When did you learn to drive?

MICHAEL: What do you mean?

REPORTER 1: They put you in the sanitarium when you were a kid. You broke out fifteen years later when you were twenty-one. Who taught you how to drive? Because you've driven several times. Do they have driver's ed in the sanitarium? What's going on?

MICHAEL: Driving's not that hard. One pedal makes the car go, the other makes it stop.

REPORTER 5: Why don't you ever run when you're chasing someone?

MICHAEL: Have you ever run before? It's awful.

REPORTER 2: Do you have a favorite kind of knife to stab with?

MICHAEL: Yes. Big ones.

REPORTER 3: What'd you think of *Halloween III*?

MICHAEL: [*laughs*] It could've used more me.

REPORTER 1: How were you able to get shot in both your eyeballs and not only did you not die, but also you didn't go blind?

MICHAEL: All glory to God.

REPORTER 3: What was going on in those middle movies where you were psychically connected to the little girl?

MICHAEL: Bro, I have no idea. I was just out there trying to get my shots up.

The moderator jumps in again. He tells everyone that this'll be the last question. All the reporters throw their hands up, calling to Michael for him to pick them.

MICHAEL, looking around, then pointing at REPORTER 2: Ehhh . . . let's go with you.

REPORTER 2: Thanks, Michael. Let's end on this: How much longer do you see yourself doing this? Everyone's got a stopping point.

MICHAEL: People ask me that a lot. I honestly don't know. I've not given it much thought. I know it's not time yet. All I'm worried about right now is making sure I'm in shape and that I'm ready to play. I just want to go out there each night and execute.

There's a pause. Everyone's silent and just looking at Michael.

MICHAEL: Get it?

A couple of the reporters laugh.

WAS ANDY DUFRESNE'S

TIME IN PRISON

WORTH IT OR NOT?

THEY BROACH AN INTERESTING SUBJECT during the final leg of 1994's *The Shawshank Redemption*. That's what we need to talk about here. First, though, a quick run-through of the movie:

The Shawshank Redemption is a prison movie that starts in 1947 and ends in 1966.[1] It stars Tim Robbins as Andy Dufresne, a cold and outwardly impersonal (but ultimately likable) banker who is wrongly imprisoned for the murder of his wife and her lover. Alongside him is Red (played by Morgan Freeman), best friend to Andy and also a resourceful veteran prisoner who oversees the group of prisoners that Andy eventually becomes friends with. There's Bob Gunton as Samuel Norton, the villainous warden of the prison who, after finding out that Andy is a banking whiz, forces Andy to launder money for him. And there's Clancy Brown as Byron Hadley, captain of the prison guards and Warden Norton's main muscle. There are others in the movie, but that's the main group.

After Andy has served nineteen years of his double life sentence, Andy and Red and their group befriend a new prisoner and career criminal named Tommy Williams. Through a wild coincidence, we find out that Tommy served time in a separate facility with the man who actually killed Andy's wife and lover. When Andy tries to talk to Warden Norton about it, Warden Norton disregards the story. When Andy assures him that if he ever got out of prison he would never say anything to anyone about the money laundering that Warden Norton is engaging in, Warden Norton becomes incensed. He sends Andy to solitary confinement for a month, then arranges for Captain Hadley to murder Tommy. When Warden Norton visits Andy at the end of his first month in solitary, Andy tells him that he's not going to launder money for him anymore. Warden Norton responds by sentencing Andy to another month in solitary to see if he'll change his mind. At the end of the second month, Andy decides he'll go back to laundering money for him. And shortly after that is the aforementioned broaching of the aforementioned interesting subject.

Andy and Red are sitting in the yard talking after Andy's gotten out of solitary. Andy asks Red if he thinks he'll ever get out of prison. Red says yes, that he'll probably get released when he's too old for his freedom to be useful anymore. Andy says that, were he given the choice, he'd live in Zihuatanejo, Mexico, "a warm place with no memory," which is a wonderful description. Then he says, "Open up a little hotel right on the beach. Buy some worthless old boat, fix it up new. Take my guests out charter fishing."

Red, who has been in prison for forty years by that point, says that he's been institutionalized; that he's spent most of his life in prison; that seeing something as big as the Pacific Ocean might scare him to death.

Andy shakes his head a little, then, while staring off into space, says, "Not me. I didn't shoot my wife and I didn't shoot her lover. Whatever mistakes I've made I've paid for 'em and then some. That hotel, that boat—I don't think that's too much to ask."

---

1. It was based on a novella by Stephen King called *Rita Hayworth and the Shawshank Redemption*.

That evening, Andy escapes from Shawshank State Prison.[2] And the next morning, pretending to be Randall Stephens, a make-believe person he created to set up bank accounts to funnel all the warden's laundered money through, he walks into a handful of banks and withdraws several hundred thousand dollars. Red, narrating the scene, says, "Mr. Stephens visited nearly a dozen banks in the Portland area that morning. All told, he blew town with better than $370,000 of Warden Norton's money. Severance pay for nineteen years."

And so there's the question: Was Andy Dufresne's time in prison worth it?

———

This is not related at all to *The Shawshank Redemption*, but let me tell you: In the next chapter, there's a list that goes over a bunch of the lessons that Robert De Niro has taught people in movies. Because of that, I had Arturo draw a picture of De Niro inserted into the scene from *Dead Poets Society* where Robin Williams stands up on the desks in front of the kids as he teaches them. We ended up not having enough room for it in the chapter, so we put it in here. Looking at it makes me happy. I hope you like it as much as I do.

———

Some stats for you:

- Andy escaped from prison in 1966.
- Adjusting for inflation, that means the $370,000 that he stole back then would be worth nearly $2.9 million in 2018, which is the number that I'm going to use going forward since we live in this general time and not fifty or so years in the past.[3]
- Andy was in prison for nineteen years.
- An easy mistake to make here is to say that that means he was, in effect and on average, paid about $152,630 per year to be in prison.
- The thing of it is, though, since Andy actually had all of the money that he withdrew, that means he didn't *gross* $152,630 per year (which is how salaries are typically advertised), he *netted* $152,630 per year.
- And, assuming (a) he was filing his taxes in Maine (which is where he was living); (b) he was filing them as a single person (because he was single when he was in prison); and (c) he was paying the standard things people have to pay within their paychecks (federal taxes, FICA, Medicare, etc.), that means his salary was likely something closer to $250,000.[4]

---

2. Here's a small but interesting thing: After the guards realize that Andy has escaped, they alert Warden Norton. As he's walking toward Andy's cell to inspect it for himself, he's shouting orders at nearby guards. One of the orders he gives is to question Red. He does so because he knows that Andy and Red are good, good, good friends, and so he's hoping that Red will have some knowledge of the escape. When Norton tells the guards to question him, you can hear in the background one of the guards say, "Open 237." It's a quick moment, and if you sneeze you'll miss it, but it's not inconsequential (or, rather, it's not inconsequential as far as small but interesting things are concerned). Turns out, the number 237 is also used in other film adaptations of Stephen King's works, including *Stand by Me* (there's a scene where the boys all pool together the money they have so they can buy some food; they have $2.37 between the four of them) and *The Shining* (it's the room number in that scene where the little boy is riding his Big Wheel through the hallways). I'd probably seen *The Shawshank Redemption* a good twenty times before I caught the 237 reference. Movies are fun.
3. This is assuming that you, the reader, are not reading this book in 2068 or beyond. If you happen to be, though, then that's cool, probably. I hope things are good in the future. Am I still alive, or did my heart crumple under the weight of a lifetime of tortillas and beans? Is LeBron James still playing basketball? I'll bet he is.
4. This assumes that Andy was not contributing any money to a 401(k), which, admittedly, does not sound very Andy-ish. It has to be that way here, though, because the money Andy withdrew from the banks was the entirety of his money. There was nothing else stashed away.

So at this point, the question is: Would you spend nineteen years in a maximum security prison if you were being paid a salary of $250,000 per year to do so?

And that's where things start to get a little fuzzy. Because it's not really just, "Would you spend nineteen years in a maximum security prison if you were being paid a salary of $250,000 per year to do so?" Because that assumes that Andy was making $0 per year outside of prison, which we know to not be true.

By profession, Andy was the vice president of an unnamed bank. Per Glassdoor, which is a website that tracks salaries across various professions, vice presidents of banks in America were paid a salary of, on average, $110,000 in 2018. In the interest of not getting too bogged down in circumstantial details, let's just stretch that across the entirety of the nineteen years Andy was in prison.

Meaning, at this point, the question is: Would you rather spend nineteen years in a maximum security prison if you were being paid an annual salary of $250,000, or not go to prison and only[5] make $110,000 per year?

—

An aside: The way Andy escapes from prison is he carves a hole through a wall in his cell. The hole leads him to an area where a large sewage pipe carries sewage from the prison and dumps it into a nearby river.[6]

It took him nearly two decades to tunnel through his wall (he was the last cell on a row of cells, so the wall was several feet thick), and so during that time he was covering the hole up with different posters of different women, the first being Rita Hayworth.

And I mention all that to tell you that the movie studio eventually ended up releasing *The Shawshank Redemption* in a bunch of different countries, several of which changed the title. My favorite one is when Finland decided to call it *Rita Hayworth: The Key to Escape*, spoiling the ending entirely. That'd be like changing the title *The Sixth Sense* to *Bruce Willis Was Dead the Whole Time!* or changing the title of *Fight Club* to *Tyler Durden Is Imaginary!* or changing the title of *The Usual Suspects* to *The Usual Suspects, One of Which (Verbal Kent) Is Not Who He Says He Is (He's Keyser Söze!)*.

—

Another thing you have to consider when you're figuring out if Andy Dufresne's time in prison was worth it is all of the other prison-related things he had to experience, not the least of which was the repeated sexual assaults that we know took place for his first two years inside. If we include that part in the conversation, then the answer seems extremely obvious.[7] But what if we could eliminate that part?

What if we could rid Shawshank State Prison not only of the Sisters (that's the name given to the prison

---

5. LOL at "only."
6. I'm certain that dumping waste into a river is against the law today, but was not against the law fifty years ago. You could basically do whatever you wanted back then. My grandmother one time showed me a picture of her driving my mom around when my mom was eight years old, and not only did neither of them have a seatbelt on, but also they were both smoking a cigarette.
7. It was absolutely not worth it, as it were.

gang that attacked Andy over and over), but of any potential sexual predators? That would certainly make things more palatable, but would it make it worth it? Because there are still just so many other threats and awful pieces in place. You've got the horrible food (which is, on occasion, maggot-infested). You've got the constant threat of physical abuse from Captain Hadley and his crew. You've got the endless lack of human intimacy. You've got the awful living conditions. You've got the billion other more subtle prison inconveniences that only people who have served time in prison know about. And you've got Warden Norton knowingly keeping you in prison even though you're innocent (this, I would guess, would be the most crushing part).

Would you choose to live with all of that if you were getting paid a handsome amount? You would have to give up the meatiest part of your alive years, but you'd be able to retire as a multimillionaire hotel owner living on a beautiful beach in Mexico.[8]

———

What's a Moment That We Know Happened in *The Shawshank Redemption* That We Weren't Shown but Would Like to See?

This is always one of my favorite things to think about when I watch a movie that I like a lot or a TV show that I like a lot. It's fun to imagine the stuff that happens (or has happened) in the background when we aren't watching (or weren't allowed to watch). A good one here would be: What was that conversation like between Warden Norton and Captain Hadley when Norton told Hadley that Tommy Williams had to be killed?

We know for sure that it happened because Tommy ended up getting shot by Hadley, so what was it like? Did it happen in Warden Norton's office? Did it happen in some back corner of the prison? Did Hadley buck back any? (I feel very confidently that he did, given that he not only seemed to like Andy, but also he seemed to be a little less morally bankrupt than Warden Norton was.[9]) Did Warden Norton have to get in Hadley's face and threaten him into submission ("You and I are both going to prison if Andy ever gets out of here!")? Did Hadley have to talk himself into doing it when he was up in the tower waiting for the signal from Norton? Did part of the conversation between Norton and Hadley include them going over what sign Norton would give when he wanted Hadley to shoot? I would like to know all of that.

What's a Moment That Maybe Happened in *The Shawshank Redemption* That It Would Be Nice to Know for Certain if It Did or Didn't?

This is also always one of my favorite things to think about when I watch a movie that I like a lot or a TV show that I like a lot, though obviously for different reasons than the previous section. A good (and dark) one here would be: Red knew that the Sisters were regularly attacking Andy. And it was definitely happening after Red and Andy had become friends. So why didn't Red have his group retaliate? There were, at most, four members of the Sisters. Red's group

---

8. Does it affect your decision at all if instead of Shawshank, we put you in that same prison that they put Ray Liotta in *Goodfellas*?

9. Inasmuch as a man we know has killed at least one man and crippled another can be, anyway.

had at least eight members in it. They could've stopped the assaults, probably. Is it possible that Red, a respected and important man in prison, gave the greenlight to the Sisters to attack Andy? Was it a situation where they asked permission ahead of time like we've seen so often in other movies with power structures similar to prison? Could that have been the case? Could that have possibly been the case? Because that makes the whole rest of the movie a lot more complicated.[10]

—

I keep trying to figure out a way to make a reasonable case that Andy's time in prison was worth it, but I just can't get there. All of the arguments for it—he had his own cell; he operated in the prison under the protection of Warden Norton and Captain Hadley; he had good friends; he had a job that allowed him at least a tiny sense of a free man's duty; he had recreational hobbies that kept him busy; he'd probably have never been able to become a multimillionaire as a regular civilian; he'd never have met Red if he weren't locked up; he might've never worked up the courage to move down to Mexico like he dreamed of doing, etc.—all get refuted by the same undeniable, unstoppable, irrefutable, unavoidable, ugly truth: "Okay, but he was still in prison, and prison is an awful place, maybe the worst place, certainly not a place anybody would choose to go to."

There's a part late in the movie where Red touches on the way that the extended stagnation of being in prison eventually shapes the way a person exists, saying, "Prison time is slow time. So you do what you can to keep going. Some fellas collect stamps. Others build matchstick houses."

A softer version of that has happened here.

I, it would appear, have written a book chapter. And the summation of it is: Andy Dufresne's time in prison was not worth it.

---

10. A smaller, less significant question I always think about near the end of *The Shawshank Redemption* is: What are the chances that Andy really fit into Warden Norton's suit and shoes that he stole right before he broke out of prison? Andy was six foot five. The warden was six foot one. I suppose there's a chance that Andy had smaller feet or the warden had oversized feet, but I don't figure there's any way that the suit could've fit in any believable way.

WHICH RACE WAS

"WHITE-SAVIORED"

THE BEST BY

Kevin Costner?

THE TITLE OF THIS CHAPTER, as you can see, is, "Which race was white-saviored the best by Kevin Costner?" The reason it's titled that is because Kevin Costner, one of my very favorite movie stars, has had many movies where he white-saviors someone. In *Dances with Wolves*, for example, he white-saviors Native Americans. In *Black or White*, for a second example, he white-saviors black people. In *The Postman*, for a third example, he white-saviors white people, which is probably the most meta level of white-savioring, I think.[1]

There's even, if you can believe this, a movie where he white-saviors Mexicans. It's called *McFarland, USA*. He plays a high school teacher in California who accidents his way into coaching the school's cross country team.[2] Watching that movie was a huge moment for me.[3] Because, I mean, I typically love any version of Movie Mexicans I can get my hands on, so imagine my joy when I found out that an actor I liked a great, great deal was going to be in a movie where he was going to try to save some of them. (I felt the same way when Michelle Pfeiffer tried to save Emilio and Raul in *Dangerous Minds* and when Hilary Swank tried to save Eva in *Freedom Writers*.)[4]

But I don't need all of the 3,000 words available to me over these eight pages to answer this chapter's prompt. I only need a handful of them. If the question is, "Which race was white-saviored the best by Kevin Costner," then I only need to say, "Kevin Costner white-saviors the Mexicans the best." There it is. There you go. Eight words. That's your answer.[5] And so, similar to what we did in *Basketball (And Other Things)* where there was an entire chapter that was made up of lists, that what this chapter is. The whole rest of this book is filled with measured, considered, fully explained answers to things. This part, however, is not. This part is just fifteen questions with only the answers and little to no explanation. It's a counterweight, of sorts.

———

WHAT ARE THE 12 BEST TINY MOMENTS FROM THE RIFF-OFF SCENE IN *PITCH PERFECT*?

1. When everyone realizes what song it is that Beca is singing and they all start singing along with her.[6]

---

1. If you get a little creative, you can say he white-saviored ghosts in *Field of Dreams*, and he white-saviored the Cleveland Browns in *Draft Day*, and he white-saviored an alien in *Man of Steel*.
2. It's based on a real 1987 cross country team.
3. This is a joke, but it's one of those jokes that's only, like, 30 percent a joke. There's a scene in *McFarland, USA* where Costner pumps the kids up before a race by telling them that the hard lives that they've lived (and that their white opponents have not had to live) give them a special kind of strength. And I wanted to roll my eyes at it. I really did. But I couldn't because I was too busy trying not to cry. I remember going into the movie hoping to only make fun of it, and then getting to that scene and being like, "Well, shit. I forgot that Kevin Costner is a fucking first class actor. I think he just white-saviored me right now too."
4. An unintentionally funny part of *McFarland, USA* is that Costner's character is named Jim White, and so the runners just call him "White" when they talk to him. ("You think you're tough, White?" "You know what these are, White?" "Somebody picked those, White.")
5. If, at this very moment, you're thinking to yourself, "Of course Shea would pick that, what with him being Mexican and all," then let me confirm to you: Yes. You are correct. That's the whole reason I picked them (us?) as the winner. That's just how it goes sometimes.
6. A quick high-five of appreciation for Anna Kendrick, who has never one single time not been great in a movie. Remember her in the *Pitch Perfect* trilogy? Remember her in *Up in the Air*? Remember her in *50/50*? Remember her in *End of Watch*? Remember her in *Mike and Dave Need Wedding Dates*? Remember her in *The Accountant*? Remember her in *A Simple Favor*?

2. Everything that Cynthia-Rose does, but especially the ad-lib she has during "No Diggity."

3. The way Bumper stomps his foot down right when he starts singing "Mickey" with the other Treblemakers.

4. When Jesse takes the lead for the Treblemakers and does that thing with his jacket.

5. When Amy gives the Treblemakers the finger during "No Diggity."

6. When Lilly pantomimes shooting the Treblemakers with a big gun during "No Diggity."

7. The face that the host makes when the girl from the stoner group first starts singing.

8. Everything that Donald does, but especially the little hand gesture he does at the beginning of "Let's Talk About Sex."

9. The ad-libs that Bumper adds in during "Let's Talk About Sex."

10. The way that Amy comes in to back up Stacie during "I'll Make Love to You."

11. Beca deciding she wants to participate in the riff-off after all and becoming very competitive about it.

12. The prize being a microphone used by Hoobastank.

WHAT ARE 7 TIMES WHERE YOU WATCHED A TARAJI P. HENSON MOVIE AND SAID, "I BET IT'D BE FUN TO HANG OUT WITH TARAJI P. HENSON"?

1. When she sings the hook in *Hustle & Flow*.

2. During that part in *Smokin' Aces* when Outkast was playing in the background.

3. When she's at the picnic with Tyrese and their son at the end of *Baby Boy*.

4. During the car trouble scene in *Hidden Figures*.

5. When she senses that the guy is about to shoot her in the back in *Proud Mary*.

6. During all of *Acrimony*, but especially the part where she pours acid on Diana's wedding dress.

7. When she was rooting for Dre in *The Karate Kid*.

WHAT ARE THE 9 MOST STATHAM-Y JASON STATHAM MOVIES?

1. *Crank: High Voltage*

2. *Fast & Furious Presents: Hobbs & Shaw*

3. *The Transporter*

4. *Safe*

5. *Crank*

6. *Snatch*

7. *The Bank Job*

8. *The Meg*

9. *Transporter 2*

WHICH OF BRAD PITT'S MOVIE LOVE INTERESTS HAD THE WORST LUCK?

1. Tracy in *Se7en*. She gets her head cut off by a serial killer and then mailed to her husband. She was pregnant when it happened.

2. Daisy in *The Curious Case of Benjamin Button*. Three main bad things happen to Daisy: Her dancing career gets ruined by a leg injury she suffers in a car crash, her husband turns into a baby (which makes her an accidental pedophile, maybe), and she eventually dies.

3. Susannah and Isabel in *Legends of the Fall*. Brad has relationships with both Susannah and Isabel. He decides he doesn't want to be with Susannah and so she kills herself. He marries Isabel and has

children with her. She ends up getting killed by a police officer.

4. Adele in *Kalifornia*. She's Brad's girlfriend in this movie. He murders her.

5. Marianne in *Allied*. She and Brad fall in love and get married and have a daughter. It turns out she's a German spy. She kills herself to save Max and their daughter.

6. Thelma in *Thelma & Louise*. Brad has a fling with Thelma. Then he steals money from Thelma and Louise. The movie ends with Thelma and Louise driving their car off a cliff.

7. Amanda in *Too Young to Die*. Brad convinces Amanda to commit a murder by telling her that since she's fifteen she doesn't have to worry about the consequences. She gets sentenced to death and is eventually executed.

8. Marla in *Fight Club*. They aren't dating. They just sleep together and talk on the phone a little. She doesn't die, but she does attempt to commit suicide.[7]

WHO WERE THE 14 BEST FIGHTERS IN THE ROCKY BOXING UNIVERSE?

1. Rocky from the end of *Rocky IV*
2. Apollo Creed from the end of *Rocky*
3. Adonis Creed from the end of *Creed*
4. Ivan Drago from the beginning of *Rocky IV*
5. Viktor Drago from the beginning of *Creed II*
6. Pretty Ricky Conlan from the end of *Creed*
7. Clubber Lang from the beginning of *Rocky III*

8. Mason "The Line" Dixon from the end of *Rocky Balboa*
9. Paulie from the middle of *Rocky III*
10. Spider Rico from the beginning of *Rocky*
11. Robert Balboa from the middle of *Rocky V*
12. Chickie from the beginning of *Rocky V*
13. Tommy Gunn from the middle of *Rocky V*
14. Union Cane from the middle of *Rocky V*

WHAT ARE THE 9 BEST JEAN-CLAUDE VAN DAMME MOVIES?

1. *Bloodsport*
2. *Kickboxer*
3. *Lionheart*
4. *Death Warrant*
5. *JCVD*
6. *Sudden Death*
7. *Timecop*
8. *Hard Target*
9. *Cyborg*

WHAT ARE THE 8 HARDEST THINGS TO CONVINCE SOMEONE OF IN A MOVIE THAT HAPPEN A LOT?

1. That you're from the future.
2. That you're from the past.
3. That you're in a body that isn't your normal body.
4. That a doll has come alive and is killing people.
5. That an apocalypse of some sort is coming.
6. That you can hear what animals are thinking.
7. That you can hear what people are thinking.
8. That a charming robot has gained true sentience.

---

7. Incidentally, Brad Pitt's wife in *World War Z*, a movie about a world war against zombies, had the best luck. She lived and her children lived, too. And I think it's important that it gets pointed out here that probably the only reason she had good luck is because she ditched Brad Pitt in the movie as soon as she could.

WHEN WAS GABRIELLE UNION THE COOLEST IN A MOVIE THAT STARTED WITH THE LETTER B?

1. When she was in *Bad Boys 2*.
2. When she was in *Bring It On*.
3. When she was in *Breaking In*.

WHAT ARE THE 11 MOST SATISFYING UNEXPECTED GUITAR SCENES IN A MOVIE?

1. When the animated hamburger plays the guitar in *Better Off Dead*.[8]
2. When Audrey Hepburn plays the guitar in *Breakfast at Tiffany's*.[9]
3. When Marty McFly plays the guitar at the end of *Back to the Future*.
4. When the guy with the new robot arms plays the guitar in *Robocop*.
5. When Cassandra plays the guitar the first time in *Wayne's World*.
6. When Howard plays the guitar at the end of *Howard the Duck*.
7. When Jim Carrey plays the guitar in *Yes Man*.
8. When Vince Vaughn plays Guitar Hero in *Couples Retreat*.
9. When Rufus plays the guitar in *Bill and Ted's Excellent Adventure*.
10. When the blind guy strapped to the car plays the guitar during *Mad Max: Fury Road*.
11. When Reed Rothchild plays the guitar in *Boogie Nights*.

WHAT ARE 12 BEST LEAD CHARACTERS WHO ARE NOT PLAYED BY JULIA ROBERTS FROM ROM-COMS THAT CAME OUT AFTER 1997?

1. Erica Barry from *Something's Gotta Give*.
2. Margaret Tate from *The Proposal*.
3. Renee Zellweger in pretty much anything she's in.
4. Hugh Grant in pretty much anything he's in.
5. Kumail from *The Big Sick*.
6. Brooke Meyers in *The Break-Up*.
7. Lara Jean in *To All The Boys I've Loved Before*.
8. Robbie Hart from *The Wedding Singer*.
9. Jerry Maguire in *Jerry Maguire*.
10. Harper in *Set It Up*.
11. Summer in *(500) Days of Summer*.[10]
12. Rachel Chu in *Crazy Rich Asians*.

WHAT ARE THE 9 BEST JENNIFER ANISTON ROM-COMS?[11]

1. *The Break-Up*
2. *The Switch*
3. *Picture Perfect*
4. *Wanderlust*
5. *She's the One*
6. *Just Go with It*

---

8. Another good one that also has John Cusack in it is when Bruce Springsteen shows up in 2000's *High Fidelity* and starts playing the guitar while Cusack is talking to himself.

9. I know there was a thing earlier in the book where I mentioned that mostly it'd be movies that came after 1980 that were discussed, but Audrey Hepburn always existed above the rule of order.

10. Zooey Deschanel is great as Summer. And I've always had a soft spot in my heart for Joseph Gordon Levitt. Which is why after Summer broke his heart in this movie I held a real and actual grudge against Zooey for it for, like, a solid two years. That's probably the best compliment you can give an actor or actress.

11. Julia Roberts is the unquestioned alpha of the rom-com genre, but Jennifer Aniston is my surprise pick for the second spot. She never was given the chance to really pin down a top tier rom-com role, but she's put together enough solid performances that I think a convincing argument can be made that, if nothing else, she at least belongs in the conversation for a second place finish.

7. *Along Came Polly*

8. *The Object of My Affection*

9. *Office Space*[12]

WHAT MOVIE LAWYER DO YOU WANT REPRESENTING YOU IF YOU EVER END UP GETTING TRIED FOR A CRIME IN A MOVIE?

1. Elle Woods from *Legally Blonde*. She successfully defended someone charged with murder before she was even out of law school. I can't even imagine how good of a lawyer she'd be after a few years of experience. If she's not available, then call . . .

2. Jake Brigance from *A Time To Kill*. Samuel L. Jackson admitted on the stand that he was guilty of the two murders he was being tried for and Tyler still got him an innocent verdict. If he's not available, then call . . .

3. Tanner Bolt from *Gone Girl*. I love how in *Gone Girl* he basically told Ben Affleck, "She's way too smart dude. You're fucked." If he's not available, then call . . .

4. Vincent Gambini from *My Cousin Vinny*. This is assuming that he has Marisa Tomei with him. If they aren't available, then call . . .

5. Joe Miller from *Philadelphia*. He sued a big-time law firm and won. You have to be some kind of special lawyer to pull that off. (The only reason he doesn't finish first here is because he was the prosecuting attorney in his movie, not the defense lawyer.) If he's not available, then call . . .

6. Lieutenant Commander JoAnne Galloway from *A Few Good Men*. You can take Tom Cruise's character if you like. But he was a little too theatric for me. Give me Demi Moore's character. She was way more experienced, more serious, more forthright. If she's not available, then call . . .

7. Fletcher Reede from *Liar, Liar*. But only either before or after he was prohibited by the universe from lying. If I catch him during that twenty-four-hour period where he had to tell the truth, then I'm probably going to need someone else. If he's not available, then call . . .

8. Erin Brockovich from *Erin Brockovich*. She was a paralegal and still went after Pacific Gas & Electric, a high-powered energy company that she knew could ruin all of her everything. I respect that kind of spirit. If she's not available, then call . . .

9. Rudy Baylor and Deck Shifflet from *The Rainmaker*. Same as with the Vincent Gambini pick, these two have to come as a duo. If one of them isn't available, then call . . .

10. Kathryn Murphy from *The Accused*. But only after she decides she wants to do the right thing, not the easy thing.

11. Kevin Lomax from *The Devil's Advocate*. But only from the beginning of the movie.

WHO WERE BEN AFFLECK'S 9 BEST MOVIE FRIENDS?

1. James in *The Town*

2. Harry in *Armageddon*

3. Literal money in *Boiler Room*

4. Will Hunting in *Good Will Hunting*

---

12. Not actually a rom-com, but there are parts that are romantic and parts that are funny so, I mean, if I cheated earlier with the Mexicans why wouldn't I cheat again right now?

5. Alyssa at the beginning of *Chasing Amy*

6. Ironhead in *Triple Frontier*

7. Superman when they finally teamed up in *Batman vs. Superman*

8. The crocodiles in *Runner Runner*

9. Gertie in *Jersey Girl*

WHICH NON-VILLAIN FROM AN ANIMATED MOVIE WOULD BE THE LEAST LIKELY TO PAY YOU BACK IF YOU LENT THEM $20?

1. Sid from *Toy Story*

2. Coraline from *Coraline*

3. Shrek from *Shrek*

4. Sid from *Ice Age*

5. The sloth who worked at the DMV in *Zootopia*

6. Joy from *Inside Out*

7. Baymax from *Big Hero 6*

8. Alfredo Linguini from *Ratatouille*

9. Zazu from *The Lion King*

10. Lumiere from *Beauty and the Beast*

11. Princess Atta from *A Bug's Life*

WHAT ARE THE NINE BEST THINGS THAT ROBERT DE NIRO TAUGHT US?

1. When he taught everyone to never let yourself get attached to anything you are not willing to walk out on in thirty seconds flat if you feel the heat around the corner in *Heat*.

2. When he taught everyone to never rat on your friends and always keep your mouth shut in *Goodfellas*.

3. When he taught everyone that cheating is bad in *Casino*.

4. When he taught everyone that sometimes lying is okay in *Sleepers*.

5. When he taught everyone to love their children unconditionally in *Shark Tale*.

6. When he taught everyone not to bet on the Eagles in *Silver Linings Playbook* and when he taught everyone that if you care too much about the San Francisco Giants you'll die in *The Fan*.

7. When he taught everyone not to walk into a place you don't know how to walk out of in *The Score*.

8. When he taught everyone that the working man isn't a sucker in *A Bronx Tale*.

9. When he taught everyone that therapy is good in *Analyze This*.

WHAT ARE 9 SITUATIONS IN YOUR LIFE THAT YOU WOULD INSTANTLY BECOME 40 PERCENT MORE INTERESTING IF MORGAN FREEMAN NARRATED THEM?

1. When you're brushing your teeth.

2. When you're standing in line at the grocery store.

3. When you're riding in an Uber.

4. When you're opening your mail.

5. When you're masturbating.

6. When you're waiting to cross the street at a busy crosswalk.

7. When you're doing that thing where you're pretending to listen to someone who you secretly don't like talk to you.

8. When you're sleeping.

9. When you're reading a book that has a chapter that ends with a list about situations in your life that would instantly become 40 percent more interesting if Morgan Freeman narrated them.

WHEN DID MICHAEL B. JORDAN

BREAK YOUR HEART

INTO THE MOST

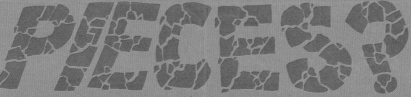

PIECES?

IT'S RIGHT BEFORE THE FINAL ROUND OF THE FINAL FIGHT in *Creed* that does it. Michael B. Jordan, who plays Adonis "Donnie" Creed, the illegitimate son of Apollo Creed, is sitting on a stool in the corner of a boxing ring. Sylvester Stallone, who plays Rocky Balboa and is acting as Donnie's cornerman for the fight, is sitting in front of him. In the other corner of the ring is "Pretty" Ricky Conlan, the light heavyweight champion of the world and a boxer so ferociously dominant that he's never even been so much as knocked down once by another fighter in any of his thirty-six professional fights. He and Donnie are fighting each other for the belt. And Conlan has just put Donnie through a goddamn torture chamber of a round.

Conlan sledgehammered him so many times across the left side of his face, in fact, that Donnie's entire left eye is swollen shut. And it's just not a regular kind of swollen shut either. It's the kind of swollen shut where it doesn't even look like an eye anymore. It looks the whole left side of head is melting away, is what it looks like. It looks like what Jeff Goldblum looked like when he was in the middle of turning into the fly, is what it looks like. It looks like a war wound, is what it looks like, which makes sense, because Donnie and Conlan were very much in a war.

Rocky asks Donnie if he's good. Donnie says that he is, but he does so while giving Rocky a look that lets Rocky know that he's really scared and really shaken up. Rocky, who was in Apollo Creed's corner thirty years earlier the night he was killed in the ring by Ivan Drago, looks in Donnie's good eye, sees the apprehension, then says, "I wanna stop this thing." Donnie yells at him not to, and before Rocky can respond the referee comes over, sees Donnie's eye, then calls for a doctor to take a look at it to determine if the Donnie should be allowed to continue. Donnie and the cornerman in charge of tending to Donnie's wounds cheat their way through the doctor's test,[1] and as soon as the doctor leaves, Rocky, who is watching Donnie's eye swell up bigger and bigger as each second passes, tries again. "I should've stopped this fight with your father," he says, "I'm stopping this one now."

Donnie tells him not to, except he's no longer yelling at Rocky, he's pleading with him. "Don't, okay. Let me finish," he says, and his words suddenly feel like they've been soaked in sadness for two decades. There's a beat of silence, then: "I gotta prove it." Rocky never breaks eye contact. "Prove *what*?" he asks, somewhat confused. Donnie takes a few heavy breaths, gathers himself, summons up all of his strength, then says, "That I'm not a mistake."

---

1. *Creed* is filled with wonderful little flourishes and nuances, perhaps none greater than here. When the doctor comes to check Donnie's eye, he does so by covering up his right eye and then holding up a couple of fingers to see if Donnie can identify them using only his swollen-shut eye. Donnie, of course, cannot. (We get this quick shot of what Donnie sees and it's basically completely black, what with his both of his eyes, in effect, being closed.) But the cornerman, who is holding a cold towel up against the back of Donnie's neck, cheats for Donnie. When the doctor holds up four fingers and asks Donnie how many fingers he sees, the cornerman, while holding the towel in place, uses his middle, ring and pinky fingers to wordlessly tap Donnie on the back of the neck four times. Donnie says, "Four." The doctor holds up two fingers. The cornerman taps Donnie again twice. Donnie says, "Two." It's an incredible moment and an unforgettable moment.

Rocky is all the way taken aback. Because he realizes right then what only Donnie had known up to that point: Donnie wasn't afraid of the fight. And he wasn't afraid of Conlan. And he wasn't even afraid of losing. He was afraid of finding out that everything he'd allowed himself to believe about himself growing up—that his place in the world was invalid; that his shoulders weren't strong enough to carry the legacy of the name he'd been running away from his whole life; that he was, as he heartbreakingly describes it, "a mistake"—was true. Rocky is totally surprised to learn that Donnie has that kind of agony in his bones. He doesn't know what to say. Donnie, who realizes this is this first time he's confronted those thoughts in front of anyone else, becomes overwhelmed with emotion.

Rocky recognizes the look in Donnie's face; he recognizes that specific type of fear. (It's a version of what he had to stare down in *Rocky III*.) And so, same as Apollo Creed did for him in that movie after Mickey died, Rocky insta-builds Donnie back up with one of those motivational speeches that always seem to make the *Rocky* movies more tender than you're expecting. Rocky pumps Donnie full of strength, full of power, full of courage, full of honor. Maybe most important of all, though: He fills him full of fire. Donnie snarls that he's about to put Conlan on his ass, Rocky tells him that he loves him, Donnie's whole everything turns titanium strong, the bell sounds, Donnie stands up, the *Rocky* theme song starts playing, and Round 12 begins.

The entire scene takes less than two minutes, but it is a true masterwork. Stallone is better than great in it. Tessa Thompson (she plays Bianca, Donnie's girlfriend) is better than great in it. Tony Bellew (he plays Pretty Ricky) is better than great in it. Even the doctor who checks on Donnie's eye is better than great in it.[2] But it's Michael B. Jordan who transcends. It's Michael B. Jordan who, without even one single misstep, manages to pirouette his way through the beats of it, emotion after emotion after emotion, all of which feel true and natural. He's perfect as Donnie, because Donnie—guarded; slightly cocky; cool but unconcerned with being cool; charming; secretly insecure; insightful; and dealing with a fundamental and profound internal struggle—is exactly the kind of character Michael B. Jordan is built to play, and has mastered playing. He's done it many, many times in his career; played a character who was built up to break your heart. And so I ask you this question:

> **WHEN DID MICHAEL B. JORDAN BREAK YOUR HEART INTO THE MOST PIECES?**

There are a bunch of times to pick from.

Was it in *Friday Night Lights* when he has the "Why do you wanna leave me by myself?" scene with his mom after she overdoses? His turn as Vince Howard, the near-orphan quarterback prodigy who just wants someone to love him and be there for him, was truly special. And at no time during his two-season run was that on greater display than when he finds his mom at home having overdosed on drugs, gets

---

2. He looks so fucking confused when Donnie correctly identifies the number of fingers he's holding up each time.

her rushed to the hospital, and then delivers a teary-eyed monologue to her about how he's not ready for her to die, that he needs her around, that he needs to not be the one who gets held and protected and loved sometimes. (Two other good ones from his time as Vince were when he asks Coach Taylor not to leave and when he blows up in Coach Taylor's office about people expecting him to be better. He ends that one by saying that he doesn't know how to be better because his absentee father never showed him how. It's very moving, and probably the second ever most crushing My Dad Wasn't Around monologue delivered by a TV character, losing out only to the Will Smith's "How come he don't want me, man?" masterpiece from the fourth season of *The Fresh Prince of Bel-Air*.) He breaks your heart into 16,000 pieces here.

Was it when he died in *Chronicle*? Michael B. Jordan is so cosmically gifted at playing characters who take all of the feelings in your chest and fucking punt them down the street that somehow, even in a movie where he becomes an accidental superhero who can literally fly, he still manages to figure out a way to die a sad death. (He gets struck by lightning while trying to talk his friend back from a nervous breakdown.) He breaks your heart into 18,000 pieces here.

Was it in *Black Panther* when he gets to visit his murdered father in the ancestral plane? He plays Killmonger here, and he spends nearly the entire movie being big and muscular and fearless and terrifying.[3] But after he defeats T'Challa in ritual combat and becomes the new king of Wakanda he gets to visit the ancestral plane, which is where the spirits of our loved ones reside after they pass. He gets to sit with his murdered father for a few moments, and Killmonger turns into a whole different person. He's no longer a mercenary looking to pull the world apart at its seams, he's just a kid who misses his dad.[4] And you'd figure that he being an adult would make it less pulverizing than when he talks to his mom in *Friday Night Lights*, but watching him have all of his strength and tenacity stripped away as an adult when he's sitting in front of his dad is somehow just so much sadder than when he does it as a kid in *FNL*. He breaks your heart in 23,000 pieces here.

Was it when Keanu Reeves told him he was too old to be on the baseball team in *Hardball*? Three things here:

1. You know the thing where you go back and watch a movie again that you'd already seen several years earlier and while you're doing so you realize that one of the people in it is someone who's grown up to be a big, big star? That's what happened to me with *Hardball*. I watched it in the theater when it first came out (2001), and then I watched it a couple times more when the DVD came out (2002), and then I'd catch it on TV every so often whenever it'd pop up on basic cable in

---

3. And smoking hot, though that seems less relevant than the other adjectives used in that sentence.
4. A very quick run-down of his situational setting: His mother dies in jail. His father is murdered by his uncle. The uncle abandons him and, in addition to leaving him to survive in the streets of Oakland all alone, he also indirectly banishes him from the rights that his royal blood should've afforded him. Also, his girlfriend gets shot and killed (though I should mention that he's the one who shoots and kills her, so I don't know if we can add this to his tally of Sad Things About Him in the movie or not).

the years since then. But it wasn't until Michael B. Jordan became a full-on movie star, though, that I realized he's one of the kids in it.

2. Let me say this very quickly about Keanu as a coach: He's very, very good. And also very, very slick. He has several tricks he does that transform his team from the laughingstock of the league position they're in when he first shows up into the league champions that they are by the end of the movie. First, he makes it so that no one is allowed to make fun of anyone else on the team for being bad at baseball. (He does this one, by the way, by making fun of a kid for being bad at baseball, which is hilarious.) Second, he invests in the lives of his players outside of baseball. (He visits them at school to check up on them.) Third, he exercises an unflinching discipline with his players. (He does this after one of his best players gets in a fight with a smaller kid on the team. He yells at the kid, the kid gets mad and runs off, and he just lets him leave. All of the other players know right then and there that it doesn't matter how good you are at baseball, Coach Keanu is not putting up with your shit.) Fourth, he establishes a reward system for good play. (Pizza!) Fifth, he recognizes and supports talent. (He figures out that one of his kids turns into fucking Nolan Ryan if he's allowed to listen to a Biggie Smalls song while he pitches.) Sixth, he offers second chances. (He lets that one kid who ran off after the fight come back to the team.) Seventh, he establishes himself as someone to look up to. (The kids on the team all have a crush on their teacher. Coach Keanu takes her out

on a date.) And eighth, he recognizes and utilizes every bit of leverage that he can. (He responds to a child on the team getting shot and killed after a win in the playoff semifinals by using it as secret fuel to motivate his players to win the championship.) Again: He's a very, very good coach. At any rate, back to Michael B. Jordan . . .

3. He plays Jamal, a total sweetheart that ends up getting kicked off the team by league officials because he's a little bit too old. When Coach Keanu tells Jamal that he can't play anymore, MBJ does that thing he's so good at where he pleads for mercy while turning his eyes into giant, terrified, devastated wet softballs. It's very sad. (He breaks your heart into about 25,000 pieces here.) Keanu fights for him to stay on the team, but the referee rules against it. Jamal starts crying and runs away. Then he joins a gang. And remember the kid I mentioned a moment ago who gets shot and killed? That happens during a gang assassination attempt that MBJ's character is participating in.

Was it in literally all of *Fruitvale Station*? He plays Oscar Grant, a twenty-two-year-old kid who gets shot in the back by a police officer while he's handcuffed and lying down on his stomach. (He dies after they get him to the hospital.) This movie was based on the real-life last day of the real-life Oscar Grant, and that murder was an actual tragedy so I don't think I want to spend any time making any sort of jokes about anything or assigning any scores or anything like that here. Just know that Michael B. Jordan is incredible in the movie,[5] and that it is extremely hard to watch.

Was it in *Creed 2* when they give his daughter the hearing test and he realizes that she's deaf? This is a monster example of how brilliant Michael B. Jordan is in these moments. He's there in a hospital testing room watching his baby daughter get her hearing tested. He sees the test start, sees that his daughter isn't responding, realizes that she's deaf, and then stands there as the full weight of the solar system lands on the back of his neck. He does the thing where you open your mouth wide and take a breath and try not to cry, but it doesn't work. The tears come, and so does that top level heartache that only he and a handful of other actors have ever been able to pull out of an audience. And what's even better about this scene is that, for the first time ever, he has someone on the other side of the screen who can match his power (Tessa Thompson is there and she plays the scene as exceptionally as Jordan does[6]). He breaks your heart into about 35,000 pieces here.

Was it during the scene from *Creed* that I was talking about at the start of this chapter? That one was tough. Really tough. I figure a big part of it is because (a) I am a dad, and (b) father-son relationships, both typical and atypical ones, are a foundational piece of the Rocky Boxing Universe. It's just easy to imagine one of my own sons in Donnie's position; lost, looking for meaning, looking for validation, looking for something—*anything*—to grab a hold of.

And that sort of disconnectedness wasn't just something Donnie was dealing with in *Creed* in regards to his relationship with the ghost of his father or his relationship with Rocky, who ended up becoming his surrogate father. There was also the whole thing where his relationship with his adoptive mother got twisted up and spun around, and there was also the whole thing where his relationship with Bianca got twisted up and spun around, and there was also the whole thing where his relationship with boxing (a thing he loved greatly) got twisted up and spun around. It hurt watching him work his way through all of that. And it really hurt watching it all smash together right in that moment where he admitted how scared he was of being viewed as a mistake. He breaks your heart into about 40,000 pieces here.

Was it when he was in *The Wire*? This is it. This is the one. He plays a sixteen-year-old drug dealer named Wallace here. And while the drug trade seems to amplify the outward toughness of many of those involved in it, it does the opposite with Wallace. Every interaction he has only ever makes him seem sweeter,

---

5. Ryan Coogler directed *Creed*. He also directed *Fruitvale Station*. He also directed *Black Panther*. Ryan Coogler knows exactly how to use Michael B. Jordan in a movie.

6. Thompson plays Bianca. In *Creed 2*, they're married. Bianca was nervous about being pregnant because she knew that the degenerative hearing-loss disease she had could be passed down to her baby. As the baby is being tested, Thompson holds her, trying to muster all of the goodwill she can to tilt the results in her baby's favor. When she sees Donnie panic and start to cry, she realizes that it's gone the other way. She turns away, looks up at nothing for a second, steadies herself, wipes a couple of tears away, then allows herself to look down at her baby, then touches her head gently. It's mesmerizing.

warmer, gentler. Take, for example, when we find out that part of the reason he deals drugs is because he needs money to take care of a group of children he's become the de facto guardian of. He makes sure that they eat, he makes sure that they go to school, he makes sure that they have a place to return to at night (they all sleep together in an abandoned apartment that only has light in it because he ran a long extension cord from a different unit to theirs). And it's not like the kids are of actual relation to him either. They're strangers. He just does it because he knows they'd be entirely eaten up without him.[7]

And that's nothing to say of the tragic way he ends up dying in the show, which is: He spots a guy that the higher-ups in his drug organization are looking for. He lets them know about it. The higher-ups kidnap, torture, and murder the guy. Wallace, realizing he was partly responsible for it, has a breakdown and finds his way to the cops. He tries to leave his drug dealer life behind (they ship him out to go live with a grandma who lives outside the city) but it doesn't stick. He realizes he doesn't know anything else. So he comes back home, starts doing drugs, asks to be a drug dealer again, then is eventually shot and killed by two of his friends. And what's more, it happens in the same abandoned apartment he'd been taking care of the kids in. He's so sweet of a person that when he gets there and sees that all the kids are gone he doesn't think, "Wait, something is wrong here. I might be walking into a trap." No. Instead, he thinks he's just walked into a big game of hide-and-seek that all the kids are playing with him. It's crushing. Watching him start to cry and beg for his life and pee in his pants is very, very, extremely crushing.[8] It's a lot. It's too much, in fact. It's the most, is what it is. This is when he breaks your heart into the most pieces. He broke it into somewhere between 50,000 and 500 million pieces, would be my guess.

---

7. A testament to the level of love and empathy he has inside of his chest: He shows up one night with dinner for all the kids. He hollers for them all to gather around, then sits down and starts handing out food. As he does so, he realizes there's a new kid there. He doesn't even question it. He asks him his name, makes a quick joke, then sees to it that he gets something eat.

8. He was only about fifteen years old when they filmed the season of *The Wire* that he was in. And he was profound in it. He was so touching, and so compelling. Everything he said felt real, and every moment felt earned. AND HE WAS ONLY ABOUT FIFTEEN YEARS OLD.

IT IS A CLEAR THING AND AN OBVIOUS THING that 1977's *Annie Hall* is the default movie to bring up when discussing Diane Keaton's brilliance. And rightfully so, given (1) she is brilliant in it; the kind of brilliant that defines a career; the kind of brilliant that somehow lives separate of all other things; the kind of brilliant so stuffed full of wit and charm and effervescence and humor that it nearly glows.[1] And (2) the film carries with it the kind of historical gravity and influence and cultural symbolism that make it inescapable.[2] And so I get that. And I understand that. And I *get* that. And I *understand* that.

But still: It is not my favorite Diane Keaton performance. Because my favorite Diane Keaton performance is the show she put on in 2003's *Something's Gotta Give*.[3]

A very quick synopsis of *Something's Gotta Give*: Jack Nicholson plays Harry Sanborn, a rich and successful sixty-three-year-old man who has a habit of dating decades-younger women. He starts seeing a twenty-nine-year-old woman named Marin Klein (played by Amanda Peet). She takes him to her mother's house in the Hamptons for a weekend getaway. Her mother, a famous playwright named Erica Barry (played by Keaton), shows up shortly after, surprising them both. Several hours after everyone meets everyone, Nicholson and Peet are in their bedroom getting ready to (presumably) have sex. Nicholson has a heart attack during foreplay and collapses on the floor,[4] and so Peet calls Keaton to help. Keaton ends up saving his life (she gives him CPR and also has Peet call for an ambulance). Peet, somehow just now realizing that her weekend boyfriend is over thirty years older than her, is wobbled by the experience and ditches Nicholson, who ends up getting quarantined in Keaton's Hamptons house until he's strong enough to travel. He and Keaton dislike each other in the beginning, but then Nicholson talks to Keaton for more than one minute and becomes enamored with her, because that's what happens when someone talks to Diane Keaton for more than one minute. And that's where things get thorny.

A real quick aside before I continue, and this will help speak to the level of sophistication and glamour that Keaton has on display in the movie: In 2018, Nancy Meyers, the writer and director of *Something's Gotta Give*, was speaking at the Tribeca Film Festival. She told a quick story about how Diane Keaton

---

1. She won the Oscar for Best Actress that year, of course. She's one of only three actresses to have won an Oscar for Best Actress in a romantic comedy in the past forty years. It's her, Cher for 1987's *Moonstruck*, and Helen Hunt for 1997's *As Good as It Gets*. (Jennifer Lawrence won the Oscar for Best Actress for 2012's *Silver Linings Playbook*, but, despite having funny parts and romantic parts, *Silver Linings Playbook* is not a romantic comedy.)
2. The most succinct explanation of *Annie Hall*'s place in movie lore came from Roger Ebert, who wrote in *Ebert's Essentials: 25 Movies to Mend a Broken Heart* that it "signaled the end of the 1970s golden age of American movies. With *Star Wars*, the age of the blockbuster was upon us, and movies this quirky and idiosyncratic would find themselves shouldered aside by Hollywood's greed for mega-hits."
3. This was actually the first movie I ever saw Diane Keaton in, which is part of the reason I care so much about it. Watching her in it was an awakening of sorts. It was one of those situations where you're like, "Oh shit. Who is this person? How do I find more of this person's work?" And so you can imagine my surprise when I found out that I had something like thirty years' worth of material to work my way through backward. Up to that point in my life, the movies I'd watched and cared about mostly featured fighting and shooting and robberies and gangsterisms and turtles that were ninjas and so forth. Keaton changed all of that.
4. I'm still not quite certain if this means that Nicholson is very good at foreplay or very bad at foreplay.

was so dazzling as Erica Barry that Jack Nicholson thought she'd really fallen in love with him. There's a scene in the back half of the movie where the two run into each other in New York (this is after they've sort of broken up following their time at the Hamptons house together) and Erica gives this great speech to Harry about how she loves him. Jack, while she was doing it, was so overwhelmed by Keaton's performance that he thought she was saying it for real, as herself, and not as her character. And so he approached Meyers and told her that Keaton had just for real, in real life, as real humans with real emotions, told him that she loved him. Nicholson is often regarded as one of the all-time greatest actors in American cinema, and Keaton still had him so spun around that he forgot that he was in a movie with her *while they were filming the movie.*

At any rate, the rest of the plot of *Something's Gotta Give*:

Nicholson's Harry falls in love with Keaton's Erica (and she's pretty sure she loves him, too). But at the same time that that's happening, the doctor who is treating Nicholson, a thirty-six-year-old Perfect Man played by Keanu Reeves, begins courting Keaton as well. And so that's what the movie is: It is, in effect, Diane Keaton accidentally making men fall in love with her, and then Diane Keaton being surprised that men keep falling in love with her, and then Diane Keaton trying to figure out which one of them it is

she wants to be with, and then Diane Keaton reacting to the reverb of all it. And it's all so perfect. As she often is.

———

Eighteen Questions about Diane Keaton, None of Which Are about *Something's Gotta Give*

What is it that makes Diane Keaton such a special actress? Is it because of how funny she is, or how charming she is, or how challenging she is, or how idiosyncratic she is? Is it because of the turtlenecks? The scarfs? The blazers? Is it her bangs? It's her bangs, right? Is it because of the way she talks about the way a bridge looks at night while sitting on a bench next to a neurotic creep-o? Is it because of the way she scans for Warren Beatty at a train station? Is it because she's so good at making applesauce?[5] Is it because of the way she tells you that her hair is a wig? Is it because she stared down the mob? Is it because of the way she kisses a frog?[6] Is it because of the way she gets out of a giant inflatable swan float when she's surprised by her daughters and the police? Is it because of the way she smiles when she's nervous, or the way she blows air out of her slightly scrunched-up nose when she's nervous, or the way her words somehow flutter around in the air for longer than anyone else's when she's nervous? Is it a combination of some of those things? Is it a combination of

---

5. *Baby Boom* is quietly a very great Diane Keaton movie. She plays a successful New York City businesswoman who becomes the caretaker of a baby from a deceased cousin. The baby, of course, derails her career, and so Keaton's character ends up in Vermont living on a large piece of property with her new little girl. She starts a gourmet baby food business almost by accident, then turns it into a multimillion-dollar corporation, which she uses to poke in the eye of the company that let her go after the baby showed up. It's fun, and the part where Keaton realizes she's not capable of giving the baby up for adoption is a perfect example of the way she can turn any moment into something grand.
6. This happens in 2010's *Morning Glory* and it's so fucking funny.

all of those things? Will there ever be another Diane Keaton?[7]

———

Does Diane Keaton make the right decision in *Something's Gotta Give*? Because what ends up happening is she chooses Nicholson over Keanu, and it's not immediately clear if that's the right thing to do.

THINGS WE KNOW ABOUT DR. KEANU:

- **He's handsome.** Keanu has always had such a great face. He's not at his absolute most handsome here (the most handsome he has ever been was in *John Wick: Chapter 2*), but he is certainly trending toward it.
- **He's tall.** A steady six foot one. (For comparison, Keaton is five foot seven.)
- **He's (likely) good at kung fu.** Immediately prior to appearing in *Something's Gotta Give*, he starred in the final installment of *The Matrix* trilogy. That means he probably had some kung fu residue still baked into his bones, which is either very important to you or not important at all to you.
- **His heart is in proper working condition.** He has zero issues with his heart in the movie, unlike Nicholson, who seems to have a heart attack every twenty seconds.
- **He's a doctor.** He works in the ER. Were I to guess, I'd say that puts his salary somewhere around $300,000. That's very good.
- **He's young.** He's thirty-six, compared to Nicholson's Harry, who is sixty-three. (Keaton's Erica is fifty-six.)

(Also: I wonder if Meyers decided to make Keanu's age and Nicholson's age a mirror of one another as a subtle way to imply that they are opposites.)

- **He's considerate.** He seems to always say a nice thing or do a nice thing, no matter the circumstances. (The biggest example is when Nicholson shows up in Paris and Keanu, rather than punching him in the nose, invites Nicholson to sit down and join him and Keaton for dinner.)
- **He's advanced.** There's a part where he reads her latest play right after she's finished it. He tells her that it's great, and then he makes a comment to her about how lucky she is that he's not intimidated by how talented she is.

THINGS WE KNOW ABOUT NICHOLSON:

- **He's handsome, but he's "for an old man" handsome.** You have to add that qualifier in there. Nicholson is handsome in *Something's Gotta Give*, yes, but he's "handsome for an old man." It's different.
- **He's taller than Keaton but shorter than Dr. Keanu.** Five foot ten.
- **He's (likely) bad at kung fu.** He was in zero of *The Matrix* movies.
- **His heart is bad.** It's like a jar full of mayonnaise and cigar smoke.
- **He's (likely) richer than Dr. Keanu.** He owns several businesses, including one of the largest hip-hop record labels in the country.
- **He's old (but only in relation to Dr. Keanu, not in relation to Keaton).** He's sixty-three. That puts him twenty-seven years older than Dr. Keanu (which is a

lot), but only seven years older than Keaton (which is not a lot if both people are older than forty-five, but is a lot if both are younger than twenty-five).

- **He's inconsiderate.** For most of the movie, anyway. Sometimes it comes off as accidentally rude (like when Keaton is excited to find out that Nicholson was briefly engaged to Diane Sawyer, and Nicholson says, "Women your age love that about me"), and other times it comes off as purposefully funny. (The single best example is when Keaton meets Nicholson for the first time. She comes home, sees him in her house, thinks he's robbing her place, and calls the cops. He says he's not robbing her, that he's there because he's dating her daughter. Right then, Peet walks in wearing a bikini and confirms it. Keaton says, "You're dating my daughter?!" To which Nicholson responds, "Now who would've thought that would be worse news?")

- **He's not advanced.** For most of the movie, anyway. It's the whole point of him dating young women.

On paper, Keanu seems like the obvious pick for Keaton. He is younger, seemingly happier, can have sex without having to check his blood pressure first,[8] and still has what I would figure to be at least forty more years of life activity ahead of him, should Keaton so choose to occupy it. But ultimately it just would not have worked, mostly for four reasons:

First, he's approaching the thickest and most intense time of his professional career. He would not be anywhere near as available as Nicholson is (Nicholson is already rich enough that he never has to worry about work again if he doesn't want to). That's important.

Second, he's not as good at being in a conversation with as Nicholson (mostly all Keanu says in the movie is how much he adores Keaton, which I imagine would eventually get old). Keaton is at her best and most lively when she has someone to swat a conversational tennis ball back and forth with. It might be her most treasured thing. Nicholson checks that box off for her. Dr. Keanu does not.

Third, the age difference is just too big. Him being thirty-six and her being fifty-six is fine right now, but that twenty-year gap is going to be a problem when he hits forty-five and she's up at sixty-five, or when he hits sixty and she's up at eighty.

And fourth, and this is the most important part of all of this, but Nicholson really, really loves her. He goes on this entire journey of self-discovery after they have a falling-out because he knows that he has to be better than what he's been if he wants to be with Keaton, because he knows that she's too smart to fall for any of his regular tricks or schmoozing. He tracks down a bunch of his ex-girlfriends, asks them how they feel (or felt) about him, and then absorbs all of that and realizes how inept of a relationship partner he is, and has been.

---

8. This will be crude, and for that I apologize, but right here feels like a good time to tell you that when my wife and I were talking about this while I was working on this chapter, I said something to her close to, "I am familiar with what a thirty-six-year-old penis looks like, because I have seen my own, but I am unfamiliar with what a sixty-three-year-old penis looks like, though I assume it would be largely terrible." She processed that bit of information, and then said that it was my responsibility to look at one, because it would be unfair of me to mark points off Nicholson's case in this conversation if I'd done no actual research on the subject. And so I looked for a few on the internet and found them and looked at them and I have to say: It's not as bad as you'd think. They're certainly not enjoyable to look at, as most penises are not, but I think that you'd have a hard time guessing a man's age based solely on his penis. While organ functionality would eventually be an issue for Nicholson before it would be for Keanu, organ attractiveness would not.

Keaton made the right decision. She mostly always does.[9]

———

Fifteen More Questions about Diane Keaton, Except This Time They're All about *Something's Gotta Give*, and Also It's Actually Only One Question, And Also This Time It Gets Answered

When is Diane Keaton the most charming in *Something's Gotta Give*? Is it the scene when she first meets Nicholson? Is it the scene when she and her daughters have dinner with Nicholson? Is it the scene when she doesn't notice any of Dr. Keanu's advances in the hospital? Is it the scene when she chats with Nicholson on Instant Messenger? Is it the scene when she and Nicholson both realize they like each other in the kitchen late that one night? Is it when she walks on the beach with Nicholson and she's wearing that hat? Is it when she stops making out with Nicholson to take his blood pressure before sex? Is it when she hears Nicholson ask to sleep in the bed with her? Is it after they first break up and she cries and cries and cries? Is it when she sees Nicholson in New York and runs out of the restaurant? Is it when Nicholson approaches her as she's getting her new play ready? Is it when Nicholson surprises her at the restaurant in Paris? Is it when she puts on Nicholson's glasses and he puts on hers? Is it when the two of them (fucking finally) meet up on that bridge at the very end of the movie?

I don't figure it's any of those. I figure it's the scene when she has to give Nicholson CPR. She's in the kitchen with her other daughter and the two of them can hear Nicholson and Keaton's youngest daughter in the bedroom listening to Marvin Gaye. Then she hears her youngest daughter calling for her. Then she runs in there and sees Nicholson on the floor, assesses the situation, and hollers at the youngest daughter to call 911. Keaton gets down on her knees, and her other daughter asks her what she's doing. "Mouth to mouth," she says, and when she says it Nicholson makes a face like he doesn't want her to do it. She sees it, and sees him, and, separate of any of the kinds of playful dizziness or eccentric quirkiness that she often packs into her lines, she says, "Ugh! Youuuu *fucking* guy."

It's all so perfect.

As she often is.

---

9. A third option here would be that actually neither Nicholson nor Keanu deserved Keaton, because nobody has ever deserved her in a movie, because she is Diane Keaton.

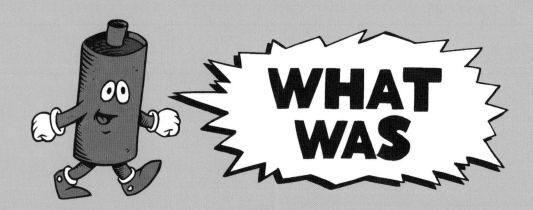

WHAT WAS

DOMINIC TORETTO'S
WIN-LOSS RECORD?

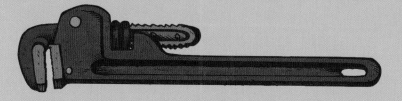

IT'S IN THE FIFTH MOVIE OF THE *FAST AND THE FURIOUS* FRANCHISE when it finally happens: Dominic Toretto, the center point of the *Fast* universe and also an unbeatable force, finally loses a race. It happens during a four-person showdown between him and three people in his crew (Brian, his second-in-command; Han, an as-cool-as-they-come social chameleon; and Roman, a loveable loudmouth). They each put up a million dollars, and then race a quarter mile for it, winner-take-all. And it seems for a bit like everyone has a chance to win—they all toggle positions for most of the race, and then end up even for the final stretch of it—but really only two of them actually do, because the franchise has, for the bulk of it anyway, always been about two of them: Dom and Brian.

Dom outmaneuvers Brian to take a late lead, but makes what appears to be a critical mistake when he eases off the throttle a little too early. Brian takes advantage, pulling ahead just as they cross the finish line, winning the race. And seeing as how he's been trying to best Dom in a street race for nearly a decade, he screams in celebration, proud to have finally gotten his win over Dom. Except here's the thing: It wasn't a win. Dom didn't lose the race; he threw it; he lost on purpose. He did so because his sister (and Brian's wife)

had just told everyone that she was pregnant and he wanted her to have the extra $3 million.

Dominic Toretto is not the overall best driver in the *Fast* universe (that'd be Letty[1]). He's not even the most precise driver in the *Fast* universe (that'd be Brian[2]). But he is the most fearless, and the most intuitive, which makes him the most successful.[3] He's also, as it turns out, the sweetest.

———

Dominic Toretto has never lost a race in a *Fast* movie that he wanted to win.[4] His legitimate movie racing record is as such:

He races three other people early in *The Fast and the Furious* (this is the first time he races against Brian). He beats them all.[5] He races Brian at the end of *The Fast and the Furious*. He beats him. He races several people in *Fast & Furious*. (They do so because they're all trying to win a spot on a transport team for a powerful drug dealer.) Brian is in that race, too. Dom wins.[6] He races a guy in Brazil for his car in *Fast Five*. This one happens offscreen, but we know he wins because he and Brian come home with the guy's car. He races Letty in *Fast and Furious 6*. (She has amnesia so she doesn't know that she's married to him.) He wins. He

---

1. The most obvious example: In *Furious 7*, when she fishtails across the edge of a cliff and saves Brian's life. (I love this one so much because after she does it she gets out her car, sees a totally spent Brian lying on the ground, and, totally unimpressed, just says to him, "You good?")
2. Remember in *Fast and Furious 6* when he swings his car out just enough to use a pole to knock a one-inch-tall electronic grenade off his car?
3. Think about any of his best or most memorable moments. They almost always involve him having to either (a) risk crashing into shit, or (b) crashing into shit.
4. There's another Brian-Dom race that happens at the beginning of *Fast and Furious 6*, but it turns out not to be a race at all. They were both driving fast to get to Mia because she's about to give birth.
5. It's heartwarming to watch him participate in this race. The Dominic Toretto we know now is of such lore and mythology that watching him compete against regular street racers for $2,000 apiece here today feels like watching Barack Obama arm wrestle a bunch of nobodies at a truck stop just for fun.
6. You can start to see right now why Brian was so excited when thought he'd finally beaten Dom in a race in *Fast Five*.

races the guy from *The Fast and Furious: Tokyo Drift* in Tokyo in *Furious 7*. This one also happens offscreen, but we know he wins because the guy says so while they talk afterward. And he races a guy in Cuba in *Fate of the Furious*. The car he uses is a clunker (so much so that the engine catches fire while he races, forcing him to finish the race while driving backward so as to avoid the flames from getting blown in his face). He still manages to win.

That's seven straight-up races for Dom, and seven straight-up wins for Dom. But Dom is a winner in nearly all categories of his *Fast* existence, not just racing. We should go over them, but first let's do the losses.

———

Here are Dominic Toretto's most substantial losses: When he does not sniff out that Brian is a cop in *The Fast and the Furious*; when he decides to try and pull off the last job in *The Fast and the Furious* without Jesse, an integral part of their team; when Vince is dangling off the truck at the end of *The Fast and the Furious* and Dom is unable to rescue him; when he sneaks out in the middle of the night in *Fast & Furious* and leaves Letty alone and she ends up dying later;[7] when he's unable to sniff out that Braga is Braga the first time they meet in *Fast & Furious*; when he gets sentenced to twenty-five years to life in prison at the

end of *Fast & Furious*; when Vince dies in *Fast Five*;[8] when Owen Shaw outsmarts him and kidnaps Mia in *Fast and Furious 6*;[9] when Giselle dies in *Fast and Furious 6*;[10] when he tries to run up on Deckard Shaw in the abandoned factory in *Furious 7*; and when Cipher kills Elena in front of him in *Fate of the Furious*. And I know that seems like a lot, but that's only ten losses in nearly two decades of a truly high stakes existence. The New York Knicks have probably lost ten times in the time it's taken you to read this paragraph.

———

Not including the races I mentioned early, here are some (but not all) of Dominic Toretto's most substantial wins, and I'm going to write them out as a numbered list because there are too many to do it in paragraph form like I did the losses:

1. **When he successfully orchestrates the robbery of another 18-wheeler at the beginning of *The Fast and the Furious*.** Here's how much Dominic Toretto loves racing: One of the law enforcement higher-ups mentions that Dom and his team have already stolen over $6 million in stuff. Even if they were selling it at half that, that's still $3 million they were splitting up between six people. So Dom had made, at minimum, $500,000 over a few months and still felt compelled to participate

———

7. At least we all thought she did. But she'd actually lived. It was just that she was in a car crash so violent that it caused her to lose her memory for several years.

8. This is the only big loss he has in *Fast Five*. He was really on his shit for that movie.

9. I'm not sure if it counts as a loss or not in this movie when Owen Shaw and his team escape the trap that Dom and his team set for them early on because it's pretty clear that the only thing Dom is interested in is confirming that Letty is alive.

10. This one might actually be more Han's fault than Dom's. But it's just that Dom is the leader of the group so any time someone dies he's going to have to share some of that blame.

in drag races that he was risking his life in just to win $6,000.

2. **When he delivers the "Ask any real racer" monologue.** In hindsight, this should've been the scene when everyone realized that we were looking at a potentially massive movie franchise.[11] Vin Diesel, an oddly charming and sincere lug, is legitimately perfect for these few minutes.

3. **When he outruns the cops in *The Fast and the Furious*.**

4. **When he delivers the "I live my life a quarter mile at a time" monologue.** Vin Diesel is a decent actor, except for when he's allowed to emote around a car, at which point he becomes a transcendent talent.

5. **When he kicks the shit out of Johnny Tran when Johnny Tran calls him a narc.** "I never narc'd on nobody!"

6. **When he smashes his car into the side of the gas tanker to rescue Letty in *Fast & Furious*.** I don't want you to think that what I'm about to write is a joke, so I'm going to do in an entirely different font so that you know how serious I am being: `Dom and Letty are an elite movie couple, and the one couple I would trust above all others to find their way back to each other no matter the circumstances.` They're better than Vivian and Edward in *Pretty Woman*, and they're better than Baby and Johnny in *Dirty Dancing*, and they're better than Rose and Jack in *Titanic*, and they're better than Nina and Darius in *Love Jones*, and they're better than Allie and Noah in *The Notebook*, and they're better than Sally and Harry in *When Harry Met Sally*, and they're better than Akeem and Lisa in *Coming to America*, and they're better than Mia and Sebastian in *La La Land*, and they're better than Westley and Buttercup in *The Princess Bride*, and they're better than Anna and William in *Notting Hill*. Pick whatever movie couple you want. Dom and Letty are better than them. And if you're like, "There's no way that Dom and Letty are better than, oh, I don't know, Romeo and Juliet in any of the Romeo and Juliet movies," let me ask you this: "Could Romeo have cannonballed himself across a giant gap between two bridges and caught Juliet mid-air as she tumbled through the sky toward her death?"[12] No. The answer is no. Romeo could not have done that. That idiot couldn't even not kill himself.

7. **When he perfectly times driving under a flipping-and-on-fire gas tanker in *Fast & Furious*.** The most underappreciated stunt in the Fast catalog.

8. **When he interrogates the one guy in *Fast & Furious* and forces him to give him answers by holding a car engine over his head.**

9. **When he interrogates the other guy in *Fast & Furious* and forces him to give him answers by dangling him out of a building window.** Dominic Toretto is fucking good at interrogating people.

10. **When he fights a bunch of bad guys after exploding his own car in *Fast & Furious*.** This was really the movie where the filmmakers were like, "You know what, let's just make Dom a bald

---

11. To date, the *Fast* franchise has grossed over $5 billion, making it the ninth most successful franchise of all time.
12. Another win for Dom.

Superman," and at no point is that more obvious than when Dom gets shot in the back at close range and doesn't even wince.

11. **When he fights Brian and beats the hell out of him in *Fast & Furious*.** I can't think of one person who could've played Brian O'Conner better than Paul Walker played Brian O'Conner. He somehow needed to be both believable as a capable hero, but also he had to always play second to Dom without it ever undoing any of his own strength.

12. **When he outdrives a bunch of bad guys in a tunnel carved through a mountain in *Fast & Furious*.**

13. **When he fucking super smashes a guy with a car and then calls him a pussy in *Fast & Furious*.** Listen, if you're going to hit me with a car then hit me with a car and let that be the end of it. Please don't hit me with a car and then call me a pussy for getting hit with a car.

14. **When he sniffs out that something weird is going on with the car heist they're participating in at the start of *Fast Five*.** I could never quite get a good read on whether or not Dom was good at sniffing things out. Because for every instance of him doing it (like here, for example, or when he finally figures out who Braga is in *Fast & Furious*), there are other times where he doesn't do it (Brian as a cop in *The Fast and the Furious*; Vince accidentally working with Reyes in *Fast Five*; Riley as a mole in *Fast and Furious 6*; etc.).

15. **When he rescues Brian off the train in *Fast Five*.** They end up driving off a cliff and falling several hundred feet to a river below. Neither of them even sprain an ankle.

16. **When he fights his way out of a torture session with Brian.**

17. **When he outruns Agent Hobbs's team (as well as the team of mercenaries that the main bad guy sends after them) in the favelas in *Fast Five*.** The most intense game of tag I have ever watched in a movie.

18. **When he talks Brian through a crisis of faith when Brian tells him that he's worried about being a dad in *Fast Five*.**

19. **When he organizes a robbery of a stash house in *Fast Five*.**

20. **When he outsmarts Agent Hobbs at the street races in *Fast Five*.**

21. **When he beats up Agent Hobbs in front of everyone in *Fast Five*.** This is the best fight we've ever gotten (or will ever get) in the *Fast* franchise. The two fights underneath it both belong to Letty. (When she fights Ronda Rousey at the party in *Furious 7* is second place, and when she fights Riley in the subway in *Fast and Furious 6* is third place.)

22. **When he saves Agent Hobbs from getting murdered in *Fast Five*.** One of my favorite things to think about with regard to the *Fast* universe is how Agent Hobbs, delivered to us as an unflinching and unstoppable bounty hunter, is no-doubt-about-it actually very bad at his job. He gets tricked by Dom into getting a tracker put on his car, he gets beat up by Dom in front of all of his men, he leads his team into an ambush that ends with several of his men getting killed, he allows a rat to infiltrate his

team,[13] and he is forced to ask Dom and Dom's team for help in catching a bad guy who eludes him one too many times.

23. **When he gives the "Salud mi familia" monologue in *Fast Five*.** I don't mind telling you that I have given this exact speech at least ten times at family gatherings when I've been asked to bless the food, and I also don't mind telling you that it has received exactly zero laughs every time.

24. **When he orchestrates the heisting of $100 million from an overlord in *Fast Five*.** This is a very small thing, but: I really like the scene when the team finally opens up the safe here and sees all the money for the first time. It really feels like they actually believe they're getting that money.

25. **When he outsmarts Agent Hobbs again at the end of *Fast Five*.** Agent Hobbs opened up that empty safe and knew there wasn't anything he could do except laugh at himself for getting duped again.

26. **When he makes sure that Hobbs is following him because he knows that Owen Shaw (the main bad guy) is going to try and set a trap for him after his race with Letty in *Fast and Furious 6*.** The way that Hobbs and Dom eventually become friends is very wonderful.

27. **When he walks out of the fire after the plane crash in *Fast and Furious 6*.** Fire cannot kill a Toretto.

28. **When he lets Letty walk away to find herself in *Furious 7*.** We're already two movies past Dom finding out that Letty has amnesia and can't remember anything and she gets really upset about it and decides to leave him for a bit. And rather than try and pressure her to stay, Dom lets her leave without protestation because he knows the strength of their love forever will eventually uncloud her brain. It's a very delicate scene.

29. **When he jumps a car out of a plane and lands it on a mountain in *Furious 7*.** I'm going to pick right here to point out how funny and how much fun Tyrese Gibson's Roman Pearce is in these movies. He's responsible for, I would guess, a solid 85 percent of the laughs in the *Fast* films.

30. **When he drives off the side of a cliff to save himself and Ramsey, a high-level hacker in *Furious 7*.** Remember the thing I talked about earlier regarding Dom's most memorable driving moments being times where he had to decide to crash into something? This is a very big example of that. And more to that . . .

31. **When he jumps a car through two skyscrapers in Abu Dhabi as he tries to steal a fancy microchip from a billionaire in *Furious 7*.**

32. **When he fights Deckard Shaw on top of a parking garage in *Furious 7*.** *Furious 7*, which is the movie that was being filmed when Paul Walker died, is the most emotional of all of the Fast movies. And I don't have any great insight for your here about that other than to say: The scene at the end when the team is gathered together all watching Brian and Mia and their son on the beach and then the transition to Brian and Dom side by side one final time in the cars is really something special.

---

13. Riley in *Fast and Furious 6*. This is more of a loss for Hobbs than it is for Dom.

33. **When he jumps a car at a helicopter, hangs a pack of grenades on the helicopter, crashes his car, and not only lives, but also jump-starts Letty's memory for her in _Furious 7_.**

34. **When he breaks into the base and steals God's Eye from his team in _Fate of the Furious_.** A cold-blooded move by Charlize Theron to purposely kiss Dom in front of Letty during this robbery.

35. **When he takes out a submarine as a heat-seeking missile is trailing him in _Fate of the Furious_.** A FUCKING SUBMARINE.

As I write this, I have a separate document open where I kept track of all of the wins and the losses compiled by Dom during all of the _Fast_ movies he's appeared in. I've only listed thirty-five of the wins here, but the full list has fifty-six on it. Dominic Toretto's overall win-loss record is 56–10.

———

Let's end this with the beginning of all of this:

The first time we hear Dominic Toretto talk happens in the early moments of _The Fast and the Furious_. Brian and Vince are in the parking lot of the Toretto grocery store fistfighting each other over Mia (Vince likes Mia; Mia likes Brian; Brian, who is undercover, has been going to the store every day for a few weeks to order a sandwich and flirt with Mia[14]). Dominic is sitting in the rear of the store with his back to the action. Mia sees the fight, then yells at Dom to do something about it. He stands up, looks at her, then jokes, "What'd you put in that sandwich?" It's a great opening line from him, and one that immediately sets in place that Dom is a better, more nuanced, more intricate movie character than maybe you were expecting to find in a movie about street racers who steal DVD players from eighteen-wheelers. The filmmakers actually set in place here all of the things that make Dom such an enjoyable figure.

They establish that he lords over everything (they do this by placing him in an office behind the deli counter of the grocery store; there's no door, though, only a screen so he can watch whatever needs to be watched). They establish that he's cool (so cool, in fact, that he unironically wears a collared shirt with the sleeves torn off and does not look like a moron). They establish that he's the leader of the group (being the one to break up the fight makes that very clear). They establish that Letty has a hold of him in a way that no one else does (he doesn't do anything about the fight until Letty hollers at him). They establish his reputation is wildly important to him (they do this by having him yell "Relax! Don't push it! You'll embarrass me!" at Vince after he pulls Vince off Brian). They establish he has super strength (he picks up Brian and throws him on top of a car). And they establish that he's savvy (he inspects Brian's ID, which we find out later on he did because he knew he was going to run a background check on him).

And it takes less than 160 seconds for all of it to happen.

It takes less than 160 seconds to establish the character than a multibillion-dollar franchise would get built around.

---

14. This, as we know now, eventually turns into a real relationship.

AFTERWORD BY DON CHEADLE

THERE WASN'T NECESSARILY A SINGLE MOMENT OR EVENT that happened early in my career that made me feel like I'd arrived, or that I belonged in Hollywood. For a lot of actors, I think it's the same thing. There's a bit of impostor syndrome where you feel like you're going to get caught; somebody's gonna go, "Hey, man. You don't belong here."

Even after you've been in a few movies or had some success, that feeling is still there. You feel like it can still happen at any point. Because acting may be meritocratic in some ways, but it's really difficult to determine what the metrics are that decide that. If you're talking about an NBA player, you have a line of thirty points, ten rebounds, five assists, two steals; you can look at that and go, "Yeah, he had a good game." There are legitimate and obvious markers like that in some professions. But I think as an actor, we don't know. You never really know. We're in a business that retires you. You don't really retire from it. At some point, people just stop fucking with you and you're like, "Oh, I guess it's a wrap."

So I never had that feeling early on where I felt like I was standing at the beginning of a decades-long career. If anything, *maybe* I can say now that I have enough of a toehold, that I have enough ancillary ways to work in this business that they can't totally shake me out. I can write, I can direct, I can produce, I can act. I can make moves. But, you know, I think actors are always trying to figure out if you've "made it" or not.

———

There's not one specific character I've played in a movie that people always ask me about. It's a variety. So when-ever someone in the street comes up to me to talk about something that I've been in, I always try to play "Who Is This Fan?" I'm trying to figure out what movie it was that they saw me in so I do a kind of demographic scan. What race are they? What age are they? Certain people come up to me like, "Oh, I love your work," and I try to guess what movie I was in that they know. Young people come up to me and I already know it's going to be the *Avengers* stuff. If a black dude came up to me and he was a little bit edgy or hood-y, like, "Man, I'm such a huge fan," I'd be like, "*Devil in a Blue Dress*," and he'd be like, "Yeah!" If a British dude walks up and wants to talk shit I know it's *Ocean's Eleven*. It always makes me laugh a little.

———

If I've ever been intimidated on a movie set, it was always because it felt like there were bigger things at work than moviemaking. *Devil in a Blue Dress* is a good example. When I did *Devil in a Blue Dress*, which was directed by Carl Franklin and starred Denzel Washington and was what I felt like an important movie, it was a big deal to me. I wanted to make sure that I was on point all the time. I stayed in character the whole time. I was very, very committed to making sure that I was doing everything I thought I needed to do to be as great as I could be.

I felt that way for different reasons when I did *Hotel Rwanda*. I felt incredibly intimidated by that material. I was very concerned that we did it right and that people who were involved felt we were doing a respectful job and servicing the material. A lot of the reason was because

Paul was there. Paul Rusesabagina, who I played in the movie, was on set the whole time. And there were survivors from the genocide that were actually in the film as extras. There was a lot of pressure to do things the right way. So there hasn't really been a time when I was standing across from another performer or actor that was intimidating to me, it was standing across from what it was we were attempting to do that was unnerving day to day.

And obviously, when I directed my own movie (*Miles Ahead*), I was wearing all the hats and sitting in all the seats. I was incredibly intimidated then for even different reasons. I was shook up every day about what it was I was doing and how it was going to turn out. There was nobody to point to if it didn't work. It was all on me.

———

I think the first time I can remember sitting in a movie theater and feeling like I was a part of something special was *Star Wars*. I was a kid and I'd gone to see it with my dad. It came out in 1977, so I was about thirteen at the time. If there was a movie that made me feel like that before then, it was *Jason and the Argonauts*. I went to see that with my dad, too. He loved those movies. He loved special effects. He was as excited to see it as I was, and I was excited to see it with my dad. It was a really special kind of spirit. And then the movie itself, you're like, "Fuck, this thing is sick."

And that's a feeling that's continued into adulthood. It doesn't go away. Movies—a great movie—can make you feel that way. When I was a senior, I saw *Gallipoli* and it hit me hard. I wasn't an adult then, but I was older and remember having that same feeling.

Spike Lee's *X* was another one that hit me hard. There have been *so* many. When I saw *Memento* I was like, "What?! You can film movies like this? You can film movies backward? And it still works forward?!" There have been a lot of them. Obviously. And lately, a movie like *Roma*, which was amazing. I could list you as many as you wanted.

Movies can be meaningful to people for whatever reason they need them to be. It's the director, it's the subject matter, it's the production value and the special effects, it's the characters. Those are the things that pull people in. It can be any one of those. A movie like *The Celebration*—that movie looks like it was shot on a Fisher-Price camera, and it kind of was, but it didn't matter. The story was so compelling and what the characters were going through was so compelling that it didn't matter that the movie looked like it was made for three dollars. You were in. You were just so in.

When you're on the other side of it, like I am now and have been for something like thirty years, it's trying to make sure that you're telling honest stories that are affecting you. You're not just trying to come up with clever things that could make someone feel something you don't feel. You're the first barometer for that when you're making a movie. If you're affected and moved, you know, water will find its level; there's a good chance that others are going to feel something watching a movie if you felt something making that movie. That's what you have to try to do. And that's what you have to try to create.

ACKNOWLEDGMENTS

Author	**SHEA SERRANO**
Muse	**LARAMI SERRANO**
Illustrator	**ARTURO TORRES**
Editor	**SEAN DESMOND**
Castaway Expert	**MALLORY RUBIN**
Coco Expert	**JIA TOLENTINO**
Star Wars Expert	**SEAN FENNESSEY**
The Red Shoes Expert	**MONICA CASTILLO**
Misery Expert	**WESLEY MORRIS**
The Notebook Expert	**AMANDA DOBBINS**
The Best Man Holiday Expert	**DOREEN ST. FELIX**
My Sassy Girl Expert	**DONNIE KWAK**
Saving Private Ryan Expert	**JASON CONCEPCION**
Fresh Expert	**JASMINE SANDERS**
Researcher #1	**ANGELICA MARIA VIELMA**
Researcher #2	**MIKE LYNCH**
Researcher #3	**BOBBY WAGNER**
Insight Guy	**SCOTT TOBIAS**
My Role Model	**LARAMI SERRANO**
The Love of My Life	**LARAMI SERRANO**
I Wanna Make Out With Her	**LARAMI SERRANO**
Bodyguards	**THE FOH**
King of Mortal Kombat	**CALEB SERRANO**
King of Basketball	**BRAXTON SERRANO**
King of Talking	**PARKER SERRANO**
I Love Them So Very Much	**BRAXTON, CALEB, PARKER**
Best Friend	**MY DOG**
Brainstormer	**GARY GUTIERREZ**
Brainstormer #2	**THE SUPER SECRET EMAIL CHAIN**
Foreword	**JOHN LEGUIZAMO**
Afterword	**DON CHEADLE**
Foreword Connector	**DAVID MINER**
Afterword Connector	**TOMMY ALTER**
Mom	**MY MOM**
Dad	**MY DAD**
Sisters	**YASMINDA, NASTASJA, MARIE**
Editorial	**RACHEL KAMBURY**
Book Publicity	**RACHEL MOLLAND**
Book Publicity #2	**PAUL SAMUELSON**
Book Marketing	**BRIAN MCLENDON**
Book Marketing #2	**ANDREW DUNCAN**
Book Production	**YASMIN MATHEW**
Book Art/Design	**JARROD TAYLOR**
Book Lawyer	**CHRIS NOLAN**
Book Copy Editor	**JUSTINE GARDNER**
Life Changer	**BILL SIMMONS**
Role Model	**SEAN FENNESSEY**
Eternal Mentor	**MARGARET DOWNING**
Eternal Mentor #2	**CHRIS GRAY**
Website	**THE RINGER DOT COM**
Favorite Movie	*BLOOD IN BLOOD OUT*
I Miss Him So Much	**TIM DUNCAN**
Magic Expert	**PAT SCHUMACKER**
Magic Unexpert	**JUSTIN HALPERN**
People I've Forgotten Because I'm Dumb	**SO MANY**